Eternal Battle against Evil

A comprehensive strategy to fight terrorists, drug cartels, pirates, gangs & organized crime

Dr. Paul R. Chabot
Military Intelligence Officer
White House Drug Czar Advisor
Law Enforcement Veteran

www.TotalPublishingAndMedia.com

ISBN: 978-0-88144-082-9

"A factual masterpiece! Dr. Chabot pulls in the reader and gives them a mission you can't say no to."
— **Calvina Fay, Executive Director, Drug Free America Foundation, Inc.**

"A courageous book by a courageous leader! Pray for our brave men and women who step forward and face this kind of terror beseeching God's children."
— **Dr. Bishop Ron Allen, Chairman, International Faith Based Coalition**

"Explosive and inspirational! Paul Chabot courageously guides the reader to an ultimate solution in the world's quest to conquer evil."
— **Mark Rusin, Department of Justice, Special Agent, Bureau of Alcohol, Tobacco, Firearms and Explosives, Executive Office of the President—The White House**

"Masterfully written - A book for the ages. The future of our world depends on how seriously we understand the very enemies Paul Chabot so brilliantly defines. This should be on everyone's reading list."
— **James J. Carey, Rear Admiral, U.S. Navy, Ret. Chairman, National Defense Committee**

"A solid winner! This is prime time material that opens our eyes to the true brutality of evil, and what we can do to fight back!"
— **Gary A. *"Rusty"* Fleming Jr., Award Winning Executive Producer of *"Drug Wars"***

"Dr. Chabot is on point and on target. His experiences of fighting terrorists in Iraq, gang members on our streets, and serving as a

Commissioner on the Board of Parole Hearings where he had to defend his decisions to keep violent offenders from being released is testament to outstanding character. Through his real-world experiences, Dr. Chabot opens our eyes to the evil in the world and lays out a masterful plan of attack. You won't put this book down."
— **Archie "Joe" Biggers – Lieutenant Colonel, U.S. Marine Corps, Ret., Silver Star, California State Parole Board Commissioner**

"The book by Dr. Chabot is a thoroughly researched and valuable document because it is based on years of practical experience shared with other professionals. It will be an indispensable addition to any university and law enforcement library and it should be widely read so that people will come to know the detailed truth about the world of drugs and the immense harm that they do."
— **Dr. Ian Oliver, Police Chief, Ret. from Scotland. International Vice President for the International Association Chiefs of Police.**

Presidential Management Fellow Dr. Chabot served with U.S. Drug Czar
General Barry McCaffrey 1999-2001

White House Advisor Dr. Chabot served with
U.S. Drug Czar John Walters from 2001-2005

Dr. Chabot led a law enforcement coalition for NYC Mayor Rudy Giuliani during his presidential bid 2007

LT Commander Paul Chabot, Intelligence Officer 2010

LT Paul Chabot, Special Operations Intelligence Officer – Mosul, Iraq 2008

LT Paul Chabot, Special Operations Intelligence Officer –
Fallujah, Iraq with Navy SEAL 2008

Dr. Chabot on televised debate 2010

Dr. Chabot with fellow U.S. Naval Personnel 2010

Dedication

To the warriors in law enforcement and the military, who
each day battle to protect the innocent.
To my late grandmother, Anna, for her overwhelming
love and guidance.

*"And thus, like the wounded oyster, he mends his shell
with a pearl."*
— Ralph Waldo Emerson

Contents

Acknowledgments

"Never doubt that a small group of committed citizens can change the world—indeed it is the only thing that ever has"
— Margaret Mead, Educator

To my family and friends, thank you for your continued support. Without your love and attention, none of this would have been possible. The long nights and time away from home were needed to accomplish this project. And I'm forever thankful for your encouragement. Thank you for staying with me through this to the end.

To the many mentors I have had through life, to my dissertation committee (Dr. David Schwandt, Dr. Michael Marquardt, Dr. Douglas Orton, Dr. Garrett Capune, and David Hagy), to my work colleagues past and present, to the many individuals who provided their stories and quotations for this book, to all of my friends who spent countless hours reviewing my work - thank you.

To all my brothers and sisters in law enforcement and the military, who each and every day fight against an element in our world that has become more ruthless, more violent, and more dangerous—thank you for all you do. You stand watch over that thin blue line that separates society from anarchy. Continue to carry the torch when a comrade falls and know that your work on earth is yet the beginning of your calling in the fight against evil. Never, ever, give up. Our freedom and way of life depend on your lasting courage to fight the good fight. It is an honor to dedicate this book to the brave men and women around the globe who have sacrificed their lives and walked their last beat on earth, watching over us.

God bless and Godspeed,
— Paul

Dr. Paul R. Chabot

Foreword

"Courage is not the absence of fear ... courage is doing what's right in spite of your fear"
—Mark Twain

Warning: This book will show you the inside of evil. Before proceeding, you must understand this is not a textbook, or a fictional thriller, or something to read simply to pass the time. By proceeding, you are venturing into a world that is the least understood, but yet remains the largest threat to humanity—the worldwide threat from evil organizations. Graphic material may be disturbing to some readers.

Civilized societies from every order are under siege from the most vicious and brutal organizations of our lifetime. Drug cartels are thriving, terrorist and pirate networks are expanding, sophisticated prison gangs manage legions of violent street gangs and ruthless organized crime syndicates breed new underworlds of horror. Like a plague, organized evil is spreading out of control; chaos is everywhere - the time to fight back is running out. Good and dark forces have locked horns; the future of the free-world as we know it is in jeopardy. This book takes you to the battlefield where you will learn firsthand the tactics and resilience of evil, and most importantly, how we can fight back and turn the tide for all humanity.

This book explores the nature of organizational resilience as it applies to these organizations. I first walk you through one of history's most notorious drug cartels, also known as a drug trafficking organization (DTO). What does it take for a DTO to remain resilient and thrive in a world of constant change and uncertainty? Why, despite a full-fledged war against the major DTOs, have the United States and

Mexico not been able to fully dismantle these organizations? An in-depth examination of the key elements of organizational resilience will help to develop answers to this question.

In particular, this will be accomplished through a brutal account of the Arellano-Felix-DTO and the dismantling efforts made by the U.S. and Mexican governments. The Arellano Felix-DTO (AF-DTO) is one of the most violent of the Mexican DTOs. Studying this period of their history will shine a light on the meaning of resilience within an organization that has experienced, and is currently undergoing, various pressures that could implode or dismantle the organization and those like them. This is the key to fighting evil of all sorts—to understand what keeps it alive so we can better replicate our successful efforts against terror networks, pirates, gangs and organized crime. Like a heat-seeking missile, the good must focus on those sustaining pillars of strength to destroy the tentacles of the serpent.

I didn't truly understand what made up these evil organizations until being sent to Iraq to work with the joint special operation forces targeting the highest level of the al-Qaeda leadership. For eight years prior, my life was immersed in studying the makeup and resilience of one of the world's most notorious criminal enterprises. What astonished me in Iraq was how similar the al-Qaeda organizational structure was to those of drug trafficking organizations. The further I explored, the more shocking the truth became: that evil does have a face, it has a body, and it has a remarkably strong structure that is built to prevent failure. I researched farther back in history looking at organized crime in the United States and around the globe, to find a number of commonalities. Time and time again, the pattern was identical. I felt on top of the world with this finding, much like a scientist might when a cure is found for a disease, well, except for one thing: I didn't have the cure to dismantle evil, but I had identified its resilient DNA components. From this point, ladies and gentlemen, is where it gets exciting. You see, in order to tear apart evil, we simply reverse-engineer our findings; we identify those evil, resilient characteristics and then correctly align our resources (i.e. military, law enforcement and civilian assets) against them, and fight like hell.

Throughout this book, you will see a number of references to Scripture. I am a Christian who believes that both God and Satan exists. I believe man is comprised of both good and evil. For humanity to survive, the good must promise eternal hostility against evil, for we have no other choice. The fight is often scary, bloody and unknown. As I learned going through a law enforcement academy, one must never, ever, ever give up. If you give up, it's the end! The bad guys win!

Serving as an intelligence officer for an elite group of joint special operations forces, I often came across a quote by George Orwell that so many of the young soldiers I met held dear to their hearts, "*People sleep peaceably in their beds at night only because rough men stand ready to do violence on their behalf.*" The courage, honor, and sacrifice of those around the globe who find themselves on the front lines and know that if their flank is taken—if their line falls—there may be nothing to prevent the spread of the enemy to annihilate those things we hold so close to our hearts. It is the resolve that these unique "super" humans have that allows us to sleep at night—and for that, I am forever grateful.

When I was a child, I often grappled with the question, "Is there really a God?" I felt horrible questioning the very existence of something I truly wanted to believe in. My childhood was not perfect by any means, and at the age of ten I began to experiment with marijuana and alcohol. I had a good job as a paperboy with two routes, made plenty of money, and found the opportunity to support my experimentation that eventually led to abuse. My grades were slipping; I often fought with other kids. At the age of 12, I made the choice to enter a youth drug rehabilitation program. That was a defining moment in my young life. I lived with older kids in an in-patient, unlocked, youth program. After 36 days of treatment, I went home. Something clicked—it was a strong inner pride of being sober and no longer allowing peer pressure to guide me. I never looked back! After 25-plus sober years, I still abstain from alcohol and illegal substances. When I laid down drugs and alcohol, however, I did continue to smoke cigarettes—it was my one main vice.

Fast forward to four years later—at 16, I lived in a small desert city in California, on a dirt road. After attending a youth Bible study program, a friend dropped me off at my house. Before going inside, I lit up a cigarette, stood in the long dirt driveway that stretched to my house, gazed up, and saw a very clear and starry night. As I smoked that cigarette and continued to look up at the stars, I felt a need to address my inner doubts about God. When I did, I again felt that uneasiness of doubting something in which I truly wanted to believe. I decided to do something that any Christian in his right mind may advise against—to test God. I had to know if He really existed. I told Him this: *"God, if you really exist, I want to see a shooting star. I don't want to see just a random shooting star. I want to see one in this particular spot, come down at this particular position (as I pointed to the sky), and finally, I want to see it when I count to three and open my eyes."* The test began. I closed my eyes and counted, *"One-Two-Three."* I looked up, and to my disappointment, no shooting star— nothing! I felt disappointed, sad, let down. I took one last drag of that cigarette, flicked it on the ground, and for some unexplainable reason, felt the urge to look up at the sky again. At that very moment, in the exact same spot where I asked God to send me a shooting star, in the exact direction and angle I asked for, the shooting star appeared! I was never so afraid and excited at the same time in my entire life! Energized, I ran into the house with an amazing sense that catapulted me into what I fight for today. Life, from that day forward, was never the same!

Since that day at age 16, so much has happened. First, I want to clear the record. I did eventually quit smoking when I turned 18-years-old; it was a few days before high school graduation. I sat in my garage on a broken-down motorcycle, reminiscing about my young life and success from rehab to becoming a high school graduate. I never dreamed I would be elected the senior class president, the prom king; living a truly remarkable senior year compared to where I could have ended up. So many of my childhood friends were not as lucky as I – drug addiction had ruined their lives. I got off the broken bike and extinguished the cigarette—and never had one again. The sense of resolve from giving up alcohol and marijuana at age twelve, and then giving up tobacco at age 18, without once relapsing, and staying strong in my resolve for myself, has led me to writing this book.

When I was a sophomore in high school, I decided to join the local San Bernardino County Sheriff Explorer Scouts program. To my surprise, I received a scholarship from them at my senior awards night. This scholarship gave me the courage to go to college and become a reserve deputy sheriff, working as a volunteer on graveyard shifts through my years in college at California State University, San Bernardino.

College was just as rewarding as high school. I started a college fraternity on campus and served as its president. Later I went on to graduate school at University of Southern California (USC) and worked as a police officer to cover tuition. In my final months at USC, I was honored with two incredible awards: the police department's highest medal for service; the Presidential Management Fellowship with the White House, and served under two U.S. presidents. These opportunities led to others, including assignments in the State Department, the Department of Justice and the Pentagon.

During my White House Fellowship, I joined the military as a reserve intelligence officer assigned to the Pentagon, Joint Chiefs of Staff, and simultaneously was admitted into a doctoral program studying executive leadership. It was the combined knowledge from school, military and law enforcement that lead to my doctoral studies of organizational resiliency and terror networks. Clearly, spending six years in the Drug Czar's office was a foundational experience as well.

In between serving in the military and working on my doctorate, I married and was blessed with beautiful children. However, a tour of duty in Iraq took me away from my family for over a year. During my time in Iraq, I served for General McChrystal, within a special operations task force targeting senior-level al-Qaeda. In Iraq, one of the strategies I developed provided suggestions to defeat the enemy. I returned from Iraq and completed my mobilization in North Carolina at Joint Special Operations Command.

Just prior to serving in Iraq, I was appointed three times as a commissioner to the California State Parole Board where I witnessed firsthand the evil of organized crime and prison gangs. In Iraq, I experienced the same with al-Qaeda.

I later ran for state assembly in California and founded a number of anti-drug coalitions as well as my international security consulting firm, Chabot Strategies, LLC.

Life, or shall I say, God, has been very good to me. I see more clearly now that my mission is to spend every ounce of energy to develop and fine-tune my skills to help turn the direction of evil.

Everybody should be aware that drug cartels run Mexico, organized crime flourishes in Europe, and al-Qaeda and other terror networks leave their ugly mark on the innocent while infiltrating Europe, Africa and creeping into Latin America. Before the terror networks align with cartels and arrive on our doorstep and cross the thresholds of other democracies worldwide, each of us must recognize the face of evil, its structure and purpose and come up with a more effective strategy for the sake of humanity worldwide. This book lays the foundation for not only understanding our enemy but also how to face and fight evil.

We cannot afford to be complacent or neutral. We need all hands on deck—one team, one fight. The Book of Psalms is one of the books from the Old Testament. *Psalm 91* is most fitting for this journey. It has tremendous meaning for today's difficult times. It's known as the *"Soldiers' Prayer"* and I hope it gives you as much strength, wisdom, comfort, and courage as it has given me.

He who dwells in the secret place of the Most High
Shall abide under the shadow of the Almighty.
I will say of the LORD, "He is my refuge and my fortress;
My God, in Him I will trust."
Surely He shall deliver you from the snare of the fowler
And from the perilous pestilence.
He shall cover you with His feathers,
And under His wings you shall take refuge;
His truth shall be <u>your shield</u> and buckler.
You shall not be afraid of the terror by night,
Nor of the arrow that flies by day,
Nor of the pestilence that walks in darkness,
Nor of the destruction that lays waste at noonday.
A thousand may fall at your side,
And ten thousand at your right hand;
But it shall not come near you.
Only with your eyes shall you look,
And see the reward of the wicked.
Because you have made the LORD, who is my refuge,
Even the Most High, your dwelling place,
No evil shall befall you,
Nor shall any plague come near your dwelling;
For He shall give His angels charge over you,
To keep you in all your ways.
In their hands they shall bear you up,
Lest you dash your foot against a stone.
You shall tread upon the lion and the cobra,
The young lion and the serpent you shall trample underfoot.
Because he has set his love upon Me, therefore I will deliver him;
I will set him on high, because he has known My name.
He shall call upon Me, and I will answer him;
I will be with him in trouble;
I will deliver him and honor him.
With long life I will satisfy him,
And show him My salvation.

With this prayer, let the lesson and your journey begin.

Law Enforcement Officer Dr. Chabot on patrol 1997

White House Advisor Dr. Chabot with LAPD hunting drug labs 2004

Anti-gang officer Dr. Chabot 2008

Dr. Chabot with U.S. Border Patrol along the Mexico border 2009

Dr. Chabot on Mexico border drug bust 2009

Dr. Chabot and U.S. Border Patrol vehicle 2009

Narcotics Officer Dr. Chabot inside of drug cartel marijuana field 2002

Narcotics Officer Dr. Chabot and team members 2002

White House Advisor Dr. Chabot with national anti-drug
trafficking leaders 2001

White House Advisor Dr. Chabot with U.S. Coast Guard in Miami, Florida
examining homeland security processes 2002

Chapter One

Critical Mass

*"The first terrorist that this county ever had, and this border
ever had, was a drug dealer. And nobody did anything about it."*
— *Betty Flores, Mayor, Laredo, Texas[1]*

Thursday, July 15, 2010, Ciudad Juarez, Mexico[2]

The man lay bleeding on the street, bound, shot, dressed in a police
uniform. First responders sprang into action. Authorities arrived
and cordoned off the scene. Paramedics went to work on the wounded
man. A news camera rolled.

Boom!

A nearby car exploded in a fiery blast, littering the street with
smoking debris. Eleven people were wounded. Three people were
killed: the wounded man, a doctor who had rushed in to help, and a
federal officer.

It was a revenge killing, performed in response to the arrest earlier
in the day of Jésus Acosta Guerrero, a.k.a. El 35, a leader of the La
Linea gang, the enforcement arm of the Juarez drug cartel. In response,
gang members kidnapped an innocent civilian, dressed him in a police
uniform, and shot him. Then they dumped his body in the street as a
decoy. A member of the gang called authorities and told them that a
member of their team had been wounded and needed help.

Watching from a distance, a gang member lurked around waiting
for authorities to arrive, then snuffed out their lives by detonating 22
pounds of C-4 that had been placed in a nearby car.

Sunday, August 21, 2010, Cuernavaca, Mexico[3]

The bodies of the four young men hung upside down from a bridge. Their genitals, index fingers and heads had been cut off. These men were not ***Blackwater*** contractors in a war zone in Fallujah,[4] they were drug affiliates in Cuernavaca, a popular resort town about an hour outside Mexico City.

A handmade sign found nearby stated *"This is what will happen to all those who support the traitor Edgar Valdez Villarreal,"* a U.S.-born kingpin known as "La Barbie."[5]

Wednesday, August 25, 2010, San Fernando, Mexico[6]

A stranger—beaten and bloody—staggers up to a Marine checkpoint. The man is Luis Freddy Pomavilla of Ecuador, the only survivor of the largest drug-related massacre in Mexico's history. Pomavilla led authorities to a ranch in San Fernando, just 100 miles from the U.S. border. Inside were the bodies of 72 people—58 men and 14 women; migrants from South America, slain by human smugglers from the Zeta drug gang when they learned their respective families were unable to pay the ransom and they refused to go to work for the cartel.[7]

Critical Mass

This is where we are, the evil we face—violence, intimidation, corruption all have steadily escalated over the years. Beheadings, mass murders, and al-Qaeda-style car bombs have become part of life in certain areas of Mexico. For America, terror is at our doorsteps and is creeping into our shadows. Without a new strategy to fight this war, drug cartels along with every other evil organization around the globe present a bleak future for the free-world. We will build a new strategy by learning from this evil. The time is at hand to fight back—not only here—but in every corner of the earth where sinister organizations raise their ugly heads. To begin, we must first examine the vile organizations known as drug cartels because, as you will learn through reading this book, there is virtually no difference between al-Qaeda operating in Iraq or the Arellano Felix Drug Trafficking Organization operating in Mexico. Eerily, they share similar traits, motives, skills, structures and personalities. Make no mistake; these are evil organizations in their purest form, stretching their claws to perfect chaos globally.

These tactics of chaos have long been used by drug lords to instill fear. This is the spread of the cancer known as "narco-terrorism." Perhaps we thought—and hoped—this evil would never rise to this level so close to home. We were taught that these things only take place on the streets of the Middle East, in Iraq and Afghanistan, maybe even Colombia. Joint governmental efforts have been battling drug lords since the early 1980s—but not in Mexico and not along the border in the measures required today. It's unthinkable that this evil trespasses into our own backyard and threatens our national security. Time is short; we must move now and fight in both the light and shadows, never ever giving up, for giving up seals the fate of humanity as we know it.

We must strike now! We have reached critical mass.

It is my hope that this examination of evil organizations, through the lens of drug cartels, will help the international communities of law enforcement, military and civilians move in lockstep forward in finding solutions to one of the most complex and pressing issues of our time.

In this book, we look evil in the eye; examine the world of the drug cartels; then microscopically examine and analyze a specific drug cartel. After examining the factors allowing them to thrive — in the final analysis, solutions are born. This book is a call to action for every citizen of the U.S., Mexico and worldwide, to help take down the mightiest of the Goliaths.

Our journey begins here by reading this book and developing a crystal clear understanding of organizational resilience. Resilience is the secret ingredient that enables humanity's enemies to thrive. For once we understand the very make up of resilience — we uncloak the veil of strength to destroy the "survivability" that persists within these organizations.

Behind the Line

In this book, you will read a number of accounts from individuals who truly have been "behind the lines." Some have witnessed terror while others have seen the goodness of mankind fighting to preserve humanity. In many cases they have seen and experienced both. Each of these accounts is told to you in their own words. It is most fitting for the opening of this book to hear from Tiffany Hartley, an American woman who lost her husband at the hands of evil.

Behind the Line – Testimonial 1: "In Loving Memory"

by Tiffany Hartley, a Wife

Tiffany and David

In Loving Memory of my wonderful husband David Michael Hartley-- my story begins:

David, my beloved husband, is with God in Heaven. I know he has won the ultimate prize in this tragedy. He leaves a legacy here on earth and I am somehow part of that plan. I will make sure David's legacy lives on.

Proverbs 3:3-6

³ Let love and faithfulness never leave you;
bind them around your neck,
write them on the tablet of your heart.
⁴ Then you will win favor and a good name
in the sight of God and man.

⁵ Trust in the LORD with all your heart
and lean not on your own understanding;
⁶ in all your ways submit to him,
and he will make your paths straight
Jeremiah 29:11-13:

"For I know the plans I have for you, 'declares the LORD,'
plans to prosper you and not to harm you, plans to give you
hope and a future.

The above two passages from the Holy Bible are my foothold and strength. Even though I do not pretend to understand why this happened to David, I know God is good and has a plan for me. He knows what my future is. I believe this tragedy happened to me for no other reason than to tell the story and build a community to fight the evil that threatens our borders, our neighbors, our families and our children.

We live in America, the greatest country in the world, and I ask, "So, when will we begin to act like it?" When are we going to start fighting for American lives and protecting them from those who are threatening the very freedom we are supposed to offer? The Land of the Free - right? We are not free if we are living in fear.

David and I moved to Reynosa, Mexico in 2007 and lived there for two and a half years. We were not naïve to the violence in Reynosa, but we certainly did not fear living there. The first two years were quiet – there wasn't the violence you see today. The viciousness escalated in the beginning of 2010 when the Gulf Cartel and Zetas divided into two groups. After that, we moved to McAllen, Texas, because David's company felt the violence warranted a move out of Mexico. We were there for *three weeks when we found out we were going to be transferred to Colorado. We were both disappointed and excited about the move. We loved living in Texas and enjoyed the warm weather and the beach. We made great friends and were part of a wonderful church. However, moving would mean living closer to family and the opportunity to start a family of our own. This is something we were looking forward to even if we did not move. Just one week from our moving day, tragedy hit us. September 30*th *was supposed to be a day of fun – when in fact it turned into a nightmare!*

Prior to that day, we heard about the pirates' violent attacks, but like most people, we never thought we would be victims of an attack. When we saw the boats heading toward us on the lake, we immediately knew who was approaching. We had talked about the pirates prior to that day, as recently as August. The border patrol mentioned the danger of pirate attacks. We talked with them about our jet skis and how fast they were, and jokingly said we could easily outrun any threat on the water.

David and I were so in love that we never talked about what we would do if pirates attacked us. But when the shooting started, David made sure that he was between me and the three cartel boats. When I saw two bullets hit the water next to me, I looked back to check on David and saw him shot and thrown off his jet ski. He was bleeding profusely. A pool of blood spread across the surface of the water.

Once I reached him, I jumped into the water, turned him over and saw where he had been shot. The bullet had entered the back of his head and exited through his forehead. This is not an image I would want anyone to experience. Some may think, "I would have never gone to Mexico, nor would I have ever gone to Falcon Lake!" Believe me - many of our friends would probably say the same thing. But we lived in that country for over two years; my husband worked there, we felt comfortable. We loved Reynosa's people who we trusted like an extended family. It was a place we often visited, much like a favorite camping, hiking, biking or vacation spot. We never gave it a second thought. We simply loved being there.

Our plans that day were to enjoy the lake and all of its surrounding beauty. This was not our first time visiting Falcon Lake. The previous month we spent about three hours there without any problems. There was simply no reason for us to expect that our final trip there would be any different.

David Hartley was shot and killed on Falcon Lake on the Texas and Mexican border on Sept 30, 2010. David was my husband. He was a man who had a zest for life and a love of history. On that fateful day, we wanted to see a partially submerged church on the Mexican side of the Falcon Lake reservoir as one last historic trip before our intended move to Colorado. It was a beautiful day to be on the lake, but in one tragic instant my life was forever changed!

While on two separate jet skis, jetting on the lake, we found the partially submerged church and took a number of pictures. Suddenly we were attacked by pirates –the Zeta Drug Cartel. These thugs shot and killed my husband!

As the events unfolded, I remember rushing to my husband's aid. The same thugs pointed a gun at me while I held David, who was bleeding to death. At that moment I thought we were both going to die without our families knowing what happened.

When one of the Zeta boats temporarily left me, with David in the water, I jumped on my jet ski and tried to pull him up and get us out of harm's way. Regrettably, I am only 4'10," 100 pounds while David is 6,' 250 pounds. I couldn't find the strength to get him out of the water! Suddenly I noticed the cartel boats heading towards me. At that moment, I heard God's voice saying, "You have to go! You have to go!" I made the most unbearable decision of my life and left my husband David behind in the water.

But on that day David truly showed his unconditional love for me. I will forever be grateful to him and always honor him in every way that I can. David and God saved my life that day so that I may live in honor of both of them.

On Sept 30, 2010, I lost my husband, my best friend and partner. Since that time, I have been judged, questioned and thrown into the spotlight. I didn't ask for this. In fact, I never dreamed something like this could happen to me. After that horrible incident I moved back to Colorado and stayed with my parents. I was without David, without a job, trying to figure out how to live my life without the one person who made my life whole. I've lost all the dreams, hopes and love that we created together. I've lost my dream of starting a family with David, raising his children and growing old with him. Those dreams have been crushed. I'm now alone to think about what I need to do for all of my tomorrows. How can I do anything when there's no end to this nightmare? I still don't have my husband's body. Our families can't even have a funeral to say our goodbyes.

Although I don't know what losses you have experienced, I ask you this: if your loved one died like this, would you want them to be taken by the hand of the devil – violently culminating in a senseless tragedy? I guess that if you had a choice you would want your loved one to die of old age, at your side. What if these same cartel groups started dominating parts of our waterways, cities, and towns? What would you do? If we don't stand up against drug cartels, we will see all of our loved ones at risk of harm or death.

Cartel members have already moved into many cities across America and it is only a matter of time before they are able to terrorize our communities as they have done and continue to do so in South American countries and along our border. DO YOU WANT TO LIVE THAT WAY? If we as Americans don't do something we will be living the same reality and fear that many Mexican citizens are living today. Even the Mexican citizens that live in America won't speak out because they fear for their lives or family members in Mexico. That is no way to live!

I believe God spared my life that day to be a voice for the people who no longer have a voice or are too scared to speak up. I believe God is going to use me to WAKE up AMERICA and our GOVERNMENT to the continuous threat that the Mexican cartels (and other cartels) pose to our country and our citizens. Too many Americans have been, and continue to be, kidnapped and murdered. Why are we turning a blind eye to those who have lost their lives, to those missing and to the reasons that this is happening? Cartels want more power. They want our country—The United States of America!

I understand that we can't change all of Mexico but we are capable of making a difference in many ways. We can change how we work with authorities, how we do business in Mexico, who we allow into our country—while implementing changes that secure our borders.

My reality today is not the reality I would want anyone else to live. I do not want any other families to go through what my family has experienced. Unfortunately this barbaric violence has happened again. On January 26, 2011 a missionary couple traveling to their Texas home from Mexico was attacked. The passenger, a wife, lost her life, and now a husband has to live this life without his loved one, his partner, his best friend. We both had to see our spouses get shot and die right in front of our eyes!

Cartel violence is all around us. I can see it so clearly now. The same day David was killed on the lake, approximately three hours from our location a college student was pulled off a bus and killed. Tell me you agree with me when I say this has to STOP! These are but just a few examples; there are a thousand more stories like mine.

I believe that we have an opportunity to fight for the ones who no longer have a voice. I believe that it is our job to educate all states, all nations, including those who are not directly affected by border issues so that they can join with us to bring changes sooner rather than later. So, I ask of you to please join with me and let's start making real change, right now. Together, let's see to it that no community is affected by the spillover violence.

Join with me in demonstrating to our fellow American citizens what this country stands for. Together we can assure that the CARTELS, GANG MEMBERS AND TERRORISTS will not be allowed to destroy our beloved country with drugs, bullets, or crashing jets into buildings. A secure border is a secure country. Let's stand together with the families who have missing sons, daughters, wives or husbands in Mexico and all the families who lost loved ones to the cartels. Tell them that we are ready to fight for them to come home and for our government to stop turning a blind eye to these families who just want their loved ones back where they belong.

Please join me – follow our story as we fight to bring David home – and fight for all the "David's" out there – past, present and future.

David's website: www.bringdavidhome.com [Please visit often for updates on the case, related media stories, and other helpful information.]

Thank you — Tiffany Hartley, a grieving widow.

Chapter Two

Faces of Evil: Dragons Never Sleep

"Submit yourselves therefore to God. Resist the devil,
and he will flee from you."
— James 4:7 ESV

Throughout history, evil organizations have sought to destroy various cultures for their own selfish greed. It is nothing new. Recent examples include the American Mafia, the Nazis, al-Qaeda, pirates, sophisticated prison gangs and organized crime.

Today we are under threat from another form of evil—drug trafficking organizations (DTOs) that are global in power and rapidly spreading. Again, this is not a new problem. DTOs have long existed from Mexico to Panama to Colombia to Peru, and to Brazil—most of the world is affected—but a new sense of urgency appears on the horizon as they fight for territory to conquer.

Four decades ago, U.S. President Richard Nixon declared a war on drugs. Seven presidents since then have made similar declarations, as well as announcements of various successes against the Central American and Mexican drug cartels. But the problem has not gone away; it's become far worse in many regions of the world as these organizations adapt to our efforts to dismantle them. The war on drug cartels has become a much bigger war, and narco-terrorism has become more violent and more widespread. Since the late 1990s, the Mexican drug cartels have gained an ever-tightening hold on the North American drug trade. We must not give up this fight. In fact, we must fight harder and smarter, operating at the speed of light with a global strategy that provides no mercy to evil. This is not a time for negotiations, as some have suggested; rather it is time to take the fight directly to the heart of the enemy and beyond—allowing no safe passages, no neutral territory. Doing so only allows evil to regroup and rebound.

When politicians describe "negotiating" with terror, they lay the groundwork for evil to grow. It shows a weakness that evil exploits because of a "perceived" weakness. President Obama, during his 2008 inauguration, described a circumstance of wanting to extend a hand to our enemies. This was largely interpreted as a message of weakness. The only thing free people should extend to evil is a sword into its heart—zero negotiation. For the good of humanity, we must fight this ugly fight. If not us, then who? If not now, then when?

While serving in Iraq as an intelligence officer with Special Forces units from our allied nations, I often came across a quote by George Orwell that these soldiers held close to their heart, *"People sleep peaceably in their beds at night only because rough men stand ready to do violence on their behalf."* These were God-fearing, unselfish soldiers who understood their mission was much bigger than any one of them, and intuitively knew the future of humanity rests on the backs of those willing to walk down that dark alley to face evil, while many others choose not to take that path. God bless these fine warriors and all those who died in defense of the good. Others around the globe are taking up similar battles. In fighting one form of terror, we can fight them all.

On December 1, 2006, President Felipe Calderón took the reins in Mexico. He vowed, in cooperation with the government of the United States, to tackle the drug cartels. Since that time, tens of thousands of people have been killed in drug/terror-related activities while the violence is spreading further into the United States, threatening our national security. There are whispers of their involvement and negotiations with terror networks like al-Qaeda, which continue to gain a footing in Africa, a doorway into Latin America.

Behind the Line

This book is honored to have a number of truly great warriors providing their personal stories. Among these is Michael S. Vigil, a good friend of mine and former U.S. Drug Enforcement Administration's (DEA) Chief– among many other highly coveted positions. During his extraordinary tenure, he served in a number of posts and worked in foreign assignments for 18 years. He was the Special Agent-in-Charge of the Caribbean and San Diego Divisions and Chief of International Operations—responsible for all DEA offices worldwide. He developed multi-national operations, such as Triangle, Unidos I and II, Liberator, Columbus, and Conquistador – well known among the international law enforcement community. The largest, Operation Liberator, included 36 countries. He was exceptional in persuading and convincing countries to work collaboratively in order to maximize the impact on international criminal drug trafficking organizations. One can imagine how difficult it is to establish a multi-national coalition and get them to put aside political differences and work towards a common objective. In many of these operations, the participating countries allowed the police forces of another country to enter their country in support of ongoing counterdrug operations. For example, Guatemala allowed Mexican police and helicopters to enter the country in support of an air smuggling operation. More importantly, the multi-national operations gave countries a sense of pride in being able to participate in such a large scale operation. This paved the way for the sharing of information which is critical to dismantling drug trafficking networks that operate in many countries and do not respect international borders and sovereignty. He received accolades from former President Clinton for his phenomenal work, and in particular Operation Triangle. He also designed and implemented "Operation Containment," a 25-country initiative to address the movement of opium and heroin from Afghanistan, subsequent to the fall of the Taliban. Participants in the operation included Russia and China. The operation has been highly successful and continues to be funded by the U.S. Congress. The operation has increased arrests and seizures in the region by huge margins. Operation Containment has been one of the most successful in the history of the DEA. Also, he is known for implementing intelligence sharing programs, such as the Unified Caribbean Online Regional Network (UNICORN) and the Regional Drug Intelligence networks which are currently worldwide. He immobilized numerous international drug trafficking organizations and was responsible for the arrests of Juan Ramon Matta Ballesteros and the former head of the Mexican Gulf Cartel, Juan Garcia Abrego. While in Mexico, he managed a large operation which resulted in the seizure of over 150 metric tons of cocaine, hundreds of millions of dollars in trafficker-aircraft, and hundreds of arrests in a four year time frame. He is the recipient of numerous awards, including the most prestigious one in law enforcement, NAPO's (National Association of Police Organizations) TOP COP award. He has been decorated by many foreign governments for efforts in combating illicit drug trafficking, worldwide. The government of Afghanistan recently made him an honorary General. He has been highlighted in several books, such as: *With Death in your Pocket; Kings of Cocaine; Silver or Lead; The Last Narco* and many others.

Michael Vigil with Sibghatullah Mujaddidi, the former and first Afghan President after the fall of the communist regime and now President of the Afghan Senate
(photo courtesy of Michael Vigil)

Behind the Line – Testimonial 2: "The Early Years"

with DEA Director of International Operations, Michael S. Vigil, Ret.

I worked in Mexico many years ago – those years were very rough times indeed. There were issues that were taking place in Mexico that called for the DEA to do a lot of extremely risky things. Despite the clear dangers, we executed operations without any type of diplomatic immunity; no protection at all! It was basically analogous to iron man football. We had no political padding. We had no protection, and we took tremendous hits on both sides of the border, politically.

DEA agent Robert Candelaria and I were transferred to Nogales, Arizona, to implement an undercover program in Mexico. It was a primary corridor for Mexican heroin and marijuana being smuggled into the United States. Our orders were basically to enter Mexico, coordinate with the Mexican Federal Judicial Police, and do as much damage to the large scale drug trafficking networks operating in the area as we could possibly muster.

However, on the Mexican side, we had one entity that was responsible for counter-drug efforts in Mexico, and that was the Mexican Federal Judicial Police. They were ill-equipped, ill-trained, out-gunned and they were having a very difficult time impeding the cultivation, manufacturing, and exportation of drugs from their country.

Many of the drug organizations in Mexico which engaged in the distribution of marijuana and heroin had already established a nexus with Colombian traffickers to also funnel large quantities of cocaine through pipelines they had established into the United States. Facilitating this cooperative criminal enterprise were cultural factors such as common language and the fact that the Colombians were having

15

problems moving their cocaine through the Caribbean. The Caribbean had a multitude of law enforcement and military assets that obstructed the Colombian transportation networks in the area. The Colombians astutely paid the Mexican traffickers a percentage of the cocaine rather than cash. This unholy alliance allowed for the Mexican drug traffickers to gain more power and become more resilient to law enforcement efforts. They had become poly-drug dealers. They also became more ruthless and violent under the tutelage of the Colombian drug traffickers.

The Mexican Federal Judicial Police also had a difficult time immobilizing the drug trafficking organizations that had already garnered extreme power. The tri-state area of Durango, Sinaloa and Chihuahua were the major areas responsible for most of the cultivation and production of opium and heroin.

Marijuana cultivation centered in the northern and central parts of Mexico. The marijuana at the time had a very low percentage of the active ingredient known as THC which was between 0.8 to 1.3 percent. Today's marijuana, which has been genetically engineered, has THC levels that exceed 30 percent. It is no longer an innocuous drug.

When assigned to Nogales, Arizona, along the Mexican border, I would cross into Mexico in an undercover capacity to negotiate with very street-wise and dangerous drug traffickers. Most often, I was alone and my only weapons were my gift of gab, ability and confidence to deal with any situation that might arise during the undercover operations. On many occasions, I negotiated with various traffickers on the streets of Nogales, Sonora, Mexico when suddenly traffickers approached me and wanted to sell me drugs, primarily heroin. They had seen me before and believed that I was a drug dealer based in the U.S. There was always danger in the air because many individuals posed as drug dealers, but would engage in "ripping off" traffickers for their money and drugs. You really had to know what you were doing – it was not a job for the faint of heart.

I remember being involved in undercover negotiations with a very significant trafficker in Mexico. I was standing on the street talking to the subject when another trafficker approached me and said, "Miguel, I need to talk to you. I just received a large shipment of heroin you might be interested in." I replied, "Listen, go have a cup of coffee at a nearby restaurant and I'll meet you there in five minutes."

Later we met. He indicated that he was in possession of several kilos of heroin that had just arrived from Culiacan, Sinaloa. Together, we shared a cab, traveled to his house out in the middle of nowhere and negotiated the purchase of the kilograms of heroin. During these operations, I had no one to provide operational security and literally took my chances alone. I always relied on a sixth sense that I had developed through hundreds of covert operations and it has always served me well and ensured my survival. When I think about the handful of individuals who ventured into Mexico to seek out and arrest these dangerous traffickers, and the only protection any of us had was a lot of intestinal fortitude and ingenuity, it was truly amazing. They were the true warrior caste of the DEA. Undercover work is a daring, dangerous, and bold activity. It's like a human chess game. If you make the wrong move, you could easily pay with your life.

I remember a raid in Caborca, Mexico. Kiki Camarena (his death inspired 'Red Ribbon Week') was working with me at this time, although he was assigned to Guadalajara while I was stationed in Hermosillo, Sonora. We planned a raid on an isolated ranch belonging to Drug Lord Rafael Caro Quintero. The tactical operation required the support of the Mexican army because the traffickers had a formidable security perimeter consisting of several armed guards carrying AK-47 Soviet assault rifles. Our plan was to rent a truck for seventy-five dollars from a local rancher in order to transport about

17

thirty soldiers since they had no transportation. The truck we rented was a large cattle truck because nothing else was available, but the Mexican soldiers did not complain. As we approached the ranch, we suddenly came under heavy fire. We had no choice but to charge the drug traffickers and force them to retreat as the bullets buzzed by our heads. Most of the traffickers dropped their weapons and fled, except one who decided to shoot it out and was eventually brought down by a heavy barrage of gunfire and died.

Our search of the area revealed several tons of high grade sensimilla marijuana worth millions of dollars. The next day, I received a telephone call from one of the Mexican prosecutors who said, "Mike, I went to the scene of the shooting to conduct an investigation on the death of the drug trafficker because I have to prepare a formal report." He added, with a chuckle, "...it was rather interesting because the trafficker who was killed in the gun battle had raw marijuana literally stuffed into his pockets." Obviously, it was a case in which the Mexican soldiers wanted to make sure that there was no question the individual killed was in fact a trafficker!

— Michael S. Vigil

Sampling of International Gangs

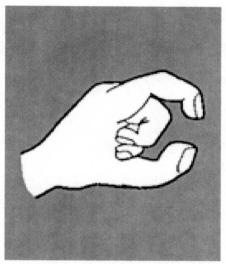

Crips – Worldwide membership exceeds 30,000 – Founded in the United States
(photo courtesy of law enforcement)

Mara Salvatrucha AKA *"MS-13"* – Worldwide membership exceeds
100,000 – Founded in Central America
(photo courtesy of law enforcement)

<u>Hells Angels motorcycle gang</u> AKA *"HA"* – Worldwide
membership is difficult to measure – Founded in the United States
(photo courtesy of law enforcement)

<u>The Mungiki</u> – Worldwide membership exceeds 100,000. Founded in Kenya –
images are limited – photo depicts their mob-style violence
(photo courtesy of law enforcement)

<u>Primeiro Comando da Capital</u> – Worldwide membership
exceeds 100,000 – Founded in Brazil
(photo courtesy of law enforcement)

<u>Bamboo United</u> – Worldwide membership exceeds 20,000 – Founded in Taiwan –
picture shows a funeral of the gang's spiritual leader
(photo courtesy of law enforcement)

Sampling of Highly Organized U.S. Based Prison Gangs with International Reach

Aryan Brotherhood, AKA *"AB"* believes in white supremacy including German and Irish ancestry. It requires an initiating-member to kill, and an exiting member to be killed. They largely focus on drug trafficking; associate with the Mexican Mafia and Hells Angels; battle against La Nuestra Familia and the Black Guerilla Family
(photo courtesy of law enforcement)

Black Guerilla Family AKA *"BGF"* consists of black inmates. Their philosophy is a mix of Maoist and Leninist revolutionary beliefs and are focused on drug trafficking. They largely align with other black street gangs and battle against the Aryan Brotherhood, Mexican Mafia, among others.
(photo courtesy of law enforcement)

La Nuestra Familia consists of rural Mexican-American inmates. To initiate into membership the new member kills – to exit the membership the member is killed. Drug trafficking is a common criminal enterprise; they share a paramilitary structure using "soldiers" with higher ranking member achieving the title of "generals." They are known to associate with the Black Guerilla Family and battle against the Mexican Mafia, Aryan Brotherhood and Texas Syndicate.
(photo courtesy of law enforcement)

Mexican Mafia AKA *"La Eme,"* is comprised of Mexican-Americans using a paramilitary structure. It's known for violent acts against anyone who crosses them. They focus on drug trafficking and associate with the Aryan Brotherhood and Latino street gangs. Their enemies include all black street gangs, La Nuestra Familia and the Black Guerilla Family.
(photo courtesy of law enforcement)

23

Texas Syndicate formed in the 1970s to largely protect Texas inmates in California prisons who were preyed upon by other gangs. Its membership is largely Mexican-American and their structure resembles that of a corporation. Drug trafficking is their primary activity - they associate with the Texas Mafia, Border Brothers and battle against the Aryan Brotherhood, La Nuestra Familia and Mexican Mafia.
(photo courtesy of law enforcement)

Sampling of Organized Crime Leaders

Semion Mogilevich, AKA the *"Brainy Don"* since he has a degree in economics giving him world-wide tentacles extending from the U.S. to the Eastern Europe involving: arms dealing, drug trafficking and violent crimes.
(photo courtesy of law enforcement)

Al Capone head of the Chicago-based Italian gang, AKA, the *"Outfit"* managed operations including violent crime, prostitution, gambling, bootlegging and drug trafficking.
(photo courtesy of law enforcement)

Charles Luciano, AKA *"Lucky"* from New York City established an Empire including a Board of Directors, is largely credited in creating the "Mafia model" – turning simple crimes into a well-orchestrated operations generating massive income.
(photo courtesy of law enforcement)

Pablo Escobar built his criminal empire in Colombia creating the well-known Medellin Cartel and developing a world-wide distribution of cocaine. Before his death, he was listed as one of the world's 10-richest people. During his reign, he was responsible for the killing of presidential candidates, an attorney general, over 200 judges, journalists, thousands of police officers, and citizens.
(photo courtesy of law enforcement)

John Gotti, AKA the *"Dapper Don"* led the Gambino crime family in the U.S and later regained the new nickname, *"Teflon Don"* for his ability to elude criminal prosecution.
(photo courtesy of law enforcement)

Hisayuki Machii, born in Korea, led a criminal empire in Japan, including prostitution, tourism and oil imports.
(photo courtesy of law enforcement)

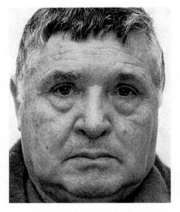

Tony Accardo, AKA *"Big Tuna"* became the head of *"Chicago's Outfit"* after Al Capone controlled it for decades involving murders, kidnappings, extortion, gambling and union racketeering.
(photo courtesy of law enforcement)

Salvatore Riina, AKA *"Toto"* was a longtime operative of the Sicilian Mafia, and wanted for more than 100 murders. He was behind Italy's 1980's *Mafia Wars.*
(photo courtesy of law enforcement)

Dawood Ibrahim, AKA *"Don of Mumbai's Underworld"* spread his influence throughout that portion of the world, starting with extortion and smuggling operations, and extended into large- scale terrorist activity, including ties to al Qaeda. He is suspected as the "mastermind" behind the 1993 terror attacks in Mumbai that killed hundreds of people and also implicated in the 2008 attacks in the same city at a prominent hotel. He travels between Pakistan and India, often in hiding, with accumulated wealth somewhere in the billions.
(photo courtesy of law enforcement)

Xie Caiping, of China, a female leader, managed illegal gambling, drug trafficking and payoffs to police and government officials. Violent crime, on her behalf, was common for anyone who crossed her organization but was protected from prosecution by her brother, a deputy police chief. She was also known to retain 16 young men for personal entertainment.
(photo courtesy of law enforcement)

Chapter Three

Inside the Cartel: We Must Learn Here for the Global Fight

"Our lives begin to end the day we become silent about things that matter."
— Martin Luther King Jr.

With the various faces of evil lurking in our midst, no single organization poses a greater threat to U.S. national security than drug trafficking organizations (DTOs) or, as they are commonly called, "drug cartels." They are already on our doorsteps, inside our communities, with tentacles spreading from Los Angeles to the state of Maine. The threat is real; it is alive and it is on the move—networking, growing and getting stronger as they align themselves with America's street and prison gangs for enhanced control and power.

Each of the most violent and powerful cartels, through their Mexican-based leadership, now operates inside the United States. In fact, according to an *April 2008 Situation Report* produced by the National Drug Intelligence Center, the Mexican DTOs are the most pervasive organizational threat to the United States. They are active throughout the country and dominate the illicit drug trade in every area except the Northeast. Federal, state, and local law enforcement agencies report that Mexican cartels operate in at least 195 cities throughout the U.S. These organizations control approximately 70 percent of the foreign narcotics that are smuggled into the U.S., including the majority of the marijuana and large portions of cocaine, heroin and methamphetamines. They distribute these drugs from

Mexico into the United States, where there is an enormous demand. A joint effort is required on both sides of the border in order to stop the flow.

At this time, despite continual efforts from both Mexican and U.S. authorities, drugs continue to flow like a river from Mexico into the United States, and the illegal organizations continue to find ways to thwart law enforcement efforts to dismantle their operations.[8] These criminal organizations generate billions of dollars of profit and have the potential to disrupt financial markets in the United States. What's more, the vast amount of money available to these organizations buys them power and influence; a significant factor in their strength and resilience.

Behind the Line

Retired Sheriff's Sergeant, Richard Valdemar, has been on the front lines against evil his entire career, and I'm fortunate to have him as a friend, mentor and contributor. Richard retired from the Los Angeles County Sheriff's Department (LASD) in 2004. For most of his 33 years with the LASD he was involved in combating Los Angeles, California, gangs. For the last 20 years he was assigned to the Detective Division, Major Crimes Bureau. In 1977-78 he was assigned to the DEA and later to the U.S. Marshals, in the "Doc Holiday - Ray Ray Browning" federal drug conspiracy case. For more than 10 years he was part of the Federal Metropolitan Gang Task Force, cross designated as an FBI agent. Since 1985 he was a member of the California (Prison) Gang Task Force. He was the "gang expert" in the U.S. Federal RICO Act (Racketeer Influence Corrupt Organization) prosecution of the Mexican Mafia in 1995 and 1999. He provided technical assistance and supervised the real Hispanic and African-American gang members used in the Michael Jackson music video "Beat It." He was a technical advisor for the movies "*Drug Wars – The Kiki Camarena Story*" and "*A Man Apart*" starring Vin Diesel and Lorenz Tate. In 2006 he was featured on the History Channel for segments on "*Military Policemen in Combat*" and the "*History of the Aryan Brotherhood*" prison gang. He was also featured on Fox News

Channel's national broadcast *"American Gangs: Ties To Terror?"* with Newt Gingrich and segments for MSNBC Scarborough Country and Fox News Hannity & Colmes on the subjects of *"Gangs in the Military"* and *"Gangs and Illegal Immigration."*

Richard Valdemar
(photo courtesy of Sheriffs' Border School)

Behind the Line – Testimonial 3: "Blood Brothers — Cartel Ties That Bind"

with Richard Valdemar, International Gang Expert

Like the unwanted dandelions that sprout in lawns, the cartel and gang partners continue to adapt and survive. The code of conduct that restrained them in the past has disappeared.

Their terrible acts of violence and cruelty continue to escalate along with their intention to corrupt our police, courts and political system. Those they cannot corrupt, they murder. That includes journalists, police, judges, soldiers, religious leaders, women and children.

When the cartel-gang alliance combines to work together they are a serious threat to our national security. U.S. street and prison gangs have done business with the Mexican drug traffickers since the 1920s. No one gang or Mexican cartel had exclusive agreements with one another. It was basically a free market with some of the larger more powerful gangs forming alliances in Mexico.

In the 1970s, California's Mexican Mafia prison gang members, such as Joe 'Pegleg' Morgan, cultivated friendships with Mexican nationals while serving time with them in state and federal prisons. One such connection was Jesus 'Chuy' Arajo, a trafficker with connections to Mexican suppliers.

Alex 'Hondo' Lechuga—a Mexican Mafia member and homeboy of Luis 'Huero Buff' Flores, the founder of the Mexican Mafia—had his own connections, and he owned businesses in Juarez, Mexico. Half-Mexican and half-Korean Mafia member, Manuel 'Mad Korean' Enerva from San Diego, also had his own connections. His father was a police officer in Baja, California.

31

In fact, several San Diego street gangs such as Shell Town, Logan Heights, National City, Pasole and Del Sol had developed strong alliances in Mexico—alliances which were often temporary and only between a few members rather than the whole gang or any single cartel. However, U.S. Latino gangs often protected Mexican cartel members while in U.S. custody or in the gang turf. Mexican cartels often employed U.S. gang members in Mexico when they were 'on the run' from U.S. authorities.

David 'Popeye' Barron was a Logan Heights gang member from 30th Street in San Diego. He was also a member of the California Mexican Mafia prison gang and crossed over the border to do business with the Arellano Felix brothers in Mexico.

On November 8, 1992, 'Popeye' Barron attended a business meeting with a few of the Arellano brothers as part of their security people. They all met in Puerta Vallarta, Mexico, at 'Christine's,' a popular discotheque.

Unknown to the Arellanos and their security, Sinaloa Cartel leader Joaquin 'Chapo' Guzman had organized an ambush with his hit men dressed like cops, much like the infamous St. Valentine's Day Massacre in Chicago.

'Chapo' Guzman led 40 men dressed like Federales into Christine's with pistols drawn and shouting like policemen. The trick didn't work. A fierce gun battle erupted with 'Chapo's' men killing many innocent patrons and only eight Arellano associates.

In the fog of the fire fight, the American gangster 'Popeye' Barron distinguished himself by grabbing a weapon and shooting several of 'Chapo's' police assassins. Risking his own life to protect the Arellanos, he moved them into the bathroom. He returned to the discotheque floor, rearmed himself with guns stripped from the dead, and again engaged 'Chapo's' hit men long enough to get the Arellano brothers to safety via the skylight. He hailed a taxi to the local police commandante to secure more weapons and then returned to the discotheque.

For his bravery and coolness under fire, the Arellanos rewarded 'Popeye' Barron with the position of chief enforcer and hoped more soldiers were like him.

'Popeye' Barron would later recruit fellow Mexican Mafia member Jose 'Bat' Marquez from San Diego's Del Sol gang along with many other members from various San Diego street gangs that he trained as Arellano enforcers.

'Popeye's' enforcers, or sicarios (Spanish for assassin), killed on both sides of the border. In 1993, 26 murders occurred in San Diego as a result of a meth turf battle between the Arellano Felix Cartel and competing organizations.

In May of 1993, 'Popeye' Barron and 20 of his San Diego gang assassins were on their way to the Guadalajara Airport on Arellano's orders to hit 'Chapo' Guzman. Told that 'Chapo' would be driving a white Mercury Marquis, on May 24th - spotting what they thought was 'Chapo's' car - they riddled it with bullets. Instead of killing 'Chapo,' they mistakenly murdered Catholic Cardinal Juan Jesus Posadas-Ocampo and six other innocent victims.

Because the drug cartels and their corruption harm every facet of Mexican society, questions remain about Cardinal Ocampo's murder being a mistake, with the possibility the Cardinal was the intended target all along. Cardinal Ocampo had told a childhood friend weeks before his death that he had been threatened when he was called to the home of Mexican President Carlos Salinas.

It is alleged that Cardinal Ocampo had uncovered links between senior politicians and the drug and prostitution trade. President Salina's brother, Raul Salinas, is currently serving a 27-year sentence for the murder of his brother-in-law and 'illegal enrichment' for his links to the drug cartels.

In a deal struck in Mexico between Benjamin Arellano Felix and the police, two Logan Heights members of the hit team were surrendered—Juan Enrique Vasconez and Ramon 'Spooky' Torres Mendez. Vasconez received nine years on Mexican weapons charges. 'Spooky' Torres was killed while awaiting trial.

Prosecutors in the U.S. charged nine Logan Heights members with Cardinal Ocampo's hit squad murder. Three pled guilty and received 18 to 22 years in prison.

My LASD Prison Gang Unit had developed an important informant in the Mexican Mafia. Ernest 'Chuco' Castro was a respected member of the Varrio Nuevo Estrada (VNE) Gang in Los Angeles and a shot caller in the Mexican Mafia. The EME (Mexican Mafia) had begun taxing and controlling street gangs in Los Angeles, Orange, and San Bernardino counties.

The EME leaders would meet once or twice a month at a motel or hotel. Unknown to them, we had formed a multiagency task force with the FBI, LAPD and California Department of Corrections. We were covertly monitoring their meetings and wire-tapping their phones.

On a sunny Saturday, June 25, 1994, at a Days Inn in Monterey Park, California, a dozen or so Mexican Mafia members met in one of the motel rooms. The meeting was recorded with both audio and video tapes. Attending this meeting was Jose 'Bat' Marquez. This is how I first heard about the Christine's discotheque shoot-out and the assassination of Cardinal Posada-Ocampo, as narrated by EME member 'Bat' Marquez.

'Bat's' purpose was to ask his Mafia brothers to assist 'Popeye' Barron and the Arellanos to find and kill 'Chapo' Guzman—the head of the Sinaloa Cartel. The Arellanos offered $2 million and their choice of any Mexican state. They also offered drugs and 'heavy artillery' and their help crossing it into the U.S.

'Bat' Marquez warned that it would not be easy. He said that 'Chapo' neither drinks nor uses drugs, takes care of his family and soldiers, has a 40-man security force, drives a tricked out four-wheel-drive armored car and does car bombings as well. 'Chapo' does have a weakness. He worships Satan. However, when his small son took ill 'Chapo' brought him to the U.S. for treatment for he doesn't trust Mexican doctors or hospitals.

'Bat' Marquez said that he wanted to start a chemical lab store and would pick up five drums of ephedrine the following week in Mexico. He would keep the chemicals on the Mexican side of the border and the EME brothers were welcome to use all they wanted. 'Bat' Marquez only asked for help on how to make the meth, not to use it personally.

Several Mexican Mafia members who attended this meeting took trips to Tijuana in the days that followed. Several returned with ephedrine or meth. But 22 of them would be arrested on April 29, 1995, and charged under federal RICO statutes. If we hadn't broken up their games, I'm sure they would have cemented a closer, more dangerous alliance with the Arellano Felix Tijuana cartel. And many more people would have been murdered.

In San Diego, January of 1995, a multi-agency task force comprised of the DEA, FBI, Federal Immigration Officers, Federal Marshals, Customs and the Chula Vista Police Officers, was formed to combat the Arellano Felix Organization (AFO). The task force would also eventually charge and convict numerous members of the U.S. street gangs and the Mexican Mafia members as well.

On November 10, 1997, the 'Popeye' Barron-Arellano hit team killed two Mexican soldiers in front of the Tijuana court house. The local Zeta Weekly news magazine named David 'Popeye' Barron as the assassin.

Angered by the accusation, on November 22, 1997, 'Popeye' Barron and his hit team ambushed the Zeta Weekly Editor, Jesus Blancornelas, seriously wounding him and killing his bodyguard and driver. In the ambush a stray round glanced off the pavement hitting 'Popeye' above the eye. David 'Popeye' Barron was dead.

In addition, because of the courageous news stories by investigative television reporter Chris Blatchford, together with the effective work of Mexican Army Major Felipe Perez-Cruz of the Office of the General Prosecutor (Procuraduria General de la Republica, PGR), the public's awareness on both sides of the border played a part in bringing down the Arellano Felix brothers and their bloody Mexican Mafia assassins.

One by one, the Arellano Felix leadership began to fall. Jesus Labra-Aviles, a cartel lieutenant, was arrested in March of 2000. In February of 2002, Arellano muscleman, Ramón, on his way to murder rival Ismael 'Mayo' Zambada in Mazatlan, was shot by police loyal to Zambada. Arellano brother Benjamin was arrested in March 9, 2002 followed by Ismael 'El Mayel' Higuera Guererro in May and Manuel 'Tarzan' Herrera, an important Arellano smuggler, a few days later.

Francisco Javier Arellano Felix was arrested by the U.S. Coast Guard off the Baja California coast, and Eduardo Arellano Felix was captured after a shoot-out in Tijuana by Mexican soldiers on October 26, 2008. Despite these arrests, the Cartel lives on.

— Richard Valdemar

In the following sections, we will examine the structure of the AF-DTO and how it operates. We will also review the previous efforts made by law enforcement to dismantle the organization and study the strengths of AF-DTO that have enabled the organization to withstand those efforts. As mentioned earlier, the structure of DTOs plays an enormous role in their success and their resilience. A winning strategy against worldwide evil organizations begins here—with a comprehensive and thorough understanding of the AF-DTO. If we examine their evolution and their resilience, we can use that knowledge globally to begin our march against the shadows.

The U.S. and Mexican governments have long had a unique relationship. Since 2008, U.S. and Mexico have sought to combat the threats of drug trafficking, transnational organized crime, and money laundering by engaging in a security partnership called the *Mérida Initiative*. These two countries, which share a common border, also share a common problem: illegal narcotics. One *consumes* large quantities of what the other *provides*. The United States consumes more illegal narcotics than any other country in the world, and the largest supply of illegal drugs into the United States (70 percent) comes across the Mexican border.[9] The supply and demand of narcotics between these countries have created an underground criminal world of drug lords. The drug lords torture and kill anyone who gets in the way of their trafficking.[10] Law enforcement, with the support of a concerned citizenry, must bring these criminals to justice and dismantle their organizations. Mexican and American citizens, through their representative governments, must fully understand the gravity of the situation, what is at stake, and what we can do about it. The average person knows little about Mexican drug trafficking organizations and this creates a challenge that must be addressed.[11] If we are to win against this certain evil, we must not place the sole burden on the backs of law enforcement and military. Rather, the burden should be shared by each of us willing to fight.

A History Lesson

Historically, the term *"cartel"* refers to a combination of independent business organizations formed to regulate production, pricing, and marketing of goods by the members.[12] Though still true to its origins, over the years the term "cartel" has come to signify a DTO or narco-terrorist organization that simply will stop at nothing to make a profit no matter how many die in the process. These organizations are under tremendous pressures from law enforcement organizations and the military trying to dismantle them (the same can be said for al-Qaeda, worldwide). But even with unrelenting pressure, the cartels are able to thrive. To substantiate this point, Rusty Fleming explains in his documentary film, *Drug Wars*, you have to ask the question: "Who's really in control of our border? The narco that gets 98 percent of his drugs through or the border agent that stops 2 percent of them?"[13]

A nation must have the political will and stomach to fight a long war. Of course, deaths will occur, and of course it will be difficult to see these images on TV. But does that mean we'll turn off the TV and forget the true world outside of the safety of our homes? For some, and some of those in power around the globe, the answer is a resounding "yes." Cowardice is exactly what feeds evil. It looks for the weakest and pounces, much like a hungry lion in the jungle. It's true what we hear— *only the strong survive*. I argue that the strength does not have to be brute muscle, but rather, mental courage and a faith in God. It's a fact that good and evil exists on our planet. They do not coexist peacefully, nor should they. No matter where we live each of us shares the same sun, the same moon and the same stars. From Iraq to Los Angeles, we are humans put on earth by our Maker for a reason. Sadly, many choose to walk the path of *darkness*. Those of us who have chosen the path of *light* must each make a personal decision: *"Will I have done all I can to make this world a better place by the end of my time on earth?"* It's a critical question and one that requires a deeper look into ourselves and into the heart of evil. By the time you have finished this book, you may see your role in this battle. Let's begin.

Until now, no in-depth investigation has been conducted to examine the vulnerabilities of these organizations and how these weaknesses could be exploited. Without sufficiently understanding the inner workings of cartels, authorities cannot do the job they are supposed to be doing—dismantling the cartels.

Dating back to the Colombian drug cartels in the 1960s and 1970s, DTOs have employed brutal tactics. This leads some to believe that cartels are merely a gang of thugs with guns and an evil predisposition. But there's much more to the story. True, cartels are made up of thugs. True, they have weapons and are not afraid to use them. True, these groups are some of the most vicious to inhabit our planet; but it's also true that these organizations are highly sophisticated. Much like al-Qaeda in Iraq, drug cartels have a highly refined system for doing business. They conduct operations in a way that enables them not only to survive but also to thrive in chaotic environments, despite heavy pressure from law enforcement agencies on a scale the likes of which we have never seen before.

When I was in Iraq, I was stunned to learn the scope of al-Qaeda's operations. While most people rightly look at al-Qaeda as a bunch of gangsters inciting violence for the sake of violence, they would be surprised to learn, for example, that their accounting practices tightly control cell operations and the use of supplies right down to the number of staples.

It's the same situation with the cartels. We are talking about organizations that hire the best financial advisors money can buy— which isn't hard to do in a country like Mexico with an already dismal (and ever declining) infrastructure and lack of good jobs—not to mention the fact they will murder you and your family if you refuse their offers of money with an utter absence of conscience!

The business behind the illegal drug trade is ruthless. Drug cartels have built empires similar to those of the early Twentieth Century U.S.-based Mafia families. In 1998, Drug Enforcement Administration (DEA) administrator Thomas Constantine provided Congressional testimony before the *Senate Foreign Relations Committee* regarding international organized crime syndicates and their impact on the United States. In his testimony, Constantine discussed four of Mexico's largest drug cartels, one of those he identified as the AF-DTO. He described these cartels as *"the 1990's version of the mob leaders U.S. law enforcement fought shortly after the turn of the century."*[14] He adds that the modern cartels are far more dangerous and influential.

He explained that the United States was able to dismantle U.S. mob organizations (home-grown) only after acknowledging the dangers they posed to the American way of life. He drew a parallel to the AF-DTO, insinuating that we, as a culture, have yet to fully recognize the dangers of Mexican DTOs and the problem in fully dismantling these DTOs is failure to consistently recognize them.

The cartels employ a pyramid structure and chain of command. This structure is not unlike that found in the military, and it was also common in the U.S. Italian Mafia families. While each cartel differs with regard to its specific structure, they all have at least one leader and, in some cases, a number of leaders, who reside at the top of the pyramid. Beneath the leaders are lieutenants, who are akin to the Italian mafia's "capos" or captains. At the bottom of the pyramid, we find the more numerous foot soldiers or enforcers.

In order to survive, DTOs have the ability to transform themselves overnight into revolutionaries. When catastrophe strikes, DTOs demonstrate "punctuated equilibrium" (rapid evolution) and understand immediately that they must change when subjected to pressure of exposure or they will die. Take, for instance, one example regarding money. As the U.S. became increasingly more effective in their efforts at monitoring electronic money transfers, DTOs quickly adapted, resorting to smuggling cash in vehicles across the border from the U.S. into Mexico.[15] This simple example also demonstrates their biggest strength—the ability to *adapt*.

Cartel Strengths

DTOs have adapted over time into transnational organizations in scope while also displaying "a degree of flexibility and adaptability in methods and modes that pose considerable challenges for intelligence, law enforcement agencies, and society at large."[16] The cartels have no choice: if they don't adapt, they will go out of business. Researchers Williams and Godson describe four types of "states"—also known as "political conditions"—that categorize most of today's countries. They theorize that DTOs survive best in the "weak state" (where there is government corruption), which allows opportunities for organized crime to grow with little interference. In the weak state, DTOs flourish, using the state as a home base.

Successful criminal networks:

- are flexible and adaptable;
- can respond quickly to market opportunities and the actions of law enforcement;
- are highly resistant to disruption, even after losses;
- can recruit new members;
- extend across national borders;
- can conduct legitimate business alongside illegal operations;

- can recruit police and corrupt politicians and judges (i.e., the decision makers); and

- possess safeguards against penetration, as well as a high degree of redundancy that *"makes them highly resilient to disruption and provides a significant capacity for reconstitution in the event that they are damaged."*[17]

Cartels employ various techniques to ensure their survival. The strategic model, also known as the Risk Management Model (Figure 1, below),[18] provides an understanding of their formula for success. The model demonstrates that these criminal organizations seek not simply to maintain their existence, but also to maximize their profits while minimizing risks with authorities.[19]

RISK MANAGEMENT MODEL: Risk management model is based on the idea that criminal organizations are in adversarial relationships in which strategy is critical	IMPLICATIONS: Criminal organizations will develop a comprehensive range of measures aimed at the prevention, control and mitigation of the risk they face from law enforcement and rivals	RESULT TO ANTICIPATE: Organized crime will seek safe havens from which to operate and will look to neutralize governments and law enforcement agencies through corruption, counterintelligence and security practices, including making greater use of information technologies

Figure 1: Criminal Risk Management Model

The theory looks at the concept of wit, with one entity attempting to outsmart the other. Criminal organizations are interested in more than just survival; they are uniquely separate from legitimate businesses. DTO members worry about going to jail or being killed. Three measures that can be considered risk-management strategies are:

(1) initiatives created for risk prevention (e.g., initiatives for protecting leaders, continued operation of the organization, and the ability to work in low-risk environments);

(2) defense measures and tactics used to minimize risks (i.e., incorporating counterintelligence and state-of-the-art technology to provide warning of law enforcement activity); and

(3) measures built to mitigate potential harm "and ensure the organization exhibits a high degree of resilience, even in hostile environments where defensive measures have proved inadequate."[20]

Other strengths of criminal organizations exist in the realm of leadership, including the following:

- obtaining safe haven;
- operating secretly;
- insisting on the highest levels of protection; and
- developing high-level disguise and concealment products.

Behind the Line – Testimonial 4: "Street Gangs & Cartels"

with DEA Director of International Operations, Michael S. Vigil, Ret.

The large scale Mexican drug trafficking organizations have traditionally used violent Hispanic gangs situated on the U.S. side of the border to provide security, conduct homicides, and distribute drugs. One of the largest and most sophisticated gangs is in the San Diego area. It is known as the Logan Heights Street Gang (LHSG) which has its origins in the oldest barrios in San Diego. The gang numbers are in the hundreds and have spread throughout many areas along the border, and they are closely affiliated with the Arellano Felix drug cartel based in Tijuana, Baja California Norte, Mexico. The Arellano Felix organization is responsible for smuggling tons of cocaine and marijuana into the U.S. on an annual basis. In 1993, the Arellano Felix brothers contracted the LHSG to travel to Guadalajara in hopes of locating and killing a rival drug trafficker by the name of Joaquin Guzman Loera AKA Chapo Guzman. They were unable to locate him and were at the Guadalajara International Airport waiting for their flight to return to Tijuana. Many of the gang members waited outside the airport terminal. By coincidence, Guzman was entering the area of the Guadalajara airport in a taxi and observed members of the LHSG huddled outside of the airport and quickly departed. Shortly thereafter, Roman Catholic Cardinal Juan Jesus Posadas-Ocampo arrived at the airport in a Mercury Marquis town car, and the LHSG members mistook him for Guzman and opened fire on him. He was killed instantly, and the gang members were subsequently allowed to board a local flight to Tijuana with the weapons used to kill the Cardinal.

In 1997, a LHGS leader named David Barron who was a ruthless killer and had been involved in the killing of Cardinal Posadas-Ocampo was contacted by the Arellano Felix organization. They instructed him to form a "hit team" to assassinate Zeta newspaper editor, Jesus Blancornelas, who regularly wrote articles denouncing the drug traffickers operating in the area. Barron crossed the border with his group of assassins and they ambushed Blancornelas as he was traveling down a street in downtown Tijuana in his vehicle. In the premeditated ambush, Blancornelas was seriously wounded, but survived the attack. His driver and bodyguard were both killed. Destiny also dealt Barron death at the hands of his own assassins. He was shot in the eye as a result of the crossfire and died on the sidewalk, propped against his shotgun with blood from his head flowing into the gutter.

During my tenure as the Special Agent in Charge of the DEA San Diego Division, we conducted numerous investigations into the LHSG and put many of them in federal prison. Unfortunately, it was my experience that many young kids idolized gang members as individuals because of their power and money. They view them as role models and want to emulate them, which tragically has created a continuous pool from which to recruit additional gang members.

I am of the opinion that we must sever the tentacles between U.S. based gangs on the border and the Mexican drug cartels by exchanging information with Mexican authorities, creating viable databases of information regarding these gangs, seeking prosecutions on both sides of the border, identifying gang leaders and organizational hierarchy in order to conduct a top to bottom dismantling of these networks, seek RICO and Continuing Criminal Enterprise (CCE) prosecutions for long term prison sentences, etc. The LHSG is but one of many that operate along the U.S./Mexico border and provide criminal support to many of the most significant drug cartels on the Mexican side. They feel that they can commit crimes in Mexico and then flee back into the U.S. to avoid capture and prosecutions.

— Michael S. Vigil

Drug Cartel Structure

The basic structure of a drug cartel resembles that of a typical legitimate organization. It consists of five main divisions with one top leadership command. Figure 2 shows the leaders of the divisions, and Figure 3 shows the functions of the divisions. The top leadership command is largely made up of blood relatives or highly trusted agents (in the case of al-Qaeda), together with a council of advisors, or core. The core is responsible for making significant decisions and directing orders to the five divisions. Although the cartel has a strong centralized decision-making process and a hierarchical structure, the family members who make up the top leadership, accompanied by a core board of advisors, help the organization continue operating.

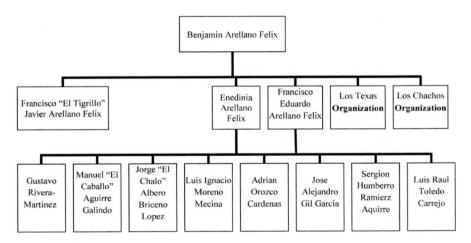

Figure 2. Historical AF-DTO Leadership Structure[21]

Figure 3. AF-DTO Functional Structure Example

Kenney describes cartels as being highly organized: "Compared with drug enforcement bureaucracies, trafficking enterprises are relatively small and flat."[22] They also contain fewer management layers, and this structure allows for quick decisions and better protection of leaders. While their counterparts in law enforcement often contain thousands of participants organized within many management levels, cartels do not. Kenney notes that in 2000, the DEA had over 9,000 employees and 4,500 special agents organized into many layers. He states, *"Information—the basic building block of intelligence—tends to travel faster when it flows through fewer processing channels."*[23] The opportunity to distort, suppress or misinterpret information increases with more channels. Hence, the small, flat structure of the cartel allows for a much faster transition of intelligence which is most effective when it is timely.

Another key hindrance to timely decision making among authorities is the "red tape" that must be dealt with before executing orders. This red tape (also known as bureaucracy) does not exist in DTOs.[24] When a cartel needs to buy a piece of equipment, it does so on the spot. If it wants to change its mission, its goals and its objectives, it can do so quickly. The ability to work quickly is essential to success. Cartels have the definite edge in this key ability, and they use it to their advantage.

DTO Operations

DTOs are made up of a number of divisions, each with a significant responsibility. The first division is charged with gathering intelligence and reporting that intelligence to the top command. The intelligence is gathered by infiltrating government institutions and police agencies. The corruption of the federal police is so rampant in Mexico that 3,200 officers, or nearly one-tenth of the force, have been fired this year under new measures to weed out corruption. Eliminating government corruption is just one aspect of President Calderon's nearly four-year-old war against DTOs. Corrupt police officers gather information to tip off drug cartels and even work for the cartels as hit men.[25] The intelligence division has a collateral duty of engaging foreign criminal organizations (largely in Colombia) to negotiate prices, shipments, routes for shipments and quotas.

The next division consists of assassins. Their primary role is the elimination of traitors, police and rivals (they operate globally.) In addition to employing their own gangs of enforcers and assassins south of the border, DTOs have extended their deadly reach into the United States by uniting with U.S. prison and street gangs such as MS-13 and the Latin Kings. The assassins' collateral duties involve protecting their top leaders and escorting drug shipments.

The third division is the financial arm of the organization, dedicated to money laundering and investments. These employees are educated, young and experienced in management and finances.

The fourth division involves distribution and ensures that shipments reach their ultimate destinations on the streets.

The fifth and final division involves spying on rivals so that the cartels can keep their competition in check.[26]

This type of structure did not happen by chance or overnight. As the DTOs faced challenges, they adapted to those challenges. The same can be said for any sinister organization still operating today— only the strong survive.

Behind the Line – Testimonial 5: "The War"

with DEA Director of International Operations, Michael S. Vigil, Ret.

Mexicans know that drug trafficking and transnational crimes are a threat to their national security and the well-being of their citizens. I remember one of the federal prosecutors in Mexico, Pedro Mireles Malpica. He resembled Ebenezer Scrooge—very old, tall and gaunt, and somewhat intolerant of certain individuals. I always had a great relationship with him and he trusted and confided in me. He carried a .45 caliber semi-automatic handgun and wore five clips on his belt. He also carried a large knife and I often wondered how he carried all that weight. Carrying multiple weapons made a lot of sense because the Mexican police were constantly under attack or engaged in arrests involving gun battles. They used all measures, and rightfully so, to defend themselves. During one meeting, Mireles Malpica, explained, "If the traffickers kill one of us, we will kill 40 of them in order to teach them that they can't do this – they will pay, and pay heavily, for their actions."

That's exactly the way justice was executed at that time. It was a very harsh rule of law; something I don't think they wanted to do, but they also understood they were playing in the big leagues -- it was hardball! The Mexican Federal Judicial Police (MFJP) at that time numbered near 2,000 strong and covered all 33 of the Mexican states.

In order to act as a force multiplier, the MFJP hired individuals who were not trained nor part of the police force—the so called "Madrinas." They were somewhat like our auxiliary police but many had shady backgrounds. They basically did the dirty work and were paid by the individual Federale agent. One of the unsavory activities by the MFJP

Madrinas included sometimes killing each other while drinking!

One of the most significant incidents we had in Mexico occurred in1985 when Kiki Camarena was kidnapped, brutally tortured, and murdered in Guadalajara. The traffickers interrogated Kiki prior to killing him and made tape recordings of the interrogation. The tapes vividly depicted the inhumane torture that he had to endure.

By the time Kiki was abducted and murdered, I had been transferred to Medellin, Colombia. However, after receiving threats from one of the insurgent organizations, the National Liberation Army (ELN,) I was forced to move to the city of Barranquilla located on the Colombian north coast, a staging area for large quantities of drugs destined for the U.S. and other countries. While in Barranquilla, a massive manhunt focused on the murderers of Kiki, namely: Miguel Felix Gallardo, Ernesto Fonseca Carrillo, Rafael Caro Quintero and their Honduran supplier, Juan Ramon Matta Ballesteros. We had numerous wiretaps that had been initiated in many different countries to locate these violent traffickers. We also had hundreds of other sources, primarily informants in Latin America, the Caribbean and Europe, providing information. This enabled us to identify an individual by the name of Jaime Garcia who lived in Cartagena, Colombia, and was associated with Matta Ballesteros.

We rented a house across the street from Garcia's residence so that DEA and Colombian police agents could conduct surveillance and monitor the activities at the house. Our strategy was not to raid the residence until we were absolutely certain that Matta Ballesteros was inside. We had a limited view of the residence and were obstructed from being able to see the front door because of the configuration of the carport. Obviously, we could not have someone standing in front of the residence, therefore we occasionally had someone casually walk on the street and attempt to determine any activity indicating the presence of Matta Ballesteros. Also making it difficult was that the vehicles parked at the house all had tinted windows. The occupants of the residence never parked on the street and would exit the residence very quickly and enter the vehicles. Hence, we could not determine with any certainty if Matta Ballesteros was actually at the residence. However, we subsequently initiated a wire intercept on the telephone registered to the residence. One day that proved interesting.

We intercepted a call in which Jaime Garcia tells the maid to get everything ready because "El Señor" is coming and everything has to be done. A couple of days later, we observed a vehicle leave the residence. It traveled to a local hotel and picked up two people. We followed the vehicle on Colombian police motorcycles to a restaurant a few miles away. The two individuals from the hotel were left at the restaurant and the vehicle then returned to the Garcia residence. Less than a minute later, the vehicle left again with a second individual from the residence and went to the restaurant and retrieved the same two individuals who had been left there a few minutes earlier. We eventually lost the vehicle as it traveled into a highly populated residential area. We knew from surveillance that what was occurring was not normal activity.

One thing was obvious; the individual staying at the residence did not want anyone to know his location. Later, we observed the vehicle with only two individuals return to the residence, but could not determine if one of them was Matta Ballesteros. I have always been a calculating gambler, and based on the suspicious activities and movement at the residence, decided that Matta Ballesteros had to be present. I then requested a force of about thirty Colombian police. We surrounded the house and knocked on the door, but no one answered. This activity continued for about 30 seconds, and suddenly, a maid appeared and opened a side window and greeted us. I told her that we were National Police and we had a search warrant for weapons. I asked her to open the door, but she refused and was visibly nervous. A moment later, Matta Ballesteros appeared at the window and inquired as to our identity. I repeated what I had told to the maid. He also refused to open the door and quickly moved away from the window. At this time, I kicked the door in and observed Matta Ballesteros running through the courtyard with a .9mm gun in his hand. He jumped on top of a wall in the backyard and fell between that one and a second wall. We wondered why he had not been able to jump the second wall.

Later, we determined that he recently had back surgery and fortunately was not able to make it over the second wall. He landed on his back and initially began to point the weapon in a threatening manner, but quickly decided to drop it. He yelled that he could get out of any prison, but not out of a tomb. Once in custody, he offered us a bribe of $3 million and added that he could have it delivered in about 20 minutes. We told him to shove it! He bragged about being able to get out of any prison. Later that night we transported him to Bogotá and placed him in the Picota Penitentiary. During the flight to Bogota, Ballesteros congratulated me on his capture and stated that no one else had been able to accomplish it in more than 20 years. Several months later, he paid over $4 million to the prison guards, walked out of prison and entered a Mercedes Benz waiting for him outside. He drove to the El Dorado Airport in Bogotá and boarded a private twin engine aircraft that flew him to Honduras, his native country. At that time, Honduras did not have an extradition treaty with the United States. Two murder charges were open against Matta Ballesteros in Honduras, but he quickly resolved them by paying significant bribes to the local authorities. Tired but not defeated, we pressed on.

After much pressure was brought to bear on the Honduran government, they graciously allowed for Matta Ballesteros to be arrested in Teguchigalpa and expelled to the United States. To this day, I still remember him getting off the plane in the U.S. with an apple in his hand displaying the most perplexed look on his face. He is now serving three consecutive life sentences!

The Camarena investigation known as Operation Leyenda continued with high intensity in order to bring justice to all of the individuals involved in this heinous crime. In 1990, the DEA abducted Dr. Humberto Alvarez-Machain, a doctor based in Guadalajara, Jalisco, who had administered drugs to maintain Camarena's consciousness during his brutal torture and interrogation. Mexico failed to arrest Machain after his earlier indictment in Los Angeles, California. As a result, the DEA paid Mexican informants to abduct Alvarez-Machain and clandestinely transport him to El Paso, Texas. This operation aroused Mexican furor, and even more so when the United States Court of Appeals ruled in June 1992 that the abduction did not violate American law. Consequently, Alvarez-Machain was ultimately released in December 1992 with a directed verdict of "acquittal."

During the same year, the Government of Mexico imposed the first written regulations that the DEA had faced anywhere in the world. The rules capped the number of DEA agents in Mexico, designated a half-dozen cities in which they must live, prohibited them from traveling without written Mexico Government consent, denied DEA agents diplomatic immunity from prosecution, and stipulated that all useful intelligence information "must be immediately transmitted to the competent Mexican authorities." They prohibited DEA agents from carrying weapons in Mexico.

I played a role in the negotiations of the "Rules of the Game." The negotiations were primarily with Jorge Tello Peon who at the time was the CENDRO Director. CENDRO was the Mexican National Intelligence Center that I helped create with Tello Peon. Tello Peon later became the head of the National Institute for the Combating of Drugs (INCD) and subsequently the Director of the National Center for National Security Investigations (CISEN). The rules were established to placate the Mexican citizens who were irate over the abduction of Alvarez-Machain. Tello Peon advised me that we should not play hard ball on the rules since they would not hold us to the strict language. I understood him perfectly. Frankly, they did not impose significant restrictions on the way we operated in Mexico.

The drug trafficking organizations in Mexico have tremendous power. Many individuals are of the opinion that Mexico could become a failed state. I am positive that will never occur because of the efforts and massive campaign that Mexico is currently waging against the drug trafficking community, and crime in general. The Mexican government continues to make many sacrifices against the drug cartels, and in the end they will prevail. One major reason, they have come a long way in professionalizing their security forces and developing their capabilities and infrastructure. Mexico fully recognizes that drug trafficking is a very insidious problem. It is their number one national security threat!

Colombia stands as an example to other countries, like Mexico, of what could happen if the drug traffickers gained too much power, as seen in the 70's and 80's. This was during the era of Pablo Escobar and other major traffickers who killed police officers and political figures on a whim. Murders in Medellin, Colombia could be accomplished for a mere $50. But Colombia waged a large and effective campaign against the drug traffickers that placed the entire country in jeopardy. Leaders like the Director General of the Colombian National Police, General Serrano and General Leonardo Gallego dismantled many of the largest cartels operating in the country. The sacrifices were huge and came with the loss of many friends. Drug trafficking in Mexico is an evil force – a force that constantly degrades economics, politics and the society of that nation, but I know that Mexico will prevail.

— *Michael S. Vigil*

Significant Sampling of Mexican Drug Trafficking Leaders

Joaquín Guzmán, AKA *"Chapo"*
(Shorty) of the Sinaloa Cartel
(photo courtesy of law enforcement)

Ismael Zambada, AKA *"El Rey"* (The King) of the Sinaloa Cartel
(photo courtesy of law enforcement)

Heriberto Lazcano, AKA *"El Lazca, Z-3"* (The Executioner) of the Los Zetas Organization
(photo courtesy of law enforcement)

Vicente Carrillo Fuentes, AKA *"The Viceroy"* of the Juarez Cartel
(photo courtesy of law enforcement)

Jorge Eduardo Costilla, AKA *"El Coss"* of the Gulf Cartel
(photo courtesy of law enforcement)

Héctor Beltrán Leyva, AKA *"El H"* of the Beltran Leyva Organization
(photo courtesy of law enforcement)

Nazario Moreno González, AKA *"El Mas Loco"* (The Maddest One), El Chayo of La Familia Michoacana Organization
(photo courtesy of law enforcement)

Juan José Esparragoza, AKA *"El Azul"* (The Blue), of the Sinaloa Cartel
(photo courtesy of law enforcement)

Antonio Ezequiel Cárdenas, AKA
"Tony Tormenta" of the Gulf Cartel
(photo courtesy of law enforcement)

Luis Fernando Sánchez Arellano,
AKA *"El Ingeniero"* (The Engineer) of
the Arellano Felix Cartel – also known
as the Tijuana Cartel.
(photo courtesy of law enforcement)

Chapter Four

The Inside of Global Evil: al-Qaeda

"Don't be afraid to see what you see."
— *Ronald Reagan, farewell address, Oval Office*

Al-Qaeda is known throughout the world as being one of the most violent and sinister organizations our planet has ever seen. While serving in Iraq, I saw firsthand just how evil the organization has become. Literally, there are no boundaries they won't cross, including the use of women and mentally challenged children to serve as human bombs.

As a military intelligence officer, I worked on a number of classified programs, and obviously, none of that information will be divulged in this book. However, I do not need top secret level clearance to understand the absolute brutality that al-Qaeda brings upon the innocent. What I found most frightening was not the level of violence al-Qaeda was willing to push throughout Iraq, but how eerily similar they were to the drug trafficking organizations in Mexico I studied for nearly a decade. Not only did both organizations use car bombs and behead victims, but their organizational structures appear nearly identical.

I arrived in Iraq in 2008 with a joint special operations task force serving under Lieutenant General McChrystal. The men and women I served with poured their heart and soul into defeating al-Qaeda throughout Iraq, while also protecting innocent Iraqis who often were the victims of al-Qaeda torture and killings. I sought and was granted permission to establish a first of its kind al-Qaeda interagency working group, which brought together joint intelligence professionals from around the battlefield to better share information as we worked together to dismantle al-Qaeda. What we learned was simple but very valuable: the harder you fight the enemy, the more diminished the enemy becomes. There is zero room to negotiate with the enemy. They respect and respond to only one thing, – an equal or high level of violence brought against them.

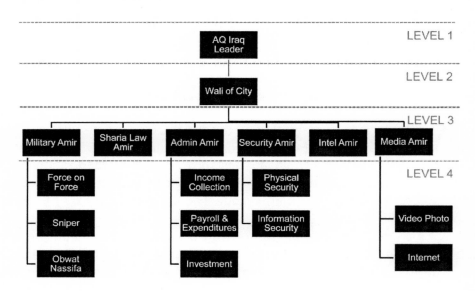

Figure 4. al-Qaeda Functional Structure

Al-Qaeda has evolved over time and refined their organizational structure. What we see today exemplifies an organizational hierarchy befitting a Fortune 500 company. Like any organization, al-Qaeda in Iraq has a leader, and under this leader are governor-like managers who run operations within a specific city/region. These managers are also referred to as *Walis*, and under the *Wali* is the second in command for a particular city, a position that goes by the name of *Naib-al-Wali*. He assists the *Wali* in all aspects of operations.

It's important to understand that while this level of al-Qaeda leaders control cities—in their mind and in their operations—they often split up geographic areas of responsibility based upon major geographic boundaries, which can include mountain ranges, large rivers and other similar geographic type boundaries. They want ultimate control and are meticulous in how they divide areas of responsibility.

We have now reached the third level of the al-Qaeda organizational structure, which is also the first operational component of the entire organization. It incorporates many leaders, also known as emirs, with significant operational control and responsibility. Each emir has jurisdictional control over a specified organizational component. For example, the *emir al-Askari* is known as the *military emir*; the *emir al-Sharia* has oversight over *Sharia law* (the law by which al-Qaeda governs itself and expects to govern others); the *emir al-Idari* is the administration leader; the *emir Amni* manages security; the *emir Istkbahrat Dahkliyah* manages internal affairs and intelligence collection; the media director is known as the *emir al-Elaami*. None of these emirs has control over the other. Each is completely independent and answers only to the *Naib al-Wali*.

The fourth level of the structure is composed of functional units where each emir has a command and control responsibility to carry out operations as tasked. Each of these emirs answers only to their emir or the *Naib al-Wali*. These functional units, for example, include the *emir al-Elaami*, responsible for photography, internet and video production. They provide promotional and propaganda materials to circulate around the globe as a form of advertisement for recruitment of fighters and for fund-raising. The *emir Amni* is responsible for both the physical security of their locations and for the security of their information. Next, the *emir al-Idari* runs the day-to-day accounting operations, which include payroll and expenditures, investment and income collection. The final emir, known as *al-Askari* is responsible for snipers and their operations, the building and dissemination of bombs, and for direct attacks on allied forces by the use of small arms, rocket propelled grenades, mortars, etc. These emir components act as the main body of operations for the entire al-Qaeda threat.

We now enter the fifth level of the organization known as "area leaders." These leaders (emirs) are subordinate to the fourth level and have specific geographic regional responsibility. While the size varies, it's safe to say that for a city the size of Bagdad, more than one area leader would be assigned to a specific portion of the city. Some areas may overlap and some areas may have no coverage at all. For those areas with coverage, each emir has operational control over a number of cells ranging from one to more than 15.

The final level of leadership is made up of cell-leaders, known as *emir al-Medjmua*. As noted above, there can be more than 15 cells or just one single cell. The typical number is somewhere between two and six. Each emir with authority over a functional unit has a number of responsibilities.

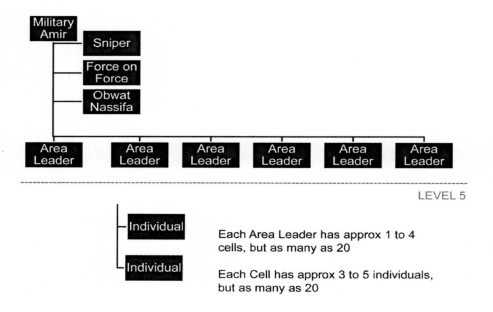

Figure 5. al-Qaeda Lower Level "Ground Operations"

- Security amir (*emir Amni*) has two separate roles. First, information security, as mentioned earlier, which involves the performance of various procedures and techniques to control orders and communications.
- Administrative amir (*emir al-ldari*) manages the administrative responsibility of the organization much like a chief financial

officer of a legitimate corporation, which includes payroll, expenditures and investments.

- Sharia amir (*emir Sharia*) acts largely alone but ensures that Sharia law is followed, implemented and enforced. This leader may act as a judge or manager over other Sharia judges.
- Media amir (*emir al-Elammi*) leads two distinct components. First, the photo and video sectors perform various types of recording of operations that include any other need for video/photo recording. The second area involves the social media sector, including managing websites and content and all information that passes through these technical means.
- Intelligence amir (*emir Istkhbahrat Danhkliyah*) oversees intelligence gathering and internal affairs. If, for example, someone was suspect in the organization, the subject(s) would be brought before either the Security Amir or Sharia Amir by the Intelligence Amir. A second component of responsibility is gathering information (i.e., intelligence) on various future targets, including people and locations.
- Military amir (*emir al-Askari*) has three primary areas of responsibilities under his command, including "direct action" operations (using the Intelligence Amir's information) known as *Houdjom*. The second is *Qanas*, which relates to sniper activities, and the final component is *Obwat Nasifa*, the building and placement of improvised explosives (roadside bombs).

This is the structure that we see within al-Qaeda. Of course, over time, they will make adjustments as we evolve in response to their threats and attempt to dismantle their structure. A resilient organization understands how important it is to adapt to its environment and its challenges. Al-Qaeda has done a very good job of doing just that, but as you have seen throughout this book, it's not only al-Qaeda which is able to adapt and be resilient. It's the nature of the beast around our globe.

Understanding how these organizations evolve into what they are is a necessary step in our global war. Everything starts from something—even evil begins small. In the following layout, you can see the progression or phases it will go through until it reaches ultimate strength—the domination phase.

Terror/Drug Organizations are Resilient Entities

They each grow in the same manner.. "Seed to Oak Tree"

1. Exist: Stay below the radar

2. Expand: Seek out like minded; co-opt the rest by bribery or force

3. Proliferate: Prove "your way" works betters

4. Dominate: Mandate "your way is the "only way"

Figure 6. Four Stages to Domination

Exist:

Al-Qaeda (AQ) in Iraq grew within this exact same context and before our very eyes. Within the first phase of "Existence," we observed the following:

- AQ Stayed below the radar; hard for others to detect.
- Dispatched security cells whose mission was to gather info through primarily human intelligence and counterintelligence, seeking out and collecting information on enemy personnel.
- This info is used to assess the physical, political, economic, security and religious environment in a specified area. From

here, you can begin to see the establishment of social networks to facilitate the arrival of other elements of the organization.

- The security cells are also gathering info on future targets, whether individuals or organizations.

Expansion:

- AQ's security cells seek out individuals or groups who share their ideology and bring them into the organization.
- These cells also co-opt those who do not volunteer using bribes or force.
- In this phase we begin to see administration, finance, Sharia and some media being established.
- AQ begins to use intelligence to conduct kidnappings for ransom as a source of funding and to use murder and intimidation campaigns to coerce the local populace into supporting their cause.

Proliferation:

- Here, AQ's cellular structure is in place and replicated in multiple locations in a hierarchical fashion. For example, admin cells at the local level report to a regional admin emir and ultimately the overall admin emir.
- AQ begins to utilize front companies and extortion as a means of financing operations.
- Media cells are functioning and facilitating both operational and strategic communications.
- Advancement of their propaganda increases as a form of providing proof of the ongoing hostility towards their enemies.
- The posting of attack claims to web forums is critical, as this becomes a key source of revenue and recruits and also serves as a warning to their enemies.

- By building a financial and personnel base, AQ message spreads and its organization grows.

Domination:

- AQ is virtually uncontested at this phase—very few threats. They have virtually complete freedom of movement with significant access to huge sums of money and recruits, which increases the speed of their efforts, initiatives and objectives.
- They become capable of building alliances with others or simply destroying them.
- The ability to incite sectarian violence is without challenge, and high profile attacks are committed at will.
- The organizational structure is supreme: a highly efficient and effective organizational structure of the various cells.
- They build operations outside of their sphere of influence to seek out new regions to conquer. In short, they are pursuing their dream of creating a caliphate—a land of their own with their own set of rules.

It is this level of refinement and dedication that remains virtually unparalleled in any "legit" industry. That being the case, it's hard for any person to fully grasp the enemy we are up against, the one that has perfected its survival by any means necessary.

Current List of U.S. Designated Foreign Terrorist Organizations

1. Liberation Tigers of Tamil Eelam (LTTE)
2. Libyan Islamic Fighting Group (LIFG)
3. Moroccan Islamic Combatant Group (GICM)
4. Mujahedin-e Khalq Organization (MEK)
5. National Liberation Army (ELN)
6. Palestine Liberation Front (PLF)
7. Palestinian Islamic Jihad (PIJ)
8. Popular Front for the Liberation of Palestine (PFLP)
9. PFLP-General Command (PFLP-GC)
10. al-Qaida in Iraq (AQI)
11. al-Qa'ida (AQ)
12. al-Qa'ida in the Arabian Peninsula (AQAP)
13. al-Qaida in the Islamic Maghreb (formerly GSPC)
14. Real IRA (RIRA)
15. Revolutionary Armed Forces of Colombia (FARC)
16. Revolutionary Organization 17 November (17N)
17. Revolutionary People's Liberation Party/Front (DHKP/C)
18. Revolutionary Struggle (RS)
19. Shining Path (Sendero Luminoso, SL)
20. United Self-Defense Forces of Colombia (AUC)
21. Harakat-ul Jihad Islami (HUJI)
22. Tehrik-e Taliban Pakistan (TTP)
23. Jundallah
24. Abu Nidal Organization (ANO)
25. Abu Sayyaf Group (ASG)
26. Al-Aqsa Martyrs Brigade (AAMS)
27. Al-Shabaab
28. Ansar al-Islam (AAI)
29. Asbat al-Ansar
30. Aum Shinrikyo (AUM)
31. Basque Fatherland and Liberty (ETA)
32. Communist Party of the Philippines/New People's Army (CPP/NPA)
33. Continuity Irish Republican Army (CIRA)
34. Gama'a al-Islamiyya (Islamic Group)
35. HAMAS (Islamic Resistance Movement)
36. Harakat ul-Jihad-i-Islami/Bangladesh (HUJI-B)
37. *Harakat ul-Mujahidin (HUM)*
38. *Hizballah (Party of God)*
39. *Islamic Jihad Union (IJU)*
40. Islamic Movement of Uzbekistan (IMU)
41. Jaish-e-Mohammed (JEM) (Army of Mohammed)
42. Jemaah Islamiya organization (JI)
43. Kahane Chai (Kach)
44. Kata'ib Hizballah (KH)
45. Kongra-Gel (KGK, formerly Kurdistan Workers' Party, PKK, KADEK)
46. Lashkar-e Tayyiba (LT) (Army of the Righteous)
47. Lashkar i Jhangvi (LJ)

Source: U.S. State Department, March 2011

Behind the Line – Testimonial 6: "The Rise of Muslim Gangs"

with International Gang Expert, Richard Valdemar

The breeding ground for all gangs begins with an excluded group who feel victimized by poverty, by the establishment, or by some other real or imagined injustice. It is fed by an anti-establishment culture of drugs, crime, hate and racial separatism.' I wrote these words to explain how gangs are formed and how they reach critical mass. Think about them as you read this.

A likely group of people that might be susceptible to recruitment by international terrorists are American gangs formed from immigrating Muslims. Rarely mentioned by the American media are gangs formed mostly of Middle Eastern immigrants. An article pointing out this phenomenon was featured in Islam On-Line (August 2009) written by Jamshed Bokan and called "In the Ghetto..? Youth Gangs and American Muslims.

The criminal gang lifestyle is immoral according to Christian, Jewish and Muslim beliefs, but the dynamics that contribute to the spawning of criminal street gangs in America affect the Muslim immigrant communities just as they have Irish, Italian, Jewish and Hispanic legal and illegal immigrants before them. The only difference is that these earlier American immigrants shared a Judeo-Christian culture; the newest arrivals do not.

The Islam On-Line article takes the point of view that these young Muslims are only mimicking the popular styles of American youth. They affect the look, attitude and behavior of the tough urbanized kids who are glamorized in gangsta' rap movies, music and videos. Some say new gangster-styled Muslims are only 'wannabes.' But this is the same denial expressed by earlier immigrant communities.

For decades now immigration patterns in Europe have established the Muslim cultures of North African and Middle Eastern immigrants in enclaves in the United Kingdom, Germany, Spain, France and the Netherlands. All of these countries have also spawned Muslim gangs.

In November, 2005, 300 French towns, including Paris, were rocked by two weeks of violent rioting. Paris was burning. The epicenter of the rioting was 'Clichy-Sous-Bois,' a suburban ghetto and enclave of Middle Eastern and North African immigrants. The fury of the angry young men 'who feel frustrated by racial and cultural problems' was blamed for the violence.

A November, 21st, 2005 U.S. News & World Report article by Anna Mulrine pointed out that French-born children of immigrants and newly arrived immigrants 'often expressed anger and civil disobedience by burning cars. As many as 80 cars were burned in France every day' before the crescendo of violence in November 2005.

Then French Interior Minister (now president), Nicholas Sarkozy called the rioters scum, dregs, or gangrene. The rioters were mostly young men of North African and Middle Eastern descent; at least culturally they were Muslims, and many were in gangs. If you saw any photographs of these French rioters you would find that they looked and dressed surprisingly like young men from tough neighborhoods in New York, Chicago and Los Angeles.

In the United Kingdom, Church of England Bishop Nazir-Ali— himself a Pakistan native—warned that Islamic extremists have created 'no-go' zones across Britain where it is too dangerous for non-Muslims to enter. Writing in the Sunday Telegraph in January, 2008, the Bishop blamed the 'novel philosophy of multiculturalism' for creating deep divisions and further warned of increasing attempts to introduce Islamic (Sharia) law in England.

In August, British citizens across the country organized protests against Prime Minister Gordon Brown's approval of the acceptance of at least 85 Sharia courts (for family law). Brown's decision provides a separate Muslim judicial system that supersedes British law.

In one of Britain's most secure prisons, Whitemoor (HM) Prison in Cambridgeshire, prison staff warned in January, 2008 that gangs of Muslim prisoners dominated several wings of the facility and a serious incident was imminent. Approximately one-third of the 500 or so prisoners claimed to be Muslims. The other inmates and staff were intimidated by the large number of Muslims, and Prison Service officials reported that they were "handing control to the prisoners."

Another taboo subject is the very emotionally volatile discussion of the practice of gang rape, which seems to be a common practice of some of these Muslim gangs. In the "Land Down Under," the cultural confrontation between Australian citizens and Muslim gangs has been clearly documented. Just before the Sydney Olympics in 2000, a group of young men and teens from Lebanese Muslim immigrant families who lived in the suburbs of southwest Sydney kidnapped, gang raped, and tortured four teenaged girls. They subjected them to racial taunts and called the girls "Aussie pigs" during the rapes.

Note: the Muslim gang culture of sexual violence and abuse against women is not expressed toward non-Muslims only; it is often the Muslim women that are victimized the most. Under Sharia law husbands are permitted to beat their wives and polygamy is sometimes permitted. There are numerous books and articles written by survivors of these practices. The rape victim is often told that the attack was her fault. Many families follow the practice of "honor killing" the rape victims for having been disgraced.

Often overlooked are the Asian and Pacific Island Muslim gangs. In May, 2007, two men were killed in fighting between warring rival gangs in Jakarta. The Betawi Brotherhood Forum and the Association of Betawi Families (both formed from the indigenous population) battled for a parking lot in this capital city and the subsequent right to extort money from motorists.

The Philippine Islands have long been a recruiting ground for many gangs. Malaysia is much the same. When these groups immigrate to the United States, they are actively targeted for conversion by more radical groups in U.S. jails and prisons.

Muslim people from many nations have immigrated legally and illegally into all of the major and minor cities throughout the U.S. The cities of New York, Chicago and Los Angeles have seen huge waves of immigrants and the criminal gangs that result. However, Michigan seems to be the center of Muslim settlers in the U.S. The city of Dearborn outside of Detroit is a Shiite Muslim enclave. From its numerous mosques the Muslim calls to worship can be heard every day.

Even before, this Detroit suburb was a dying city with an auto industry moving out, unemployment at more than 28 percent, the crime and murder rate climbing, the school system in receivership, and the treasury $300 million short of funds for even the bare bones municipal services. This is the formula for disaster, and it's also the perfect storm condition to spawn more gangs.

One of Detroit's most infamous gangs is the Five Percent Nation or the Nation of Gods and Earths/Five Percent. This is a very violent street gang that was spun out of the Fruit of Islam, more commonly known as Black Muslims. Like Chicago's El Rukins street gang, they bear little resemblance to any orthodox Muslim belief system but claim to be religious adherents. Recently a Federal Magistrate judge, Steve Whalen, told Michigan Prison authorities to drop the ban on the Five Percent gang's inflammatory recruiting material and to treat the group like any other religious organization.

African Muslims are also becoming a presence in America's cities. The country of Somalia is primarily Muslim and seriously broken. Before and after the "Black Hawk Down" raid, Somalia fell apart in civil war and gangs and warlords took over, starving the people. Gangs of young children roamed the streets carrying AK-47s and chewing on 'khat,' a stimulant.

In 2001, large numbers of Somali immigrants began migrating to Maine bringing their clan rivalries and their love of khat with them. Since then these Somali rival gangs, or "clans" as they prefer, have taken root in such far flung U.S. cities as Lewiston (Maine), Minneapolis-Saint Paul, Kansas City and Garden City (Kansas), and San Diego.

So far I have not seen the growing Muslim gang threat covered at any length by the mainstream media or discussed by many in law enforcement. Why not? What happened to our pro-active mission to prevent crime and criminal gangs before they reach crisis proportions? In this politically correct society are we forbidden to address this situation without being admonished for 'hate speech' or 'racial profiling?'

— Richard Valdemar

Top 10 Wanted Terrorists
(historical examples)

Osama Bin Laden – According to the FBI, wanted, *"in connection with the August 7, 1998, bombings of the United States Embassies in Dar es Salaam, Tanzania, and Nairobi, Kenya. These attacks killed over 200 people. In addition, Bin Laden is a suspect in other terrorist attacks throughout the world. Bin Laden is left-handed and walks with a cane."* Killed in 2011
(photo courtesy of law enforcement)

Ayman Al-Zawahiri – According to the FBI, *"has been indicted for his alleged role in the August 7, 1998, bombings of the United States Embassies in Dar es Salaam, Tanzania, and Nairobi, Kenya. Al-Zawahiri is a physician and the founder of the Egyptian Islamic Jihad (EIJ). This organization opposes the secular Egyptian Government and seeks its overthrow through violent means. In approximately 1998, the EIJ led by Al-Zawahiri merged with Al Qaeda."*
(photo courtesy of law enforcement)

Dr. Paul R. Chabot

Fahd Mohammed Ahmed Al-Quso – According to the FBI, *"was indicted in the Southern District of New York for his role in the October 12, 2000, bombing of the USS Cole in Aden, Yemen, in which 17 American sailors were killed."* *(photo courtesy of law enforcement)*

Husayn Muhammad Al-Umari – According to the FBI, *"was indicted in the District of Columbia for his alleged role in the August 11, 1982, bombing of Pan Am Flight 830, while it was en route from Japan to Hawaii. He is alleged to have prepared the bomb that was placed under a seat on Flight 830, resulting in the death of a 16-year-old passenger and injuring 16 other passengers."* *(photo courtesy of law enforcement)*

Ahmed Mohammed Hamed Ali – According to the FBI, *"was indicted in the Southern District of New York, for his alleged involvement in the bombings of the United States Embassies in Dar es Salaam, Tanzania, and Nairobi, Kenya, on August 7, 1998."* *(photo courtesy of law enforcement)*

Anas Al-Liby – According to the FBI, *"was indicted in the Southern District of New York, for his alleged involvement in the bombings of the United States Embassies in Dar es Salaam, Tanzania, and Nairobi, Kenya, on August 7, 1998. Al-Liby recently lived in the United Kingdom, where he has political asylum."* *(photo courtesy of law enforcement)*

Wadoud Muhammad Hafiz Al-Turki – According to the FBI, *"was indicted in the District of Columbia for his alleged role in the September 5, 1986, hijacking of Pan American World Airways Flight 73 during a stop in Karachi, Pakistan. The attack resulted in the murder of 20 passengers and crew, including two American citizens, and the attempted murder of 379 passengers and crew, including 89 American citizens."* *(photo courtesy of law enforcement)*

Ahmad Ibrahim Al-Mughassil – According to the FBI, *"has been indicted in the Eastern District of Virginia for the June 25, 1996, bombing of the Khobar Towers military housing complex in Dhahran, Kingdom of Saudi Arabia. Al-Mughassil is the alleged head of the "military wing" of the terrorist organization, Saudi Hizballah."* *(photo courtesy of law enforcement)*

Abdul Rahman Yasin – According to the FBI, *"is wanted for his alleged participation in the terrorist bombing of the World Trade Center, New York City, on February 26, 1993, which resulted in six deaths, the wounding of numerous individuals, and the significant destruction of property and commerce."* *(photo courtesy of law enforcement)*

Jamal Saeed Abdul Rahim – According to the FBI, *"was indicted in the District of Columbia for his alleged role in the September 5, 1986, hijacking of Pan American World Airways Flight 73 during a stop in Karachi, Pakistan. The attack resulted in the murder of 20 passengers and crew, including two American citizens, and the attempted murder of 379 passengers and crew, including 89 American citizens."* *(photo courtesy of law enforcement)*

Chapter Five

Arellano-Felix DTO: A Case Study

The Unites States and Mexico have had a mutual extradition treaty since 1980, yet the DEA reports the major cartels in Mexico, the Arellano-Felix organization continues to expand their powers and operate with virtual impunity.[27]

In order to fully understand the drug cartel as an organization, it is helpful to be specific and zero in on one cartel; so let's continue our discussion by diving deeper into the underworld and exploring the Arellano Felix Drug Trafficking Organization (AF-DTO). This organization, although no longer as strong as it once was due to drug-cartel infighting in Mexico and the good work of authorities targeting its leadership, the AF-DTO still remains a threat. What you are about to read is one of the most exhaustive studies ever performed on a specific drug cartel – you will learn a great deal in this chapter that will prepare you well for the second half of this book.

Historical Overview of AF-DTO / Arellano Felix Organization / Tijuana Cartel

"The most prominent Mexican drug trafficking organization that impacts the United States is the Arellano Felix Organization (AF-DTO)."[28] That was, at least, until recently. Now, all the cartels that have survived are severely impacting the U.S., but it was the AF-DTO that set the stage. The AF-DTO is one of the most powerful criminal organizations that has existed. The AF-DTO officially formed in the 1980s after the arrest of an uncle of the AF-DTO family, Felix

Gallardo.[29] Felix Gallardo was an ex-cop who became the first Mexican drug lord to ally himself with Colombia's cocaine cartels in the 1980s. As a result, he became head of the powerful Guadalajara cartel. Upon Gallardo's arrest and subsequent imprisonment, the Guadalajara cartel fragmented into the AF-DTO (or Tijuana Cartel) and the Sinaloa Cartel. Such fragmentation of the major cartels continues to occur today and is something that will be examined in greater detail in a later chapter. The organization grew into what has become today an international drug trafficking organization. An investigative reporter with *Time Magazine*[30] reported in her story, "Border Monsters," the brutal strength of this organization:

> ...so few boundaries—national, moral, legal—constrain the border's worst bad guys, Benjamin Arellano Felix, 49, and his kid brother, Ramon, 36. The two baby-faced playboys head the Tijuana cartel, which sits atop Mexico's $30 billion drug-trafficking underworld and may be the most powerful organization in the country of any kind. Each year, they smuggle to the U.S. hundreds of tons of cocaine, marijuana, heroin and methamphetamine ferried on ships, planes and inside truckloads of legitimate merchandise. The Arellanos are thought to have hundreds of millions of dollars stashed away, and that's after bribing Mexican officials, cops and generals to the tune of some $75 million a year.

The AF-DTO ultimately reached the attention of the White House. On November 26, 2002, President George Bush stated, "As head of DEA, Administrator Hutchinson has focused his efforts at dismantling high-profile drug trafficking organizations, including the Arellano Felix organization."[31] Nine months earlier, on March 20, 2002, President Bush had been interviewed on Mexico's Television Azteca and was asked, "Benjamin Arellano Felix, the head of the cartel, suspect in Mexico, was apprehended there. Are you going to ask for extradition—for an extradition of this guy to the United States?"[32] President Bush responded by explaining the current U.S. indictment against the AF-DTO and the cooperation in place with the Fox administration. It was extraordinary to have a president not only mention a DTO by its name, but also reference specific efforts used in targeting the organization. The fact that the AF-DTO had caught the attention of the leaders of Mexico and the U.S. showed the significance of the organization.

Historical Overview of Past Attempts to Dismantle the AF-DTO 1997-1999

Federal Officials Target the AF-DTO

A 1997 DEA press release announced a $50,000 reward for the arrest of Ramon Eduardo Arellano Felix, a key member of the AF-DTO. It was drafted by the FBI after Ramon Eduardo was placed on the FBI Ten Most Wanted Fugitives list. This small reward continued to grow as the U.S. government realized the complication and sophistication of the AF-DTO. In that same year, a high-level target was arrested in Mexico as a result of U.S. information and efforts to dismantle the DTO.[33]

In July 1998, the transportation chief of the AF-DTO was indicted, with little impact on the organization.[34] In that same year, then U.S. Attorney General Nora Manella stated, *"The indictment...will significantly disrupt the domestic operations [of the AF-DTO]."*[35] However, the organization continued to operate, even as they dealt with other competing organizations. Attempts by other powerful DTOs to take over or infiltrate the AF-DTO failed repeatedly because of an inadequate understanding of the region.[36] According to researchers Dettmer and Maier,

> *...successfully infiltrating the system requires a deep knowledge of the region, particularly with regards to the idiosyncrasy of the people, their culture, and the weak and strong points of the Mexican judicial and political system...it is necessary to know whom to bribe, when and how.*[37]

U.S. Congressional Hearings

In 1999, the assistant secretary for International Narcotics and Law Enforcement Affairs for the U.S. Department of State testified before the House Government Reform Oversight Committee stating that Mexico had instituted a comprehensive national counter narcotics program that included the following:

- A three-pronged interdiction program aimed at detecting and deterring the illegal entry of drug shipments into Mexican territory, airspace or waters;
- A longstanding eradication campaign that has destroyed more illicit drug crops than any country in the world;
- New specialized investigative units that build cases against the most significant drug traffickers and DTOs in close cooperation with U.S. law enforcement;
- A treasury ministry to better detect suspicious transactions and combat money laundering; and
- Law enforcement and health agencies working to detect and deter smuggling or diversion of chemicals used in drug production.[38]

Beers's testimony explained that Mexico had reported the following significant accomplishments in combating the AF-DTO:

- Sentencing General Alfredo Navarro to 20 years in prison for bribery;
- Sentencing assassin Francisco Cabrera to 40 years in prison for killing a federal police commander;
- Formally indicting two AF-DTO brothers;
- Arresting key security and money launderers; and
- Approving a key lieutenant for extradition to the United States.[39]

In 1999, Ronald Brooks, then president of the California Narcotic Officers Association (and current director of the Northern California

High Intensity Drug Trafficking Area Program), provided congressional testimony to the House Subcommittee on Criminal Justice, Drug Policy and Human Resources. Brooks' testimony was specific to the hearing topic regarding the importance of a drug kingpin's extradition. Brooks testified that several murders in San Diego County had been directly linked to the AF-DTO and that the Mexican government

> *...had not made an honest effort to eliminate the powerful drug Mafias.... The United States and Mexico have had a mutual extradition treaty since 1980, yet the DEA reports the major cartels in Mexico, the Arellano Felix...organizations, continue to expand their powers and operate with virtual impunity.*[40]

2000-2003

Investigative Reporting

In 2000, PBS's *Frontline* conducted an interview with the FBI agent who supervised the AF-DTO Task Force. Agent De La Montaigne[41] provided valuable insight into the organization's strength, as well as possible factors leading to the organization's resilience. The organization uses violence to get things done. They will kill anyone who gets in their way and will make their own employees watch as they torture others, as a way of letting them know that if they are not trustworthy, they too will be tortured and killed. The organization is a family business which trusts only the family. Their top leaders are very intelligent people, and they know how to isolate themselves and prevent capture. Intimidation is a key to stopping others from testifying against the organization. They will go after neighbors, grandparents, and friends to ensure that no one testifies. Despite government efforts in arresting key members of the organization, their activities have never been fully disrupted. The AF-DTO is also good at recruiting U.S. gang members to work for them in the United States to traffic narcotics, torture and kill. The organization also recruits young adults who are wealthy and indoctrinates them into the drug trade. An example of the ruthlessness of the AF-DTO appeared in the *U.S. News and World Report* (1998), describing the organization's killing of 19 people, including six children and two babies who were dragged from their residences, shot and killed on their patio in Tijuana because a family member crossed the AF-DTO.

In 2000, the British Broadcasting Corporation (BBC), through reporter Jose Baig in Tijuana, Mexico, reported that the AF-DTO handled almost all the marijuana, much of the cocaine, and a good part of the amphetamines trafficked into the United States, representing a monopoly over the drug products. Baig's research showed that approximately 20 years ago, the AF-DTO was a small group smuggling cigarettes and alcohol to and from Mexico, but then grew into a very powerful DTO. He explained that most of the junior officers of the DTO are either dead or in jail, but the family organizations of the DTO remain strong because of the DTO's ability to use violence to keep competition, authorities and the media away. Within the last decade, this DTO, according to Baig, has been responsible for murdering two police chiefs and has networks of cocaine extending from Mexico to Colombia to the streets of the United States. "Their communication and interception equipment is, in many cases, more advanced than the Mexican authorities. The money laundering operations are carefully planned."[42] Despite all of these advantages of the AF-DTO, Baig predicted that the entire DTO would be dismantled by the end of the year (2001), but he was mistaken.

Nations Working Together

In 2001, the *Washington Crime News* reported information relayed from the DEA stating that the brothers of the AF-DTO were looking into moving the center of their operations into Arizona due to police crackdowns in both Mexico and the United States. The AF-DTO was apparently, according to an anonymous source, looking at small-time dealers and gangs without widespread controls over their narcotic trafficking. In that same year, it was reported that "*Bush, on March 1, 2001, certified Mexico as fully cooperative in drug control efforts, citing the arrest of key members of the AF-DTO, the aggressive eradication programs, and continuing cooperation with the United States in a number of areas.*"[43] The report also cited criticisms, namely, that Mexican authorities failed to weed out corruption and arrest major drug traffickers and to extradite Mexican citizens to the United States. However, praise was given regarding the Mexican Supreme Court's 2001 ruling that Mexican citizens could be extradited to the United States for drug charges, so long as they were sentenced under Mexican guidelines. This measure, of course, would help in dismantling the DTOs, but Mexico still would not extradite its citizens if it knew the United States would press for capital punishment.

High-Intensity Drug Trafficking Area Program

The White House Office of National Drug Control Policy (ONDCP) manages the nationwide High-Intensity Drug Trafficking Area (HIDTA) program, a unique effort that mandates equal domestic law enforcement participation for local, state and federal agencies. To date, 28 HIDTAs are in existence throughout the United States and its territories. A review of each HIDTA's annual reports and strategies revealed that a number of HIDTAs had the AF-DTO on their list of top organizations to dismantle. The Southwest Border HIDTA, which covers the entire border area from California to Texas, mentioned significant milestones in past-cases involving the AF-DTO,[44] stating that the AF-DTO has been seriously disrupted by unprecedented law enforcement efforts by both the United States and Mexico. The California Border Alliance Group (CBAG), however, made tremendous headway in leading efforts to fight AF-DTO. But the efforts to fight the AF-DTO were not isolated to the border – looking back historically, the ONDCP Oregon HIDTA (2005) listed the AF-DTO as a primary target of its law enforcement operations – but again, I must emphasize that it was the HIDTAs along the border – San Diego region specifically, that took on a leadership role – and they had to –the AF-DTO's leadership was in their backyard.

Not far away, the ONDCP Los Angeles HIDTA (2004) had the AF-DTO on its list of annual significant accomplishments, and their Southern California Drug Task Force (SCDTF) conducted regional investigations into cocaine distribution directly linked to the AF-DTO in 2002. This task force initiated 43 wiretaps over a 22-month period, revealing that AF-DTO activities stretched throughout the United States. Many of these cells were dismantled: in Los Angeles alone, 85 subjects were arrested, and $2.2 million in cash was seized. Shortly thereafter, the investigation and arrests led to an all-out offensive, with over 400 domestic police officers targeting the states of New York, Minnesota, Connecticut, and California. The national effort led to 234 arrests of members or associates of the AF-DTO. Despite these arrests, the organization remained intact and operational, albeit little more than a remnant of its peak.

In 2002, the U.S. Federal Government began a nationwide program with the HIDTAs, asking each HIDTA to identify priority targets (also known as CPOTs).[45] These CPOTs represented the largest DTOs trafficking in their area of responsibility. The Los Angeles HIDTA listed the AF-DTO as one of its top three targets and requested nearly $1.2 million in funding from the White House for law enforcement equipment. This equipment was to be used specifically in operations aimed at dismantling AF-DTO operations in its region (i.e., travel, equipment and personnel). In this same report, a HIDTA in the other corner of the country, the New England HIDTA in Boston requested $245,000 in funds specifically to target marijuana operations run by the AF-DTO. The New England HIDTA described the AF-DTO as being one of the:

> *...most powerful, aggressive and arguably the most violent of the drug trafficking organizations.... [It] orchestrates the transportation, importation, and distribution of multi-ton quantities of cocaine, marijuana, and large quantities of heroin and methamphetamine into the U.S.. Violence, intimidation and corruption are the AFO trademarks.[46]*

The Midwest HIDTA headquartered in St. Louis, Missouri, requested $150,000 to target the AF-DTO operating in its region. The Nevada HIDTA requested multiple expenditures to target the AF-DTO within its region, as well as operations existing in its investigations stretching to Nebraska. The Northern California HIDTA requested $222,000, while the Oregon HIDTA requested $100,000. The operations of the AF-DTO spread all throughout the United States, thereby demonstrating the AF-DTO's ability to expand operations while under significant pressure from law enforcement. Fortunately, the overall HIDTA program benefited greatly from border leadership – much concentrated near the San Diego region – targeting the AF-DTO just miles from their offices. As such, these leaders credit strong cooperation with Mexican authorities and the U.S. agreeing to non-death penalty cases for extradited suspects from Mexico.

Attempts of Mexican Authorities and Prosecutors to Attack Evil

In 2002, Mexico's top organized crime prosecutor, Jose Luis Santiago Vasconcelos, *disclosed that the cartels in Tijuana and other areas were currently working together to rebuild a network of gunmen to defend their drug territories.*[47] In an ironic twist, after law enforcement arrested top AF-DTO and leaders from another DTO, these rival DTOs forged alliances in prison to work together to help strengthen their cartels. This was confirmed by the Mexican and American governments.[48] In that same year, an article in the *Economist*[49] referenced the demise of the AF-DTO subsequent to the capture of an Arellano Felix brother and the killing of another. The article claimed that greater trust among Americans and Mexicans had led to closer intelligence teamwork that was key to the success against the AF-DTO. Indeed, there was a good working relationship, but the AF-DTO was still operational, although perhaps more decentralized. In fact, the article acknowledged new data stating that, although the AF-DTO appeared to be dismantled, other organizations had taken the lead.

Efforts after September 11, 2001

After the terrorist attacks in 2001, the AF-DTO, operating largely in Tijuana, increased its kidnapping operations. In 2003, over 500 kidnappings were reported in that area and experts began to see frightening similarities to activities that had taken place in the early stages of Colombia's drug trafficking formulation.[50] In 2001, the AF-DTO was one of the most powerful and violent of the Mexican DTOs;[51] it created new ways to produce funds after initially believing that U.S. borders would be much more difficult to penetrate. Shortly after 9/11, however, the AF-DTO found that border security remained at relatively the same levels as before 9/11, and the DTO stepped up its drug trafficking into the United States.

Governments Offer Significant Rewards

In 2003, an anonymous reporter[52] found that the United States DEA was offering millions of dollars for the arrest of specific targets of the AF-DTO. The DEA was reportedly offering an additional $2 million for information leading to the arrest and conviction of the AF-DTO's top lieutenants (Gilberto Higuera, Gustavo Rivera Martinez, Efrain Perez, Manual Aguireer Galindo and Jorge Aureliano). This offer was issued in large part because the AF-DTO brothers were operating an army of assassins used to shield the organization's smuggling operation.[53] In that same year, the DEA reported that the Fox administration arrested key members of the AF-DTO and credited increased cooperation between U.S. and Mexican authorities since 2000.

Limited Success

Even so, the DEA[54] reported that despite some success against the AF-DTO in Mexico, the organization remained powerful because it was well organized, had large amounts of financial resources, and was good at corrupting and intimidating public officials. Nevertheless, the DEA attributed its partial success against the AF-DTO to not only the increased cooperation between U.S. and Mexican authorities, but also to a more serious attitude from Mexico about drugs in that nation. Time and again, the DEA reported that the arrests that were made would not have been possible without the cooperation of both governments.

Interestingly, the report also attributes the AF-DTO's strength to its cooperation with other entities. The AF-DTO worked with criminal organizations thousands of miles away in Canada, Europe, Asia and the Far East to obtain chemicals used in the production of illegal narcotics. The DEA also attributed the AF-DTO's success in smuggling drugs into the United States to the DTO's use of various innovative ways to conceal and transfer the narcotics (e.g., using carbon paper to pack drugs to conceal them from x-rays).

The DEA detailed the arrest and killing of key AF-DTO members but concluded that "the organization continues to operate."[55] A White House report[56] cited a number of factors that helped to partially dismantle the AF-DTO: indictments, arrests, extraditions for higher ups, and unprecedented cooperation with the Mexican authorities. The report emphasized that the organization was under significant pressure and had moved into alien smuggling and kidnapping as a form of generating funds to substitute for lost drug smuggling revenue. This adaptation or organizational learning ensured the safety of the organization.

Evil Remains Operational

In September of 2003, the U.S. Department of State[57] released a poster and press release listing seven key AF-DTO members and offering a total bounty of $20 million. This was done in cooperation with the DEA just one year after the key arrest of the AF-DTO leader, Benjamin Arellano Felix.[58] This press release cited improved cooperation between U.S. and Mexican law enforcement agencies. It is unknown how effective the bounty was regarding the capture of some of these men, but just one year later, two of the seven listed by the U.S. State Department were in police custody.[59]

The DEA is not the only U.S. federal agency focusing large amounts of resources on the AF-DTO. In 2003, the U.S. Federal Bureau of Investigation (FBI) released a press statement detailing its efforts to dismantle the AF-DTO by announcing a Federal RICO case—an anti-criminal organization prosecutorial tool—indictment against each of 11 top leaders of the organization. The article also detailed the prior arrests of two AF-DTO brothers in 2002 and 2003 and the killing of a third related brother in the same timeframe. Yet, the Defense Intelligence Agency reported in 2003 that, although the AF-DTO had lost a significant amount of its influence due to recent arrests, the cartel continued to control large portions of the drugs transiting from Mexico into the United States. In short, the organization continued to operate, demonstrating a profound resilience. And resilience, as you will read later, is what we must focus upon. We must identify the characteristics of resilience and break those down to better fight the enemy and weaken their pillars of strength.

2004-2007: Limited Progress

In 2004, there were various progress reports regarding the attempts to arrest and dismantle key DTOs in Mexico. In a four-year time span, 2000-2004, the Mexican press reported that the AF-DTO had suffered from 7,376 arrests, including two top leaders, five financiers, ten top aids, 43 gunmen, 33 corrupt government officials, and 7,293 street-level drug dealers.[60] Also in 2004, Mexico's attorney general announced that five members of the AF-DTO would stand trial on organized crime charges.[61] In that same year, a Mexican court upheld the indictment of a known AF-DTO member.[62] And again in 2004, Mexico's state attorney general office sought the arrests of five violent men with links to the AF-DTO. Shortly afterward, an anonymous tip led authorities to all five suspects, who were found in possession of AFI (Mexico's equivalent of the FBI) badges, bulletproof vests, and handheld radios tuned to police scanners.[63] This is a remarkable accounting of the organization's ability to acquire sophisticated equipment.

A 2004 DEA press release described key arrests in the AF-DTO and credited the successes to combined investigative efforts of both governments. Additional arrests were made against the AF-DTO in the United States, and the pressure was kept on the AF-DTO by a U.S. government reward of $5 million leading to the arrest of two of the DTO's key brothers. The DEA administrator was quoted in the press release as stating that the organization was "in ruins." However, this kind of optimistic statement had been made many times before, only to be proven wrong when the AF-DTO bounced back as strong as ever.

In 2004, the Mexican press[64] reported that another cartel in Mexico's Tijuana region was attempting to gain influence. Meanwhile, the arrest and death of two key AF-DTO members initiated a string of kidnappings and retribution assassinations against those within the AF-DTO who had betrayed them. This included Mexican police officers. The report detailed serious corruption issues within the Mexican government and Mexican elections, all reflecting the AF-DTO's influence despite serious setbacks, arrests and deaths of its members. More perplexing, though, was the investigative reporter's findings that the AF-DTO was being reorganized under the leadership of other dominant Mexican drug traffickers in the region. In short, the head of the organization was cut off, but the organization grew another head in its place. As usual, the AF-DTO demonstrated great resilience.

Violence continued throughout 2004. Authorities believed that the AF-DTO killed more people to gain control over its respective territories, including a rival drug lord in a region south of the AF-DTO's former area of control.[65] A report by *Mexico City Reforma*[66] revealed that the AF-DTO had joined forces with the brothers of the Osiel Cardenas DTO to smuggle drug shipments from South America into the United States. The article referenced a new type of cooperation between these two DTOs that led to the successful trafficking of 30 tons of cocaine into the United States.

Backup Arrives for the Battle

Mexico uses a considerable amount of its military to combat drug production and drug trafficking. Approximately 30,000 soldiers are involved in these efforts in the air, water and ground. Each month, they use an average of 88 airships, 370 bases and 18,000 military units located nationwide. Approximately 12,000 units are responsible for preventing drug trafficking on roadways. Some nine amphibious groups, made up of 1,512 units and 250 vessels, work jointly in this endeavor.[67] However, the military has been no more successful than the police at dismantling the AF-DTO. Although the military was effective in surrounding the Tijuana offices of the State Attorney General's Office and capturing Estrada Sarabia, who had been working in the offices as an undercover operative of the AF-DTO,[68] the AF-DTO was able to work in the shadows during heavy military presence.

White House Presidential Designation

On June 1, 2004, the White House, through a presidential designation of the Foreign Narcotics Kingpins Initiative, announced additional names as high-priority U.S. targets. Of the ten additional international targets announced, two were key leaders in the AF-DTO and a third was the AF-DTO organization itself; all three were at the top of the list. In the release, the White House announced that the action underscored the President's determination to do everything possible to pursue drug traffickers, undermine their operations, end the suffering that trade in illicit drugs inflicts on Americans and other people around the world, and prevent drug traffickers from supporting terrorists.[69]

The Kingpin Act provided further support for law enforcement agencies targeting the AF-DTO. However, these agencies have been targeting the AF-DTO for decades and, until recently, have made very little impact on the organization's ability to traffic drugs. In 2004, the U.S. Department of Treasury announced a list of significant foreign traffickers, and the top three traffickers listed were members of the AF-DTO. A $2 million bounty offered by the U.S. State Department[70] did not help in the eventual capture of one of the DTO's top leaders, Benjamin Arellano Felix, and the organization remained operational despite the U.S. government's best efforts to arrest these key figures.

Lessons First Learned in Evil

A former undersecretary for border security at the U.S. Department of Homeland Security, Asa Hutchinson (also a former DEA administrator), was reportedly credited with the first indictment of known terrorists for drug trafficking and oversaw the arrest of the head of the AF-DTO when leading the DEA in 2003. Hutchinson stated in 2004 that Mexico's President, Vicente Fox, "greatly enhanced the law enforcement cooperation and the rule of law in Mexico…the Mexican government has been very supportive from a different context."[71] Hutchinson describes Mexico's reasoning for combating DTOs: "They look at it from the standpoint of how the smuggling organizations are treating the Mexican citizens…abusing them and endangering their lives…they want to address it from that perspective—more of a safety perspective."[72] Hutchinson acknowledged that the U.S. perspective is different in the sense that we want to secure our border, stop the flow of drugs, and convict DTO leaders. According to Hutchinson, the two countries are targeting the same group for very different reasons.

Despite some failures, there have also been successes in dismantling the AF-DTO. In 2004, the *White House Office of National Drug Control Policy's Annual High-Intensity Drug Trafficking Report* stated:

The dismantlement of the Arellano Felix Organization (AFO) continues with indictments, arrests, and extradition proceedings for the upper echelon, and transportation and enforcement cells of that cartel, as well as unprecedented cooperative efforts between U.S. and Mexican law enforcement. Multiple intelligence sources tell us that the remaining cells of the Arellano Felix Organization are having difficulty getting cocaine from the source countries, and have been forced to turn to other sources of income, such as alien smuggling and kidnapping. Of course, a lack of drug income makes the AFO even more vulnerable to the pressures being exerted by the Zambada-Garcia Organization (ZGO), currently making a play for the Tijuana plaza.[73]

This statement was released by one of the 28 HIDTAs, the Southwest Border HIDTA, which covers the entire southwest border area between the United States and Mexico. This HIDTA has intimate knowledge of the inner-workings of the AF-DTO because the DTO is one of this HIDTA's top strategic priorities. Nevertheless, the annual HIDTA strategy[74] also stated that the AF-DTO is still operational and may be on the rebound.

In May of 2005, the *LA Times* reported: *Much of the violence [in Tijuana, Mexico], say experts and law enforcement authorities, results from the continuing battle for control of the drug trafficking corridor through Baja, California. With the Arellano Felix drug cartel weakened by arrests and killings, other organizations have been trying to gain control...the Arellano Felix organization is struggling to maintain its power base.*[75] In essence, this article describes what can be interpreted as either the weakening of the AF-DTO or the resilience of the organization as it maintains its power in the drug trafficking world.

It All Boils Down to Resilience

In 2000, PBS reported on the AF-DTO and the organization's involvement in the murder of two Tijuana police chiefs, and dozens of prosecutors, police, lawyers and journalists. AF-DTO members torture its victims as a means of intimidating others, while also getting information on law enforcement drug units. Two agents who endured torture were then killed. They had their skulls crushed slowly. One of the AF-DTO's survival mechanisms is to instill fear—to have others spread the word about its ruthlessness. This fear tactic almost worked with the U.S. authorities. The U.S. considered pulling its agents out of Tijuana after many assassinations of authorities in that region. That same level of fear had been experienced a few years prior in the United States in 1997. The *U.S. News and World Report*[76] narrated that federal drug agents in San Diego were increasingly concerned about safety after intelligence intercepted raised alerts that members of the AF-DTO wanted to kill U.S. agents for their role in confiscating drug shipments.

In 2001, Dettmer[77] described sweep operations disrupting key cross-border smuggling routes. High-profile arrests were common, and seizures of cocaine were breaking records. These efforts placed pressure on the DTO to adapt. In late 2004, the Mexican press[78] reported that DTOs in Mexico were forming alliances in order to preserve control over their own jurisdictions for trafficking. For example, the AF-DTO formed an alliance with the Gulf Cartel. This alliance influenced other DTOs in Mexico to form similar alliances to balance the power of other competing DTOs.

The AF-DTO employs strict rules with all of its employees and those wishing to do business with them. Traffickers in their regions can carry only small amounts of drugs (fewer than 10 kilograms of cocaine or 500 kilograms of marijuana) and must pay the AF-DTO a commission in order to do business in their regions. Anyone caught with more than the allowed amount of drugs is killed. The AF-DTO has also imposed high tariffs to deter others from the drug business.[79] With its base in Tijuana, it controls one of the most significant drug corridors into the United States.[80] This level of control helps ensure the AF-DTO's monopoly and power, thereby ensuring its survival.

In order to understand the DTOs, one must look at the geography and demographics of the production, trafficking and end use. While the types of illegal drugs consumed in the United States are extensive, not all of these narcotics arrive from Mexico. Cocaine and marijuana make up the majority of drugs trafficked into the United States over the border of Mexico.[81] Behind the efforts to traffic these substances into the United States exist wealthy, violent and highly organized DTOs. The AF-DTO, in particular, has built relationships with existing street gangs in California, Texas, Illinois and many other states to help distribute narcotics throughout America. This new cooperation with U.S. street gangs has furthered the organization's ability to build its business through violence and control and also makes it more difficult for U.S. law enforcement to counteract the spread of the organization.

According to the DEA,[82] Mexican law enforcement officials who were friendly to the AF-DTO were often rotated from their assignments. However, in these cases, the corrupt Mexican officials would often assist with the corruption of the incoming official. These meetings took place between the highest levels of the AF-DTO.

The corruption covered all levels of government necessary to allow for a smooth order of the drug trafficking business without interruption. Monthly payments to high-level officials could range up to $500,000. The corruption eventually led to Mexican officials traveling with AF-DTO shipments and personnel in order to ensure safety from detection or arrest.

Legitimate Mexican officials attempted to circumvent the corruption by moving the military into place to assist with taking down drug shipments. However, the AF-DTO simply adapted by paying off the Mexican army and navy commanders. The AF-DTO leadership expanded its scope by creating a position to supervise the logistics of maritime shipments. The AF-DTO was also successful in having the corrupt law enforcement partners receive promotions from the Mexican government, which only furthered the success of the AF-DTO.

A significant success of the organization was the corruption of the former Mexican president's personal secretary, who agreed to assist the AF-DTO. The secretary received a bribe of $1.5 million. This level of bribery exemplifies the organization's ability to infiltrate the highest levels of government in order to ensure the organization's success and survival.

Reports[83] describe Mexican troops helping the AF-DTO bring illegal narcotics into the United States, while other reports[84] detail standoffs with U.S. law enforcement at border locations. Mexican military personnel were driving hundreds of pounds of marijuana across the U.S. border (with the situation escalating to a standoff with U.S. police) before Mexican militia retreated back. And yet the Mexican military was thought to be very difficult for the AF-DTO to infiltrate.

The AF-DTO relies on technical assistance from law enforcement and uses around-the-clock wiretapping teams to wiretap offices throughout Mexico. "These wiretaps enable the cartel to eavesdrop on rival traffickers, federal and state police, prosecutors, and the American DEA's operations in Tijuana."[85] The AF-DTO was also successful in corrupting at least one U.S. official, a U.S. immigrations agent, who was later convicted. Caldwell, in his research report titled "Cold-Blooded Killers," states:

> To facilitate its continuing drug trafficking, it's certain that the AFO continues to lavish huge bribes, always paid in U.S. dollars, on Mexico's corruption-riddled law enforcement agencies and on important Mexican government officials at the local, state, and federal levels. The resulting corruption must be counted as the primary reason…leaders are still at large, operating with seeming impunity under the noses of Mexican law enforcement in Mexico's largest border city, a scant 25 miles south of San Diego.[86]

Caldwell analyzed the efforts undertaken by the AF-DTO to ensure its survivability through sheer brutality and intimidation. He states, "The total number of killings committed by the AFO likely will never be known... [and] surely reaches into the hundreds over the AFO's blood spattered, 20-year history."[87] According to Caldwell, a U.S. investigation documented direct evidence of 23 such killings between 1989 and 2000. Five of these killings took place in the United States, which further demonstrates the organization's disregard for international boundaries.

Documents show that those killed included informants, associates of the AF-DTO, rival traffickers, members of the Mexican military, police, a businessman, and a Mexican prosecutor. These murders were extremely sadistic. A woman in San Diego was slain in her home in front of her teenage daughter. A Baja prosecutor was shot 120 times in Tijuana because he was investigating the AF-DTO. An AF-DTO enforcement team massacred 19 members of three families, including women and children, who were shot to death in execution fashion. The organization kidnapped, savagely tortured, and executed a number of Mexican federal agents investigating the organization. Caldwell pointed out that the killing is just another cost of doing business.

According to Caldwell's investigative work reviewing court documents,[88] once a brother was captured or killed, another family member simply stepped in to take on the reins of leadership. Francisco Javier Arellano Felix was the youngest of the brothers, and documents state that he inherited leadership after his brother Ramon was killed and his brother Benjamin was captured in 2002. It wasn't long, though, until Francisco was captured; he was arrested by the U.S. Coast Guard in 2006 and brought to San Diego.

The leadership structure included members from outside of the family as well. Ismael Higuera-Guerrero served as the cartel's director of operations, confirming that the AF-DTO had a solid business structure. He and his brother, Gilberto Higuera-Guerrero, were arrested in Mexico and extradited to the United States in 2004. According to court documents, both admitted to being lieutenants of the AF-DTO and pleaded guilty to bribery, kidnapping, torture and murder ordered by the AF-DTO brothers. In 2006, they both stated that the youngest of the brothers, Francisco Javier Arellano-Felix, had been leading the organization until his recent arrest. After these arrests, the organization continued to find replacements ready to take the helm. Caldwell described a number of front-runners, including an AF-DTO senior partner, Aguirre-Galindo. However, as of the date of this study, it is unclear who is now running the organization.

A 2002 U.S. indictment[89] listing multiple AF-DTO family members and lieutenants as defendants provided additional insight into the criminal activity of the organization, which in many respects supports the resiliency characteristics discussed in this study. The indictment described the AF-DTO as an "enterprise" made up of multiple defendants who have violated U.S. law. The following charges were made: affecting interstate commerce; racketeering; illegal trafficking of drugs; laundering of drug proceeds; kidnapping, torture, and murder of informants, rival traffickers, law enforcement and other perceived enemies of the organization; and methodical bribing of Mexican law enforcement and military personnel. The AF-DTO was described as operating not only within Mexico, but also in the United States and Colombia.

The U.S. government uses Title 18 to define the organization as an "enterprise," based on its composition of leaders, members and associates working together and functioning as a continuing entity for the common purpose of achieving the goals and objectives of the organization. Such goals and objectives include enriching members through the trafficking of drugs into the United States; preserving and protecting the enterprise's power over Tijuana and the Mexicali region through the use of threats, intimidation and violence—including kidnapping, torture, and murder; instilling fear in others, including the Mexican media, law enforcement, rival traffickers, probable informants and the Mexican public at large; and enhancing and promoting the activities of its members and associates.

The indictment supported the premise that the AF-DTO has a business-like structure: "The Enterprise operated within a well-defined hierarchical structure."[90] The indictment also listed the organization's top tier leaders, as well as the second-level managers. It listed the activities of the organizational leaders and included the hierarchical structure and the roles associated with each level. The top leader has responsibility for overall decisions, including the organization, transportation and distribution of drugs, as well as enforcement activities undertaken by other members. The indictment listed Alberto Benjamin Arellano-Felix as the top leader, followed by his chief advisor and brother, Eduardo Ramon Arellano-Felix, "who was involved in, and consulted about, all major enterprise decisions."[91] A third brother, Francisco Javier Arellano Felix, served in a leadership role within the organization, participated in most enterprise decisions, and was put in charge of operations after the apprehension of Ismael Higuera-Guerrero in 2000.

A second layer of leadership includes the senior partners, who participated in most major decisions, encompassing decisions of murder. The indictment identified the senior partner as Manuel Aguirre-Galindo and claimed that he was retained by the organization due to his close connections to Colombian DTOs and due to his law enforcement and military contacts assisting with drug-trafficking operations. A second senior partner was Jesus Labra-Aviles, who was retained for the same reasons as Aguirre-Galindo.

The third layer described in archival documents includes the organizational members labeled as lieutenants. Ismael Higuera-Guerrero was the AF-DTO's top lieutenant who was responsible for the day-to-day operations throughout Mexico, including the receipt of drugs and the importation of those drugs into the United States. He had collateral duties of collecting the drug proceeds, policing the Tijuana area of Mexico and kidnapping, torturing and killing enemies of the organization.

Higuera-Guerrero's brother, Gilberto, was not described in documents as having an official title; however, he was appointed by his brother to supervise the Mexicali, Mexico operations, which included identical collateral duties as his brother, but only within a specific region of responsibility. Efrain Perez, who worked for Ismael Higuera-Guerrero, was tasked with organizing large shipments and supervising the shipments of drugs into the United States. Efrain's assistant, Jorge Aureliano-Felix, was strictly responsible for the safe storage of drugs in Tijuana and for collecting proceeds. In short, the leadership is concentrated in the family and then branches out to "trusted others" to take lower level supervision duties.

The structure also had a type of ambassador assigned to Mexico City, Rigobeto Yanez, who served as the initial point of contact for Colombian traffickers wishing to do business with Ismael. He also transported money to Colombian traffickers and supervised drug shipments outside of the Mexicali area. The organization's chief of security and chief enforcer was Armando Martinez-Duarte, a former high-ranking Mexican law enforcement official. He was charged with protecting the shipments from Mexican law enforcement. Under the direction of Gilberto, he would manage the kidnapping, torture and murder in the Mexicali region.

The strengths of the organization's structure are apparent in details found in court indictments describing the method and means of the organization.

Evil's Operational Strengths

1. Negotiate with Colombians for purchase and transportation of drugs.
2. Arrange for transmission of U.S. currency—in the form of wire transfers, cashier's checks and bulk shipments—to Colombia to pay for drug shipments.
3. Negotiate with Mexican marijuana growers for product to purchase and traffic.
4. Use commercial fishing boats, commercial airlines, private planes and cargo containers for shipments.
5. Convoy large shipments of drugs overland throughout Mexico to the Tijuana region through a variety of concealment measures.
6. Smuggle drugs into the United States using a number of methods, including trunks of vehicles, secret compartments located in commercial vehicles, helicopters, backpacks and small boats.
7. Obtain vehicles to be used to transport drugs and cash, and recruit drivers for the vehicles.

8. Arrange for smuggling to Los Angeles and other regions in the United States.

9. Smuggle proceeds from the United States into Mexico.

10. Bribe law enforcement and military officials in order to: protect the enterprise leadership and drug shipments; halt the arrest of enterprise members; have law enforcement seize drug shipments from rival DTOs and provide those drugs to the enterprise for their control.

11. Use codes and sophisticated equipment to communicate in order to disguise identities and conversations.

12. Use armored vehicles specially equipped with guns, bulletproof glass, smoke, oil, and/or nail dispensers to evade law enforcement and rival drug traffickers.

13. Obtain houses in Mexico and the United States to store drugs, guns, money and armored vehicles and to serve as regional headquarters for operations.

14. Operate houses, known as nests or caves, to conduct wiretap operations and to monitor communications and operations of rival DTOs and law enforcement.

15. Purchase hundreds of assault rifles, Uzi machine guns, high-caliber handguns and rifles, and bulletproof vests for the use of the enterprise enforcement teams.

16. Obtain law enforcement and military uniforms, credentials, and equipment to conduct assassinations of enemies.

17. Have "rules" of the organization, including not cooperating with law enforcement and punishing (possibly murdering) those who violate the rules of the organization to make examples of them.

18. Direct the kidnapping, torture and murder of enemies, including law enforcement, rival drug traffickers, military personnel and members of the media who write unfavorable stories.

19. Negotiate with Colombia's Revolutionary Armed Forces of Colombia (FARC) for drugs and weapons.[92]

Mortally Wounded? Not so Fast!

In 2002, an *LA Times* investigative reporter, Kraul,[93] wrote an article, "The Collapse of Mexico's Invincible Drug Cartel," detailing the killing of Ramon Arellano-Felix and the capture of his brother, Benjamin. Kraul interviewed the former head of the DEA's Mexico Unit, Michael G. Garland, and believed that these deaths would lead to rivals fighting with one another to take the lead. Kraul explained, "*You can expect a period of violence, first to settle vendettas and then as people try to position themselves to take over.... [The AF-DTO]...has been mortally wounded.*" *(p. 1)*[94] The Federal Attorney General's delegate in Baja California, Arturo Guevara Valenzuela, doubted that drug shipments into the United States from Mexico would lessen. Kraul credited Mexico's President Fox with success against the cartel because of his efforts to quietly move 1,300 special police (army soldiers) into Baja, Mexico. Kraul cited Mexico's State Attorney General, Antonio Martinez, who believed that these units made a huge difference in antinarcotic enforcement. Kraul also cited Erroll Chaves, the special agent in charge of the DEA's San Diego office, who gave credit to the Mexican government. Kraul's investigation revealed previous strengths and a strategy behind the AF-DTO's continued survival.

The AF-DTO learned to be brutal back in the 1980s through its leader, Miguel Angel Felix-Gallardo, who was imprisoned in 1985 for the kidnapping, torture and killing of DEA special agent Camarena. Before Felix-Gallardo went to jail, he divided up his smuggling regions among his family. The family quickly learned that, although it had control over land throughout Mexico, its success depended on control of the Tijuana-San Diego region, a key smuggling platform into the United States. The family employs "mules" (i.e., drug smugglers) to move drugs into the United States, not through large border towns, but rather in isolated areas of the border where they can blend in with Mexicans entering the United States illegally. The AF-DTO collects money from rival suppliers who want to move narcotics through the AF-DTO controlled regions, and rivals who don't contribute money are killed.

As the AF-DTO grew, it became more businesslike. AF-DTO members flew to Peru, Colombia and Panama to make deals in purchasing drug products. In doing so, the organization created a monopoly for heroin, marijuana, methamphetamine and cocaine. Shipments of drug supplies to the AF-DTO were orchestrated through specialized waterways along the Pacific Coast. The waterways were so specialized that they had refueling points and logistical support along the routes. The organization also corrupted U.S. immigration and customs agents, but this tactic became much more difficult after the United States prosecuted those who were caught. The AF-DTO suffered a significant blow in 2000 when its key accountant and chief operating officer, Ismael Higuera Guerrero, was arrested.

But despite this arrest and the 2002 arrests of high-level members, law enforcement officials admitted at the end of 2002 that the organization was continuing its operations as before; now it was being run by the two lesser-known brothers, Javier and Eduardo.[95] The White House stated that, despite all efforts to attack and dismantle the AF-DTO, "the organization continues to operate."[96]

In 2006, U.S. authorities uncovered the largest underground drug smuggling tunnel they had found since the tracking of the tunnels began in 2001. The tunnel, first noticed by Mexican authorities, contained over two tons of marijuana and was under the border between Tijuana and San Diego County. John Fernandez, the DEA special agent in charge of the San Diego area, stated that the AF-DTO was responsible.[97]

The Investigative Reporting

Robert Caldwell, a Vietnam Vet and retired editor of the "Insight Division" (an investigative component) of the *San Diego Union Tribune*, had been investigating the AF-DTO for over a decade. In addition to including him as one of the ten interviewees for my doctoral dissertation on drug cartels, I have consulted his publications because they are highly significant to this book and our understanding of evil.

In July 2007, Caldwell published the most extensive investigative report on the AF-DTO ever done by a media outlet. His four special reports, all published in the same month, provided by far the most significant findings in this overview of AF-DTO resilience. Caldwell described the AF-DTO's 1993 accidental assassination of Mexico's highest Roman Catholic cleric as the organization's single biggest blunder, one that should have pushed the organization into near extinction. He said, *"Unless AFO leaders could pre-empt that response [government action] they [the AF-DTO leaders] and the cartel would be in grave jeopardy."*[98] Caldwell described the account of a senior AF-DTO lieutenant, Everardo Arturo "Kitti" Paez-Martinez, provided as testimony to a grand jury in San Diego. The account explains how the organization acted quickly to prevent possible extinction by moving its personnel into immediate action.

Within hours of the assassination, the AF-DTO began colluding with Mexican officials and providing significant payoffs. The AF-DTO leaders began at the top, using two AF-DTO lieutenants, along with one of its leaders, Benjamin Arellano-Felix, to pay Rodolfo Leon-Aragon, chief of the Mexican Attorney General's Federal Judicial Police, $10 million. The Federal Judicial Police, now called the Federal Investigative Agency, was the Mexican equivalent of the FBI and Mexico's lead law enforcement component in investigating the DTO.

In exchange for the $10 million, Leon-Aragon was to do what he could to protect the AF-DTO. Later on that same day, a local commander was summoned for a meeting with the leadership of the AF-DTO. Following that meeting, Benjamin Arellano Felix, his top lieutenants, and Mexican officials created a plot to protect the AF-DTO by allowing the Mexican government to find several AF-DTO safe houses in Tijuana, but only after any incriminating documents were removed from the locations. The AF-DTO also offered a small number of scapegoats from the squad who had killed the cardinal.

The AF-DTO leadership then temporarily fled their Tijuana stronghold, only to return months later and rebuild the business in that area. Years later, Leon-Aragon, the Federal Judicial Police chief who had accepted the $10-million-bribe, was arrested for accepting a $1-million-bribe from another DTO.[99]

Caldwell states that,[100] *until recently, the U.S. government has had little knowledge about how the organization operates, its chain of command, the degree of its drug trafficking, and its operational techniques, including how profits are laundered and what smuggling methods are used.* It wasn't until 2002 that major breakthroughs were made by the U.S. government due to federal prosecution efforts in San Diego and the help of law enforcement experts. The information can be found in what Caldwell describes as thousands of pages of court documents, which were later assembled to support the extradition of key AF-DTO leaders to stand trial in the United States.

Much of the following analysis is based on key findings from Caldwell,[101] who writes, *"These documents, contained in the extradition packages for eleven AFO principals in custody in Mexico, were delivered to the Mexican government beginning in 2005. The documents were subsequently obtained by The San Diego Union Tribune."*[102]

Paez-Martinez, the senior lieutenant arrested and placed in U.S. custody in 2002, became the first senior AF-DTO figure to cooperate with the U.S. government against the organization. The details that he provided shed light on how the AF-DTO operates and survives. Paez-Martinez was closely associated with the family members of the organization and they trusted him. His tenure with the organization lasted twelve years, during which time he witnessed the daily activity of moving tons of narcotics across the border. Once the drugs arrived in the United States, they were shipped throughout Southern California and to other locations across the country. Paez Martinez described his work as supervising this distribution network. He developed business relationships with the DTO's counterparts in Colombia, who provided the AF-DTO with cocaine to sell.

In 1990, according to Paez Martinez, the AF-DTO improved its products and its distribution efforts and built an alliance with Colombia's Revolutionary Armed Forces (FARC). Under the agreement, FARC gave the AF-DTO cocaine for cash and weapons. Paez Martinez had witnessed the most brutal aspects of the AFO operations, including kidnapping, torture and murder. He admitted personally setting up several killings, some of them in San Diego. He had monitored AF-DTO radio communications, which ordered the killing of rivals, and witnessed the torture and killing of an AF-DTO associate at the hands of another associate who suspected the individual of cooperating with U.S. authorities.

Paez Martinez also outlined the significant corruption initiated by the AF-DTO, including bribes that involved millions of dollars per month. The AF-DTO "made Baja California's local and state governments and their corrupt police agencies de facto collaborators in the Tijuana cartel's drug trafficking."[103] The corruption reached as far as Mexico's Attorney General, who received a bribe of $3 million. As mentioned earlier, the personal secretary of former Mexican president Ernesto Zedillo also accepted bribes. Nor was the Mexican military immune. The AF-DTO found ways to bribe members of both the army and the navy. In short, the AF-DTO relied on an extensive day-to-day bribe system to ensure consistency of operations.

A DEA overview of the bribes, as reported by Caldwell, describes a payoff system providing bribes to sustain all areas of business, which includes:

> …the protection during the arrival of cocaine shipments and marijuana shipments within Mexico, the transportation of that cocaine and marijuana to locations within Mexico near the United States/Mexico border, the storage of that cocaine and marijuana before being transported into the United States, the transportation of that cocaine and marijuana to United States ports of entry and points in between, and even sometimes the transportation of that cocaine and marijuana into the United States.[104]

The DEA identified operations in which leaders of the AF-DTO were provided with key details about law enforcement's efforts to attack the AF-DTO, as well as with information on the DTO's drug trafficking rivals. Corruption allowed the AF-DTO to obtain radio frequencies and codes used by the authorities, so that the AF-DTO could monitor law enforcement efforts. These operations exemplify the AF-DTO's ability to gather intelligence and counterintelligence—a significant strength associated with the DTO's resiliency.

Unclassified research on the AF-DTO published in October 2007 by Strategic Forecasting Incorporated (a firm that produces intelligence reports, many of which are used by the federal government, law enforcement and the military) describes an organization in flux, due to a high number of arrests, and theorizes that the organization has "largely abandoned the drug trade in favor of other criminal enterprises—mainly kidnapping, according to a Mexican attorney general's report."[105] If true, this change demonstrates the ability of the AF-DTO to move from one business to another in order to remain operational.

As mentioned, the AF-DTO is highly structured and has been consistently dependent on its family membership. With a family structure of seven brothers and four sisters—all of whom have, or have had, varying degrees of responsibility within the AF-DTO[106]—the organization has had typically ample access to replacements, but they are now relying on just one family member, Francisco Eduardo. All of the other members have been killed or arrested, or have fled. As of the date of this study, the actual leader is unknown, but the organization remains operational with Francisco Eduardo and other lieutenants, including Enedina, who is responsible for money laundering.

Beyond that, little is known of AF-DTO's current operations. The organization's movement away from drug trafficking may be the result of a new vulnerability, due to a shortage of family members. Because the organization has always relied heavily on strong leadership, especially from family, the diminishing leadership may be responsible for an inability to sustain drug trafficking operations.

Constantine[107] states that the AF-DTO is one of the most powerful, violent, and aggressive drug trafficking groups in the world. And more than any other Mexican drug trafficking organization, it extends its tentacles from high-echelon figures in the Mexican law enforcement and judicial systems to street level individuals in the United States. He describes how the AF-DTO has killed Mexican law enforcement officials, informants and journalists, as well as how it has threatened the DEA and the FBI and a U.S. prosecutor. The AF-DTO uses Tijuana and San Diego street gangs as assassins. It uses high-level communications equipment, conducts counter surveillance, and has a well-trained security force.

Constantine[108] substantiates his testimony by describing large bribes to Mexican police, and approximately $1 million every week to

Mexican officials, to ensure no interference from the authorities. *Mexico City Contralinea* reported that the Mexican army seizes approximately 80 percent of the total drugs seized because the PGR (the Mexican equivalent of the office of the attorney general) does very little and has been suspected of selling "protection" to drug traffickers.

Resa-Nestares, a University of Madrid research professor specializing in drug trafficking and also a member of the International Association for the Study of Organized Crime, found that although the PGR is good at dismantling organizations, it fails miserably in securing important intelligence that other Mexican government agencies, including the Army, could use to make bigger gains."[109]

Resa-Nestares also highlighted other issues. For example, Mexico currently combats drug trafficking by splitting the country into seven drug trafficking sectors. But nobody seems to be in charge of these areas, too many groups are acting alone. He also pointed out a key problem with the Mexican army's involvement. The PGR's Office of the Deputy Attorney for Special Investigation into Organized Crime (SIEDO) has been unable to build a single case since the beginning of mapping drug territory in 2003. SIEDO's efforts now go primarily toward protecting witnesses. Resa-Nestares stated that the PGR needs to do police work. "It's very simple: gather information and then act."[110]

Behind the Line

For a number of years, Rusty Fleming has been traveling along the U.S.-Mexican border investigating the drug cartels. In his recent documentary, he describes the eye-opening experience, full of horrifying revelations and life-changing consequences. He is the award-winning producer of this acclaimed movie and has authored a book by the same title, "Drug Wars." I was so impressed in meeting with Rusty and his stories that I feel a strong need to include one in this book.

Behind the Line – Testimonial 7: "Drug Wars: Narco-Warfare in Twenty-First Century"

with Rusty Fleming, Film Executive Producer

The truth is the war is about all of us. It's not just a Mexican problem or a Colombian problem. It's an American problem, it's a Canadian problem, and it's a truly massive problem. It is far bigger than anything a single government, nation, or legal system can handle—bigger than any one solution, and far worse than any of us realize.

To cross these guys is a death sentence, and it doesn't matter who you are. Look at the killings that have taken place just this year. They have beheaded police officers, lawyers, and judges. They will kill anyone who gets in their way. They have killed journalists for digging too deep. They have killed cops for cooperating with rival gangs and killed them for not cooperating at all. They have killed the wives and children of rivals, of police officers, and of anyone else they wish to send a strong message to. They have no compunctions whatever about doing it, and because they are almost never caught or punished, they operate with virtual impunity.

There is not one single voice out there telling us, 'It's okay now; we've got a handle on this.' And I am not referring to the problem of illegal immigration. I'm referring to the security of our nation's southern border being in the hands of the Mexican drug cartels that control the entire region of our country—and they will hold on to that control by whatever means necessary.

In regards to the training cartels put their members through. It starts out as any other military boot camp with physical training, running and obstacle course drills, and then classes later in the day, 24 hours a day, seven days a week, for six months; the same training that is given to the most elite special-forces anywhere in the world is given to these teenagers, all in the concerted effort to build a generation of narco-terrorists better than their predecessors.

The armed attacks and threats by drug traffickers against media organizations have made Mexico the world's most dangerous country, after Iraq, for journalists, according to the French media advocacy group Reporters Without Borders. During my filming, I had no idea where I was taken for the meeting, because I rode for six hours in the back of an SUV with a hood over my head. But finally I had an opportunity to ask my contact about what it was like to be a boss of one of the most powerful criminal enterprises on earth. My contact's last words to me sounded like a prophetic warning: "Be careful when you get here, Rusty." he said. "They're killing reporters down here just for asking the wrong questions.'

In years past, the U.S. and Mexico governments have engaged in a lot of finger-pointing back and forth, which has diverted our attention from the true situation. The harsh reality is that the Mexican side of this war against the narcos has been brutal and costly. Being at close range with these drug lords and the narco-insurgents they employ is no picnic. Some of the things we take for granted in this country are the very things almost entirely lacking in Mexican society today. A safe and secure living and working environment is just one of the basic needs that have virtually disappeared.

The fact that they have not unleashed the same levels of wholesale violence as the Colombians does not mean they haven't the capacity for such violence; it simply means they have had no reason to use it yet—they will not escalate the violence until they are faced with escalated threats. Such restraint is no different from that exercised by countries with nuclear weapons—just because they are not using their armaments to wreak mass destruction does not mean that they won't if sufficiently provoked. The Mexican narco-insurgency's full capacity for violence has yet to be tested.

It appears that the Cartels' political objectives begin and end with the ability to maintain their operating authority in a country that corrupt government officials have made a safe haven for them—their political aspirations are simply to keep insulated from foreign governments seeking to bring them to justice.

A U.S. Federal Agent once told me, "Mexico may not be Colombia yet, but you can damn sure see it from here." No matter how it is spun, the situation is closer to being out of control than under control.

This much is painfully obvious: we need to pay closer attention to Mexico and the deterioration of its society because the next step in the "Colombianization of Mexico" could very well be the "Mexicanization of the United States." This is not as far-fetched as some may think. The evidence is mounting, and the trend shows no signs of slowing down.

Groups such as the Zetas are mainly responsible for transporting and securing the loads of drugs coming into the United States from Brownsville, Texas; San Diego, California; and all points in between. They have cell groups in United States cities such as Dallas, Houston, Atlanta and Chicago, and they can kill, kidnap and extort at will. According to intelligence sources, cross-border abductions of American and Mexican Nationals are now reaching twelve per day.

They come across the border with orders to kill police officers and any other law enforcement personnel who cross their path to send a simple message: "Stay out of our way." They have more resources than any law enforcement group fighting them, and no rules of engagement when it comes to completing their mission.

It's easy to write stories or talk on television about these drug dealing terrorists once they are locked up or dead, but our story is about the ones who are still in the game—and you can be sure they won't sit idly by for very long. Not many people would see this project as worth risking their lives for, but here's why, for some, it is: "I have met the people who have been terrorized by this situation—people with the most heartbreaking stories I've ever heard—and I can only pray that I never know what it's like to be in their shoes."

The subject of my film still has a certain amount of hysteria attached to it. When we went to South Texas to hold a private screening of the final production for the journalists, victims' families, and law enforcement people who had helped us make the documentary, the theater owners in San Antonio made us agree not to allow the press to disclose the location where we were showing it. We agreed, and even then, three weeks before the event, they canceled on us, fearing retaliation from the cartels. Pretty amazing to think that the narco-terrorists can wield that much power 200 miles inside our border.

This merits some careful pondering in assessing whether the Mexican government can get the job done—even with nearly a billion and a half dollars in aid. The Gulf Cartel has been taken over by its Zeta enforcers and now, more than ever before, is at the top of the government's hit list. In the year since President Calderón declared all-out war, his government has barely put a dent in public enemy number one, while arresting or killing a scant handful of ranking members. Will he really do that much better if we throw a wad of money at the problem? On the other hand, Mexico is certain to lose the fight if it has to do it with no help from the United States.

I have come to know men like border Sheriff Arvin West, D'Wayne Jernigan, Rick Flores and 'Sigi' Gonzalez, Jr. and, along with their fellow border sheriffs, they constitute the front line of defense this country has with regard to border security. I take nothing from the men and women in other agencies like Border Patrol and ICE, but these men and women are out there almost completely on their own with almost no help from the federal government whose responsibility it is to do this job in the first place.

I cannot stress this point enough and, if you come away from reading my book and there is only one thing you remember, please let it be this: I have traveled this border region, I have seen this enemy at close range and, without question, there is no solution to this problem without men like these being part of that solution. They live on this border, their families live on this border, they have insight and far more at stake than all the bureaucrats in Washington put together. I have seen them fighting this war hamstrung from the lack of support from our government, and it is nothing but politics.

That fence was no surprise to the Cartel members; they knew we were going to build it three years before we did it. I am not saying that the fence is not a good idea; in fact I think it will serve a very good purpose in specific portions of the border. But some in America have lulled themselves into a false sense of security thinking that this was going to be the answer to the security issues along that border, and I assure you it is not. The narco-terrorists who control our border had that fence clocked before the first bucket of cement ever showed up in the desert.

It is the very assets we have that make our communities so appealing to them. Everything positive for us is a positive for them, too. Our vast, vigorous and diverse cities serve as their protection and their profit base; our international commerce system and our superhighways serve as high-speed conduits for their goods; and they see our children as customers and potential recruits. Our steadfast denial of the situation makes it all possible for them.

— Rusty Fleming

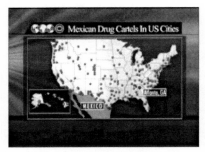

Cartels operating in the U.S.
(photo courtesy of law enforcement)

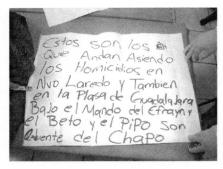

Warning letter from Mexican drug cartels
(photo courtesy of law enforcement)

Bodies dumped in a Mexico
neighborhood *(photo courtesy of law
enforcement)*

Bound heads of drug cartel victims
(photo courtesy of law enforcement)

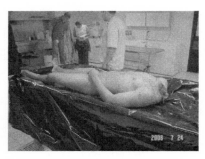

Mexican headless body *(photo courtesy
of Gary "Rusty" Fleming)*

Mexican drug cartel victim head *(photo
courtesy of Gary "Rusty" Fleming)*

Drug cartel tunnel into the U.S.
(photo courtesy of law enforcement)

Violence on Mexico's streets
(photo courtesy of law enforcement)

Counterfeit U.S. money produced by
Mexican drug cartels *(photo courtesy of
law enforcement)*

Wanted poster of drug cartel leaders
(photo courtesy of law enforcement)

Mexican drug cartel members
(photo courtesy of law enforcement)

Mexican soldier stands guard as
confiscated drugs are burned
(photo courtesy of law enforcement)

Saint Malverde – Mexican drug lord
(photo courtesy of law enforcement)

Heavily armed Mexican police/military
(photo courtesy of law enforcement)

David Barron, drug cartel hit-man killed
(photo courtesy of law enforcement)

Mexican police stand guard in busy city
streets *(photo courtesy of law
enforcement)*

Cartel victims dissolved in barrels of
acid called *"pozole."* A threatening note
is left by those who committed this
crime *(photo courtesy of law
enforcement)*

Heads of rival drug cartel members
(photo courtesy of law enforcement)

Cartel victims
(photo courtesy of law enforcement)

Cartel victims
(photo courtesy of law enforcement)

Cartel victims laying near large warning
letters from the cartel responsible for the
murders *(photo courtesy of law
enforcement)*

This victim's body shows significant
signs of torture
(photo courtesy of law enforcement)

Rival cartel members shown purposely
on video *(photo courtesy of law
enforcement)*

Rival cartel members heads placed on the
hood of a vehicle, with a warning note
from a cartel *(photo courtesy of law
enforcement)*

Mexican military and police build up their forces *(photo courtesy of law enforcement)*

Cartel members display a victim in front of cameras *(photo courtesy of law enforcement)*

Cartel members display a victim in front of cameras *(photo courtesy of law enforcement)*

Citizens of Mexico, at times, protest the government's fight against cartels. These citizens are often paid by cartel members *(photo courtesy of law enforcement)*

Cartel members often bind their victims before killing them to prevent the spread of blood during interrogations, torture and killing. Killers have left behind a note. *(photo courtesy of law enforcement)*

Children in Mexico are instructed on how to cover on the floor when drug cartel violence occurs *(photo courtesy of law enforcement)*

Cardinal Juan Jesus Posada-Ocampo is
executed by cartel members
(photo courtesy of law enforcement)

DEA Special Agent Camarena working
in Mexico was kidnapped in 1985,
tortured and killed by cartel members.
His killing led to the creation of *Red
Ribbon Week*
(photo courtesy of law enforcement)

Mass grave in Mexico
(courtesy of the El Paso Times)

Mexico cartel car bomb – a tactic seen in
Iraq *(photo courtesy of law enforcement)*

Mexico cartel car bomb
(photo courtesy of law enforcement)

Cartel members kill two victims and hang them from a bridge in a resort city – a tactic seen in Iraq
(photo courtesy of law enforcement)

In Iraq, two bodies are hung from a bridge after being drug through the streets *(photo courtesy of law enforcement)*

U.S. vehicle destroyed in Iraq – Mexico cartels replicate this tactic *(photo courtesy of law enforcement)*

al Qaeda mass killing in Iraq
(photo courtesy of law enforcement)

Terrorists in Iraq *(courtesy of Fox News)*

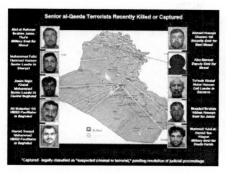

Example of al terrorist leadership chart used by U.S. to identify targets *(photo courtesy of law enforcement)*

al Shabaab terror organization based in Africa *(photo courtesy of law enforcement)*

Russian gangs
(photo courtesy of law enforcement)

Hells Angeles
(photo courtesy of law enforcement)

Gangs in Africa
(photo courtesy of law enforcement)

Latin American gang members
(photo courtesy of law enforcement)

The spread of terrorist organization in Africa *(photo courtesy of CBS)*

Nazi terror during WWII
(photo courtesy of U.S. Government)

U.S. organized crime terror in the 1920s and beyond *(photo courtesy of law enforcement)*

Hitler
(photo courtesy of U.S. Government)

Bin Laden
(photo courtesy of U.S. Government)

Troops connect with youth. Key to winning our eternal battle against evil *(photo courtesy of U.S. Government)*

Chapter Six

Santa Muerte: Angel of Death

"The Angel of Death hears prayers from dark sources."[111]

Behind the Line – Testimonial 8: "The Dark Side"

with International Gang Expert, Richard Valdemar

*L*et no one be found among you who sacrifices his son or daughter in the fire, who practices divination or sorcery, interprets omens, engages in witchcraft, or casts spells, or who is a medium or spiritist or who consults the dead. Anyone who does these things is detestable to the Lord, and because of these detestable practices the LORD your God will drive out those nations before you. -- Deuteronomy 18:10-13

International Gang Expert Richard Valdemar explains:

Throughout the long history of gangs, their members have flirted with the dark side of evil. On the one hand, they claimed to be defenders of their race and neighborhood; on the other, they acted in league with the devil, both metaphorically and literally. This conflict can be seen in the mixture of religious and demonic symbols depicted on their tattooed bodies.

While most street gangs were not driven by evil spiritual motivation, in the ugly manmade hell of prison some of these gangs clearly turned to the dark side, with escalated violence being the result. The Mexican Mafia actually forbade its members from "picking up the Bible" or espousing any form of

Christianity. Some members of the Aryan Brotherhood were followers of pagan witchcraft or worshipers of the devil.

In taking on these new belief systems many gang members eschewed the moral codes they had previously ascribed to as part of their religious/superstitious upbringing.

In the 1980s, Cuban "Marielitos" brought Afro-Cuban cult beliefs into the Los Angeles drug and gang culture. Santeria, Voodoo and Palo Mayombe followers became some of the most violent criminal gang members Los Angeles had ever seen. Across the city, small altars with caldrons or 'gangas' of fruit, rum and cocaine, as well as animal blood sacrifices, dotted the map. "Botanicas" (occult pharmacies) that sold the paraphernalia required for these rituals sprang up in every community.

Drug cartels from Mexico practiced their own rituals. "Brujeria" (witchcraft) altars with figurines of the bandit saint "Jesus Malverde" or "Santisima Muerte" (holy death) were common in cartel drug houses. Cartel members wore amulets and placed figurines of occult symbols in their cars. Some openly worshipped Satan.

Of all the criminal groups that I have worked over the more than three decades in law enforcement, the most credible attempts on my life have come from these occult true believers. Be aware of these trends and beliefs. Gang members who take the occult seriously can be truly dangerous.

— Richard Valdemar

Santa Muerte, or the "Saint of Death," is also known as the "Angel of Death." In appearance, she is the Grim Reaper with a grotesque skull; long, grasping skeleton hands; and a body draped in black or white shrouds. Of the many patron saints in the Mexican drug underworld, she is the most powerful.

It has long been a part of Hispanic culture and customs that people pray to many saints and icons to intercede with God on their behalf.

Many of these saints, Mexican or otherwise, are sanctified by the Catholic Church, and many are "folk saints" not recognized by the Catholic Church but an integral part of Mexican folk culture. All of the various saints and icons are well represented not just in churches and on home altars, but also on amulets, bracelets, and myriads of decorated candles and images that are sold in every market. Altars often feature many saints and icons together; more is often considered better.

Like the majority of the Mexican population, drug lords, drug dealers and drug traffickers pray to saints and icons, particularly to those who are known to provide protection and safety. Robert Almonte, a retired deputy chief of the El Paso Police Department who has been on the frontline of the drug war for many years, conducted extensive research on the Mexican drug trade and also on what he calls the "drug saints." Currently he runs a law enforcement training academy focused on the drug trade.[112] One of the courses he offered is "Patron Saints of the Mexican Drug Underworld." His video of the same name[113] illustrates the widespread use of saints and icons in the Mexican drug trade. Over the years these "saints" have become particularly popular in the underworld of the drug cartels. Understanding their importance and wide use in the drug trade is critical in helping law enforcement officers discover and arrest drug traffickers and others working with the cartels.

Highly popular among drug traffickers is Jesus Malverde, the "Robin Hood" of Mexico and the patron saint of the poor and of generous bandits. He is easily recognizable by his black hair, heavy black eyebrows, and mustache. Law enforcement officials see him often, particularly when Mexican traffickers cross the border with drugs wearing Jesus Malverde amulets and bracelets, and on the dashboard statues are seen for anticipated protection.

Other saints who offer protection and safety to those in the drug world are San Simon, the patron saint of undocumented aliens and gamblers; Juan Soldado, the patron saint of safe passage; and San Jude, the patron saint of hopeless causes and difficult situations. San Ramon is the patron saint of secrets and silence. Drug dealers ask for his help in keeping their dealings and their information secret. And there are many more.

Most powerful of all, however, is Santa Muerte, the Angel of Death. Santa Muerte is not recognized by the Catholic Church, but she has become immensely popular in the last 60 years and has a strong following in certain areas of Mexico. She is the patron saint of outcasts, outlaws and the criminally minded, but she has also become the patron saint of those who feel desperate or desperately poor and who may feel deserted by the government or the church.[114] Perhaps their supplications to La Virgen Maria (the Virgin Mary) or the Virgen de Guadalupe have not been successful, so they turn to the Angel of Death for help.[115]

In the drug underworld Santa Muerte is considered a powerful protector, and she is not only fervently worshipped but also offered sacrifices in the hope that she will grant special requests. When the homes or offices of drug dealers or drug traffickers are searched, there are often altars with candles and offerings for Santa Muerte. In the drug cartels, where murder and torture are commonplace and where the key feature of the culture is violence and fear, people are often killed in front of statues of Santa Muerte, or their body parts or burned heads are given to Santa Muerte as offerings.[116] In the dark underworld of drug cartels, where the forces of darkness and death are everywhere, Santa Muerte may be a powerful protector for some, but she is indeed the Angel of Death for others.

My friends, this is the evil we are up against. It is remarkably shocking to imagine an entire underworld culture that praises evil and know that their ranks are growing. If such evil can flourish in Mexico, one of the staunchest Catholic nations on the planet, it can flourish anywhere—and it has.

Behind the Line – Testimonial 9: "Patron Saints of the Mexican Drug Underworld"

with Richard Valdemar, International Gang Expert

Recently it has been my privilege to travel and teach with the Border Sheriff's Posse in El Paso, San Diego and Ontario, California. This organization supports the National Border Sheriffs' Coalition and puts on a conference called Border School. The conference is intended to provide local law enforcement, public servants and community leaders with information about the border issues that are not being presented by the national media.

The highly effective instructors include Sheriff Arvin West of Hudspeth County, Texas, and Sheriff Sigi Gonzales of Zapata County, Texas, but the coalition is made up of sheriffs from Texas, Arizona, California and New Mexico. These sheriffs represent law enforcement in the counties along our border with Mexico. They are honorable, frank, plain-talking men who speak with one voice, unlike our politicians.

In the El Paso Border School, I met Diana Washington Valdez, a journalist for the El Paso Times, who is also the author of "The Killing Fields: Harvest of Women." Her presentation dealt with the hundreds of unsolved murders of Mexican women in the Juarez border area. She is considered an expert in the Juarez femicides. I highly recommend this book.

Finally, I met retired Deputy Chief Robert Almonte of the El Paso Police Department. He served three terms as president of the Texas Narcotics Officers Association and was also the vice president of the National Narcotics Officers Association. After 25 years with El Paso Police Department, he became a consultant with General Dynamics and started a law enforcement training company. Robert Almonte has recently been appointed as a U.S. Marshal for Texas.

I was most fascinated with his training video, "Patron Saints of the Mexican Drug Underworld." I have had some experience in this dark spiritual world during some of my own investigations in Los Angeles involving the Cuban Marielitos and Mexican cartels.

In a strange way, it ties together much of the evil perpetrated by the gangs that are trafficking in drugs and human beings and their violent inhuman behavior. There is a spiritual dimension to their madness, and recognition of the signs and symbols of their belief system can help you identify them. As Almonte says: "This is presented for the officers' safety and to help the law enforcement officer identify traffickers and make larger seizures."

When the Spanish explorers first visited Meso-America, they found the great culture of the Aztecs and other indigenous natives flourishing. But there was also much tribal warfare and even human sacrifice to the female god of death, Mictecacihuatl, near what is now Mexico City. The Spanish conquistadors were determined to convert the pagan natives to Christianity. However, this was not always done in a Christian way.

Orthodox Catholicism involves a multitude of legitimate saints invoked by pious Catholics to intercede for them. Some of these saints have specific attributes that make them patron saints for specific requests. For instance the Archangel Michael, who defeated Satan, is the patron saint of the police, the airborne, and the protector of the state of Israel and the Church. For this reason a believing soldier or law enforcement officer might legitimately petition Saint Michael for intercession and protection or wear a medal of his likeness.

Some requests and the invoking of the saints might have less than noble intentions. We see this often in Mexico among the poor, undereducated and superstitious. The Mexican criminal elements often invoke both the recognized and even non-

recognized or folk legend "saints" to protect the drug smuggler, bandit or human trafficker.

The Lady of Guadalupe

In December, 1531 on Tepeyac Hill near Mexico City, the miraculous appearance of the Virgin Mary known as Our Lady of Guadalupe almost overnight converted millions of Mexico's indigenous natives to Catholicism. This was partly due to the fact that she is said to have appeared as a native in native dress and first appeared to a simple indigenous man named Juan Diego. This appearance is said to have occurred near the spot where human sacrifices had once been made to the pagan god Mictecacihuatl. The Lady of Guadalupe became the patron saint of Mexico and of the entire American continent. Her image is found throughout Mexico and in both Central America and South America.

Both pious orthodox Catholics and superstitious criminals often utilize statues and images of the Lady of Guadalupe. She is invoked by criminals who are believers in magic for protection and to identify with Mexico. She can often be found in their cars and homes along with unorthodox folk saints and good luck charms.

Scarface and Tweety

For some reason two common "good luck" images among Narco traffickers are the movie character from "Scarface" and the cartoon character "Tweety Bird."

Al Pacino's Scarface is admired and invoked because the movie depicts him as a highly successful narcotics kingpin. I have seen posters from the movie in countless gang members' homes and even a "Scarface" doll owned by a Mexican Mafia member arrested in Orange County, Calif.

Tweety can be thought of as a pollo (baby chick), which is Mexican slang for an illegal border crosser, and a pollero is slang for a smuggler or coyote. The Tweety decal on an automobile is another hint about its owner's occupation.

Orthodox Catholic Saints

Saint Jude is a recognized Catholic saint. He is considered the patron of hopeless or desperate causes. Comedian Danny Thomas built a hospital in his name for people with terminal diseases. In the criminal underworld, Saint Jude is invoked to protect smugglers and bandits because of their desperate situation.

Saint Toribio Romo was a Catholic priest who was martyred in 1928 during the persecution of Catholics by the Mexican government in the Christero War that followed the Mexican Revolution. In the 1990s, illegal immigrants crossing the Sonora desert into the U.S. began reporting that they were given food and water by a stranger who resembled the image of Saint Toribio. Subsequently, he became the patron of immigrants or illegal immigrants. He is invoked by both coyotes and border crossers who must cross the dangerous border area.

Santo Niño de Atocha (Holy Child of Atocha) came to Mexico from 13th Century Spain. During this time, the city of Atocha fell under the control of Muslim invaders. The males of the town were imprisoned and denied food and water. Only very small children were allowed to visit these men. The women pleaded and prayed for divine intervention to a statue of the Virgin Mary who held in her arms the Christ child. A small child appeared in the prison carrying a pilgrim's staff with a gourd of water and a basket of food. This was assumed to be the Christ child. Santo Nino became the patron of prisoners and travelers. Because of this, his image is often used by prisoners and by human smugglers.

San Ramon was a saint who was born by Caesarian operation. He is known for exchanging himself to free Christians warriors held hostage by the Muslims in Algiers. He was tortured for preaching to convert his captors. A hot iron rod was used to pierce his lips and a lock was used to seal his mouth. He is invoked as the patron saint of midwives and of silence. Drug dealers especially invoke San Ramon to prevent the telling of secrets. It is common to see his image with a coin or tape placed across his lips to ensure silence.

A Prayer to Jesus Malverde

Today before your cross prostrate,

Oh, Malverde my Lord,

I beg your mercy to relieve my pain.

You who dwell in glory,

And you who are so close to God,

Listen to the suffering of this humble fisherman.

Oh, miraculous Malverde,

Oh, Malverde my Lord,

Concede this favor and fill my sprit with joy.

Give me health Lord,

Give me rest,

Give me wellbeing,

And so let it be.

We now look at how the Mexican underworld has appropriated and perverted the iconography of Mexican culture and the Catholic faith.

Unorthodox Folk Saints

San Juan Soldado (Saint John the Soldier) was a real person, Juan Castillo Morales, a soldier in the Mexican Army. In 1938, he was convicted for the rape and murder of a young girl in

Tijuana. Believers claim that he was an innocent man. He was sentenced to face a military firing squad, but he was allowed to run. If he could reach the distance of a thousand meters or so without being killed, he was a free man. Juan was shot running through a cemetery toward the U.S. border.

Later, blood mysteriously began to appear in the spot where Juan was shot. This was witnessed by numerous people. He is now invoked as the unofficial "saint" of illegal aliens, fugitives, and for people seeking safe passage.

"Brother" San Simon was a drunkard and a gambler from Guatemala. He is depicted as a mustached man dressed in a black suit and hat sitting in a chair. Sometimes he holds a staff or cane, smokes a cigar and has coins in his hand. In Guatemala, he is slightly more colorfully dressed and is often crudely carved from wood. He represents a man of the Twentieth Century enjoying worldly things. He is the patron of drunkards and gamblers.

The image of Jesus Malverde comes from the city of Culican Sinaloa, Mexico. There are two different folk stories explaining Jesus Malverde. The first version of the tale is that he was a bandit who was caught by the Federales (Mexican Federal Police). Without a trial he was hung from a tree, cursed, and left to be eaten by vultures.

A poor peon rancher happened to pass the rotting corpse he recognized as Juan Malverde. The poor rancher was looking for his only cow which had wandered away. He invoked the intervention of the bandit promising to give him a proper burial if he would help him recover his prized possession. The cow returned and the poor rancher buried Malverde as he promised, building a small shrine over his grave.

Another folk tale is that bounty hunters shot the "Robin Hood" like bandit. Jesus had been nicknamed Malverde because he employed the tactic of dressing in green camouflage and hiding in the brush to surprise his victims. Mal in Spanish can be translated in English to "bad" and verde to "green." Though mortally wounded he escaped the bounty hunters and returned to his rancho. He pleaded with his friends to turn in his dead body and split up the reward with the other villagers. This is what they did.

Bandits and drug smugglers soon began visiting his shrine and invoking his intervention to protect their illegal cargo and other criminal enterprises. They brought gifts of tequila and flowers and hired expensive mariachi bands to serenade his image.

Some drug dealers even observe the "Sabbath of Jesus Malverde" by doing no trafficking on Thursday because they believe this is the day Malverde was killed. Malverde is by far the most common folk "saint" that I have encountered among the Mexican drug traffickers in Los Angeles.

A caution here, Jesus Malverde has become so popular that he has been accepted as a saint by many Mexicans who are not necessarily drug dealers. He is depicted as a mustached young man with black hair wearing a white shirt. He is also sometimes depicted with a noose around his neck. Sometimes he is shown wearing a white cowboy hat.

Afro-Caribbean and Mexican Brujeria Influences

The Afro-Caribbean influences of Haitian Vodou, Santeria, and Palo Mayombe have many devoted followers in Mexico. In these systems, Catholic saints are substituted for the African deities. These belief systems are often mixed with local folk magic and brujeria (witchcraft).

And not all believers are poor, uneducated, superstitious peons.

In the 1940s, the "Evangelist of Satan" Aleister Crowley and his associates studied the dark arts, including brujeria, in Mexico. One of his associates was rocket scientist Jack Parsons who worked at the Jet Propulsion Laboratory in Pasadena, Calif. Crowley would pick Parsons to lead his occult church, the Ordo Templi Orientis (O.T.O.), in Pasadena, California. Parsons was also an associate of L. Ron Hubbard, founder of the Church of Scientology.

Santa Muerte

In Mexico's District Federal, the cathedral was filled with smoke and the smell of burning marijuana. The large icon was surrounded by burning candles, flowers, and offerings of money and tequila. A well-dressed middle-aged man knelt before the shrine. He was followed into the cathedral by a band of mariachis. "Play for her" he ordered, and the mariachis began to play one of Mexico's popular narcocorridos (ballads) by Chalino Sanchez.

A larger than life figure stood before them, a smirking skeleton dressed to look like what Americans would recognize as the grim reaper, complete with the soul-harvesting scythe. The figure was similar in dress to the grim reaper, except this figure was female. Her long tufts of hair hung from her gruesome skull. She was Santa Muerte, the "Holy Angel of Death."

Santa (or Santisima) Muerte is worshiped in Mexico like the evil sister of the Virgin of Guadalupe, and today she has converted thousands of souls to her dark world. Some say she had her beginnings in a Mexican prison in the 1960s. She is sometimes affectionately called "La Niña Blanca" (The White Child) and dressed almost bride-like. Her colors have significance—white for good luck, red for love, and black for protection.

Santa Muerte is invoked by smugglers, bandits and drug dealers for health, happiness and successful "business transactions." She is also said to protect the drug load in its journey across the frontera and the smuggler from the police. There are small shrines, churches and cathedrals dedicated to Santa Muerte all over Mexico and a few in the U.S.

Mexican Sinaloan Drug cartel boss Joaquin "Chapo" Guzman as well as Armando "Chato" Garcia, the murderer of Los Angeles County Sheriff's Deputy David March in 2002, are both worshipers of Santa Muerte.

What is far more disturbing is the growing acceptance of this perverse idol worship among the general Mexican population. Thousands attend processions and celebrations to honor Santa Muerte, and the traditional Catholic saints are ignored.

Some human sacrifices to Santa Muerte have been claimed in Tijuana and Nuevo Laredo in 2006. In 2008, eleven headless bodies were found in the Yucatan and the heads were said to have been burned in honor of Santa Muerte. Perhaps Mexico is returning to the practice of human sacrifice to a new Mictecacihuatl, the female Aztec god of the dead.

— Richard Valdemar

Santa Muerte: Angel of Death

A worshiper blows marijuana smoke onto the face of the Saint of Death
(photo courtesy of law enforcement)

Candles of Santa Muerte, called "tapadas" are sold throughout Mexico
(photo courtesy of law enforcement)

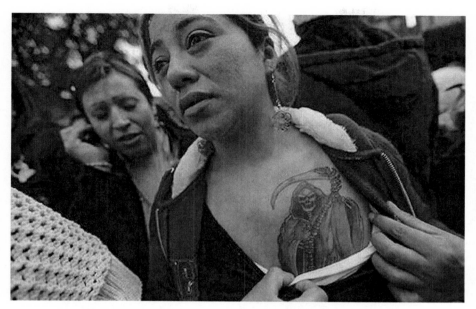

A woman displays her tattoo of Santa Muerta
(photo courtesy of law enforcement)

Large crowd gathers for worship with statues of Santa Muerta.
(photo courtesy Washington Post)

Dr. Paul R. Chabot

Santa Muerte prominently displayed on a busy street.
(photo courtesy Las Vegas Sun)

134

Chapter Seven

Resilience

"At a moment's notice everything that was left unprepared becomes a complex problem, and every weakness comes rushing to the forefront."
— Patrick Lagadec

The AF-DTO and Resiliency

In previous chapters, I have presented an historical overview of organizational resiliency within the AF-DTO (Arellano Felix Drug Trafficking Organization) with two objectives in mind: first, to analyze significant research to determine if the AF-DTO is a resilient organization; second, to set out and identify the core resiliency factors sustaining this evil. Through this journey, I have identified a number of core resiliency characteristics, as well as two environmental factors, which, as you will see in later chapters, are the foundation for our attack strategy to fight the ultimate evil.

The historical overview provided valuable information concerning the AF-DTO's successes, setbacks and failures. They revealed an understanding of factors sustaining the organization over time, and allowed me to create a framework upon which to build. In beginning this building process, I came across a brilliant researcher and theorist by the name of Karl Weick who has written extensively on a topic called mindfulness,[117] which really opened my eyes to how simple resilience is to understand.

Karl Weick proposed a mindful infrastructure for high reliability, and I used this in the creation of a new model for organizational resiliency specific to the AF-DTO. In order for me to wrap my arms around the why and how of resilience, I set out to answer two general questions:

Question 1. *What role does organizational resilience play in the prevention of organizational failure within highly volatile organizations?*

While it is uncertain what role organizational resilience plays within volatile organizations, it is clear what role organizational resilience plays within the sustainability of the AF-DTO. It became apparent in the course of this study that generalizing resiliency characteristics to organizations as a whole would not be appropriate. The AF-DTO operates in a much different environment than other organizations, including other criminal organizations.

The AF-DTO has developed core resiliency characteristics that explain how the organization has learned to sustain itself within a volatile environment. Organization resiliency has prevented organization dismantlement. The organization was able to learn from failure and apply methods to counter future attacks that exploited its vulnerabilities.

Organizational resiliency was not an end state, but rather an evolutionary and, at times, revolutionary cycle. It allowed the organization to improve itself based on its ability to apply newly learned traits to its way of conducting business. Organizational resiliency, as it turns out, is not in itself an applied technique; rather, it is something an organization develops as it fights back to prevent failure. This study reveals that organizational resiliency within the AF-DTO is applicable only when the AF-DTO applies its resiliency characteristics to situations that, if left unchecked, could lead to organizational failure. For example, when the United States changed tactics for drug detection and interdiction at the border points, the AF-DTO adapted to this change, thereby allowing its narcotics to flow, relatively freely, into the United States. If the AF-DTO failed to adapt to the changes, it would lose its ability to traffic narcotics—that is, it would lose its financial lifeblood.

Organizational resiliency is achieved only by cycling through several phases described in the AF-DTO resiliency framework (this becomes crystal clear for you at the end of this book). Organizational resiliency does not prevent organizational failure. Rather, organizational resiliency is the phase reached by implementing any number of AF-DTO resiliency characteristics. The AF-DTO became resilient as it fought numerous efforts that were made to destroy the organization. From each of these efforts, the organization's leadership learned how to adapt and implement the necessary changes to survive.

The role that organizational resiliency plays within the AF-DTO can be described by examining episodes of organizational hardship and the actions taken by the AF-DTO to counteract them. Therefore, organizational resiliency does not prevent failure; rather, it is a concept used to describe organizations—like the AF-DTO—that are able to survive when extreme conditions present a likelihood of organizational failure.

Organizational resiliency can best be described and understood through the lens of human beings. Resilient human beings are not resilient simply because they bounce back time and again from significant hardship; rather—and more importantly—it is because they *take actions that lead to* their resiliency.[118] These actions—for both human beings and organizations—are the essence of resiliency. This understanding leads to the study's second (and final) question.

Question 2. *What is the essence of the experience of resilience from the perspective of law enforcement and justice personnel who were assigned to dismantle the DTO? In short, what can we learn to improve our fight on the battlefield?*

The perspective of law enforcement and justice personnel assigned to the AF-DTO shows an organization demonstrating 14 core resiliency characteristics and two environmental factors, with each characteristic made up of core themes. The core resiliency characteristics include adaptability, business acumen, compartmentalization, corruption, international reach, loyalty, monopoly goal orientation, optimism, recruitment, reputation, self-reliance, situational awareness, technology and trust. Collectively, law enforcement and justice personnel provided several these similar to those contained in the archival documents.

The AF-DTO's resilience certainly frustrates those charged with dismantling the AF-DTO. Despite law enforcement efforts over 20 years, the organization continues to find ways to sustain itself. Simply stated, the organization is able to do whatever is necessary for survival far beyond the normal boundaries of legitimate businesses. Those providing the data emphasized that although the organization certainly has many of these resiliency characteristics, the reason it is able to maintain that resiliency is because it operates within a region of the world that has little regard for the rule of law. Second, the AF-DTO has a vast consumer base of drug users in the United States. The framework shows two environmental factors vital to the organization's survival.

The organization has free rein to operate with near impunity and a constant flow of money from its success in selling drugs to American drug users. With these two environmental factors in place, the organization simply has to bounce back from setbacks when attacked. These setbacks enable the organization to develop strengths, which then become characteristics of the organization—part of its organizational memory—allowing it to apply its knowledge, adapt, and act.

Adaptability occurs through the organization's ability to respond to any number of adverse situations and find creative ways to endure. The organization is creative in its tactics and strategies when it comes to addressing danger and finding ways to survive. While the AF-DTO is not a typical company, law enforcement describes a leadership structure highly concerned about its bottom line. The structure, as described earlier, contains a well regarded hierarchy with a centralized management structure under the direction of an implied transactional leadership arrangement. The organization looks for ways to increase its profits, which leads to additional activities like kidnapping for ransom and methamphetamine trafficking. It also threatens other organizations and individuals to achieve its goals.

Those charged with leading the organization delegate responsibility to lieutenants, each of whom manages a component of the organization's structure. This business platform has worked well, despite a number of ranking members and family leaders being killed or arrested. The AF-DTO simply mentors and trains new members to take the reins when a void is apparent.

AF-DTO compartmentalization is one of the largest headaches for law enforcement. The AF-DTO separates its activity into what is referred to as "cells." Each cell operates independently and only shares information with others on a need-to-know basis. This isolation of the cells prevents one cell from accidentally bringing down other cells when under attack from authorities, thereby representing a "loosely coupled system"[119] and a "highly reliable organization."[120] Each leader of a cell is highly protected by a number of well-armed men. The leadership protection allows the organization to remain operational during turmoil.

Law enforcement points out that the AF-DTO leadership strongly believes that, no matter what occurs, the organization will find ways to survive. This optimism carries through from its senior leaders down the chain of command to its core members, who are leading efforts on the ground level. Robb[121] notes that a resilient organization begins with the organization's culture. For the AF-DTO, part of the culture is the significant family control. The family members inspire a level of confidence throughout the organization which is endemic. The long history of sustained organizational success further fuels the sense of confidence and entitlement.

Certainly, the organization's ability to corrupt and blackmail officials is a foundational resiliency characteristic. The AF-DTO uses its significant cash flow to pay off those individuals in Mexico who would be potential problems or who could help to reduce problems. Those unwilling to take bribes are often blackmailed or killed. Those receiving payments include high-level members of city and state government, elected officials, police and the military. United States authorities have also been convicted of accepting bribes from the AF-DTO.

The AF-DTO has a reach well beyond the borders of Mexico. The organization networks with criminal organizations in Latin America, the United States and other nations, and it depends on international support for the lifeblood of the organization—drugs and the products used in the production of drugs (i.e., methamphetamine). The AF-DTO also depends on violent U.S. gang members to serve as enforcers of the organization both in Mexico and the United States.

The loyalty of those within the organization and those who cooperate with the organization remains a vital component of the organization's success. The AF-DTO demands loyalty from its members and its business partners, and this loyalty must be given without question, often out of fear. This level of loyalty makes it difficult for law enforcement to infiltrate the organization and also limits the number of members defecting to help authorities. The few defectors who are caught by the AF-DTO are severely tortured and killed as an example to others.

The AF-DTO has a monopoly mentality regarding its operations. Law enforcement describes the AF-DTO as an organization that is intolerant of competition and that inflicts serious damage on competitors. The organization has control over vital geographic regions required to conduct its operations. It kills competitors, infiltrates trade lines, and cooperates with adversaries of enemies for the sole purpose of remaining the dominant force in its region of control.

The AF-DTO is an incredible recruiting machine. It not only recruits gang members, as described earlier, but also college graduates and non-drug-users to facilitate its business operations. It recruits in great numbers and can easily replace members killed or arrested. The AF-DTO offers much higher salaries to recruits compared to legitimate employment wages in Mexico. It also recruits members who possess "street smarts," that is, who understand violence and can function in an organization based on violence because they grew up in violent neighborhoods and found ways to get through their adolescence by developing a criminal mentality.

The reputation of the AF-DTO is known around the world. The organization prides itself on fear and intimidation and uses its reputation to create advantages. This reputation is based on its ruthless attacks on police, elected officials, members of the media, even women and children. It undoubtedly prevents victims from pressing charges or becoming witnesses during a prosecution. The AF-DTO has branded itself internationally and uses its violent reputation for sustainability.

The AF-DTO does not greatly depend on others for its success. It has evolved into a self-reliant organization that, like a bear in winter, has fattened up to survive scarce times. It has such a significant cash flow that the loss of capital due to law enforcement confiscation does little to affect the sustainability of the organization. The AF-DTO buys legitimate businesses to diversify its funds and uses some of these businesses to launder drug money. It is also able to readily change its lines of business (e.g., kidnapping, drug production, trafficking patterns) to sustain its bottom line when any of its activities are disrupted.

Situational awareness is a frame of mind for the AF-DTO. The organization is constantly aware of its surroundings and has backup plans in place when authorities attack. The AF-DTO collects both intelligence and counterintelligence. It can foresee problems and act accordingly. Like a turtle sensing danger, the AF-DTO can withdraw until danger is gone; it rarely gets surprised by authorities. The organization pays attention to the smallest of details and works at preventing errors. An aura of diligence is apparent. Weick's[122] work on sensemaking and Schwandt and Marquardt's[123] work on organization learning are relevant components in helping to better understand AF-DTO success. Simply put, organizations act like human beings. They make sense of their environment; they learn and grow.

The technology possessed by the AF-DTO is far superior to those of the authorities, especially in Mexico. The organization uses sophisticated surveillance and communication equipment, as well as an array of dangerous weapons and high-tech methods for transporting drugs. The AF-DTO is able to make purchases of new technology more quickly than authorities, who often must await bids and navigate often slow channels of bureaucracy.

Trust is a unique component of the AF-DTO. It is largely a family-run business, rarely allowing non-family members to rise to high levels within the organization. The business develops trust with lower level members (i.e., lieutenants) and provides them with greater control over operations only when trust has been earned. The leaders do not trust others and do not allow lower level members to know any more than what is needed to get the job done.

In July, 2007, Caldwell published an investigative report, titled *The Evidence,*[124] in which he provided government verification, describing the operations of the AF-DTO. His report supports findings from this study's interviews, describing aspects of an organization that used legitimate businesses as fronts for money laundering, murders, extortion, bribery and racketeering. It also supports the notion that the organization's resiliency is partly dependent on trust and intimidation because, once its former high-ranking members struck deals with U.S. officials for lenient sentences or witness protection in the United States, both trust and intimidation were removed from the AF-DTO arsenal. As a result, officials were able to discover operations of the AF-DTO. When officials learned of these operations, U.S. efforts to minimize AF-DTO efforts were strengthened. Caldwell stated, "Taken together, the extradition documents provide the most detailed and hitherto secret information yet available on the Arellano-Felix Organization."[125] The cooperating AF-DTO leaders included assassins and business leaders who truly understood the organization's capabilities and strengths. From their testimony, we have learned about aspects that helped the AF-DTO survive times of stress.

The AF-DTO has developed a massive process of systematic bribes when it comes to dealing with officials. This process is funded through the DTO's lucrative cash flow from illegal narcotics and from laundering money. The process is also assisted by the DTO's ruthless reputation of using force against anyone it felt to be a threat to its survival.

The Narco Bosses,[126] another investigative report by Caldwell, highlights the AF-DTO's structure, business operations and leadership. The report was created from thousands of pages of court documents, including sworn affidavits from former members of the AF-DTO, most notably the organization's top lieutenant, Everardo Arturo "Kitti" Paez-Martinez, who identified Alberto Benjamin Arellano-Felix as the cartel's leader (Alberto is now in Mexican custody awaiting extradition to the United States). "Kitti" was described as a CEO type, "[more] an astute businessman and manager than the criminal boss."[127]

This report confirms that the organization operated as a ruthless business. Court documents detailed Benjamin's account of sending his most ruthless assassin to murder a prosecutor and, time and again, describe Benjamin as the leader who authorized many killings. Benjamin's brother, Eduardo Arellano Felix, was shown to be a close and constant advisor who eventually signed off on the cartel's killings with no remorse. The late Ramon Arellano Felix was the cartel's primary enforcer and was known for his ruthlessness in the killings of others. He was portrayed as a sadistic killer who threatened to kill his common law wife if she made any mistake that resulted in his apprehension. The documents demonstrated the disregard for human life and how the organization's leaders used threats and fear to gain compliance from those around them. In fact, the disregard for human life and the use of threats and fear are likely reasons for the DTO's initial success.

What you have witnessed up to this point is the evolution of evil. It has adapted rapidly to an ever changing environment and not only survived, but thrived. In doing so, the organization gained confidence. This confidence was felt not only by the members of the DTO, but also by similar organizations replicating virtually identical successes. In short, it became a virus that spread throughout the underworld and strengthened its resolve.

Behind the Line – Testimonial 10: "Who do you Trust?"

with DEA Director of International Operations, Michael S. Vigil, Ret.

Mexico is evolving and professionalizing its security forces. When I went to Mexico City in 1990, I managed a very large and complex international drug initiative in coordination with the Mexican government. This was a very significant operation that incorporated resources from a multitude of agencies—the Navy, the Coast Guard, U.S. Customs, U.S. Southern Military Command (SOUTHCOM), the Mexican Attorney General's Office, and the DEA. We tracked trafficker-aircraft along the Eastern Pacific and Western Caribbean transit zones. When we acquired the suspect aircraft-targets, based on an existing profile we used, i.e., no flight plan, flying without lights, using an altitude of 8,000 to 1,200 feet, and bearing a false registration number, SOUTHCOM scrambled jet fighters to identify and observe the suspect aircraft. We used other radar platforms, both aerial and ship borne to continue tracking the aircraft into Mexican airspace.

In Mexico, we had four Cessna Citation jet aircrafts equipped with F-16 radar and Forward Looking Infrared (FLIR) systems. We launched these resources whenever the suspect aircraft began to enter Mexican airspace. In 1990, most of the trafficker aircrafts landed in northern Mexico. Our initiative was very successful, since we accomplished significant seizures and arrests. Later, in 1991 we built upon our success as trafficker operations shifted to the southern part of Mexico. We delivered massive strikes to the Mexican and Colombian traffickers and disrupted their illicit activities—again!

In 1992, they began to shift to maritime operations. Our Mazatlan office, under the direction of Jose Menendez, investigated a group of international drug traffickers who were making arrangements to smuggle and import a multi-ton shipment of cocaine into Mexico and eventually into the United States. We identified two potential fishing ships they used for the smuggling venture: the Daniel Torres and the Mardoqueo were docked in Mazatlan. We also identified several individuals who were meeting and planning the smuggling venture, including a Swedish citizen. The Swede coordinated the drug operation with the Cali Cartel headed by Gilberto and Miguel Rodriguez-Orejuela. They were the rivals of Pablo Escobar and the Medellin Cartel. When the two fishing ships departed the area, we used U.S. assets along the Eastern Pacific to track them as they made their way to the Galapagos Islands- a commonly used staging area. The fishing ships loitered in the area for a few days and then began to make their way back to Mexico. A day or so later, I received a telephone call from a Naval Admiral asking for permission to intercept and board the two ships due to fear that tracking assets might lose them. I advised the Admiral that we opposed that tactic since it would only result in a drug seizure and we would not be able to arrest the key players in Mexico. His response was, "This is on your head." Again a calculated risk, but combating the drug trade requires hard decisions. In this kind of work, there is no room for indecisiveness (i.e. paralysis of decision making). It requires risk-taking and bold action.

When the two ships approached Mexican territorial waters, they were followed by a U.S. Coast Guard ship. The Coast Guard could not legitimately enter Mexican waters. Realizing this, I contacted a Mexican official and requested permission for the Coast Guard to enter their national waters. Within 20 minutes, authorization was provided from the highest levels of the government. The Daniel Torres anchored in the Mazatlan Bay, a couple of miles from shore. The Mardoqueo continued north to the Sea of Cortez.

We launched a very slow yacht boarded with Mexican police to seize the Daniel Torres. It took several hours to reach the ship.

145

In the morning, the local Mexican Police Commandante told me that they had been unable to find any cocaine. I told him that he should interrogate one of the individuals on board the ship—a local bartender—who would find the hidden cocaine. Shortly thereafter, the cocaine was located in the hold of the Daniel Torres, covered with heavy steel plates. An opening the exact size of the cocaine bales had been cut through the floor of the hold and the cocaine had been loaded, one bale at a time. A day later, we intercepted the Mardoqueo near the Mexican state of Sinaloa. It was also carrying a large amount of high grade cocaine. The total seizure was approximately 13.5 metric tons of cocaine. One for the Gipper!

On November 7, 1991, we had a very tragic situation occur in Mexico during an operation. We were tracking a single engine aircraft flying very low and approaching from the Eastern Pacific. As it entered Mexican airspace we intercepted the aircraft and followed it veering to the east across southern Mexico. It eventually went into an area in the state of Veracruz on the Caribbean side of the peninsula and landed in a pasture surrounded with trees. The area is known as Los Llanos de las Viboras. Two of our Cessna Citation aircrafts were in close pursuit.

The suspect aircraft landed and a male and female disembarked the aircraft leisurely walking away abandoning the airplane. Shortly thereafter, one of the Cessna Citations landed which had two PGR (Mexico's Attorney General's Office) pilots and eight armed PGR agents. The second Cessna Citation continued to circle above the area recording through FLIR as the PGR agents approached the trafficker aircraft. When the agents began to inspect the aircraft, they came under heavy gunfire from the tree line adjoining the pasture. Radio communications were transmitted reporting that the Mexican Army was firing at the agents. Emergency telephone calls were rushed to the commanding Army General of the region to advise him that his troops were shooting at PGR agents and for them to cease and desist. The General refused to take any action. A second telephone call to the General resulted in his only response, "We will see how this turns out." He and his company-size force stormed into the area surrounding and killing all eight of the PGR agents. The military, after massacring the agents, located the PGR pilots hiding in a hole near their aircraft. According to statements by the pilots, the military was threatening to kill them; and the only thing that saved their lives, was the other aircraft circling above. The General demanded that the pilots order the plane to land realizing that the Army's murderous actions were recorded. Obviously, this was not about to happen, even after trying to force the issue.

The General later claimed that the massacre of the PGR agents was a case of "mistaken identity" despite the fact that the Cessna Citations were painted in the blue and white PGR colors and that many of the agents had jackets with large PGR lettering on them. However, the most damaging evidence came as a result of the autopsy reports. Several of the PGR agents had their heads bashed in with rifle butts. One individual had a gunshot wound to the roof of his mouth. It was not a case of mistaken identity: it was obvious that the Mexican Army was protecting the smuggling operation. One of my PGR friends told me that the General had told him during the investigation, "This will teach you not to mess with us!" Considering all the damaging evidence, two Mexican Army Generals went to jail along with other assorted rank and file officers. This event created a massive rift between the Mexican Army and the PGR for quite some time. The cooperation and coordination are still a work in progress—and continues today.

— Michael S. Vigil

Chapter Eight

The Good Fight: Take the Shot

The time to take counsel of your fears is before you make an important
battle decision. That's the time to listen to every fear you can imagine!
When you have collected all the facts and fears and made your
decision, turn off all your fears and go ahead!
— General George S. Patton

Strengths of Knowing the Enemy

The framework I developed for battling evil is partially based on
Weick et al.'s study on mindfulness[128] that proposes a
mindfulness infrastructure for high reliability. Mindfulness, I believe is
the process whereby any resilient organization begins the process of
adaptation. But so many other components of researching evil were
evident. I remember sitting down before my dissertation defense
committee and going over the years of research I had compiled on this
subject. I understood from the onset that this unique level of
examination—never looked at in this fashion before—radiated with a
strong sense of validity and reliability because of the research design,
peer review, member checks, richness of documentation, willingness
of participants, access to relevant archival data and my significant
professional experience in law enforcement, the military and
government policy. It was, if you will, a culmination creating a perfect
storm that led to the final approval of the academic work. It was then
that I knew that I could not simply rest on leaving this data to sit on a
shelf. Rather, I wanted it to be told as a story so that others could share
in what I learned, but more importantly, to also build upon the

148

foundation of findings to help humanity devise a way to corner evil and then tear it apart.

Answers to questions emerged quickly from the records and interviews. As additional data was gathered, the findings converged into patterns that remained steady through the end of the study. Some of the data collected was represented in the initially proposed framework, and other data collected had resiliency characteristics specific to the AF-DTO (Arellano Felix Drug Trafficking Organization). The interview data was collected after the review of archival records, and it quickly became clear that saturation of the data had been reached as very little new data emerged from the ten in-depth interviews; only supporting and reinforcing data were gathered. In both sources, the findings were tied to the identified organizational resiliency characteristics, and these are indeed the resiliency characteristics of the AF-DTO.

The most significant strength of this book and its recommendations for fighting evil is that the participants interviewed have significant experience with doing just that—fighting or reporting on the most sinister of organizations. A number of the participants are undercover agents who for years focused their work on the AF-DTO, and others have prosecuted high-level AF-DTO members. Some of the participants hold high-level or secret positions within agencies targeting the AF-DTO and its members worldwide, and the reporters interviewed have spent years doing investigative reporting. I finally felt as if I had exhausted my sources and was at a point where I could cut through the DTO (Drug Trafficking Organization) and predict their very next move.

Behind the Line – Testimonial 11: "Racketeer Influenced & Corrupt Organizations Act"

with International Gang Expert, Richard Valdemar

One morning in May, 1992, Ana Lizarraga hurriedly packed a few things into her van as she prepared to drive to the funeral of her mother. Lizarraga was a 49-year-old gang counselor for the Los Angeles Community Youth Services. She was an exceptional counselor, having relatives who were gang members in both Sureño (Southern California) and their rivals, the Norteño (Northern California) gangs.

Lizarraga's gang knowledge had landed her a position as a technical advisor on the Edward James Olmos film, "American Me." She had even played a small part in the film.

However unknown to most of Los Angeles, Olmos' movie had disrespected and offended the Mexican Mafia prison gang by depicting the fictional prison rape of one of its respected founders. This was cause enough for the other two technical advisors, both of whom were Mafia members, "Rocky" Luna and "Charlie Brown" Manriquez, to be murdered. Later, in covertly monitored Mexican Mafia meetings, I would learn that Olmos himself was marked for death.

On Lancaster Avenue, in the shadow of the Los Angeles General Hospital, Lizarraga stood on the driveway near the driver's door of her van. Her son was on the passenger side getting ready to open the door. They were startled to see two males walk quickly up her driveway and approach Ana. The men were dressed in dark clothing and their faces were covered with stocking masks.

Before Ana Lizarraga could react, she was cut down by multiple shots from both gunmen. The masked shooters stood over her and fired point blank, hitting her 13 times. Like the death scene in some gangster movie, Lizarraga's body jerked and twisted in slow motion as the bullets ripped and tore through her body.

Los Angeles Police Officer, Thomas Lira, happened to be passing by in his patrol car and witnessed the cold-blooded shooting. As the two masked suspects fled, one of them fired at the officer. Units responding to Lira's request for assistance captured one of the shooters, Jose "Joker" Gonzales, a Big Hazard gang member. But the unidentified second shooter escaped.

"Joker" Gonzales was eventually convicted of the murder. Since the killing was ordered by the Mexican Mafia prison gang, his conviction later became one of the predicate acts used to convict 21 of 22 Mexican Mafia Members and associates in a 1995 federal criminal conspiracy trial. This was the first time the Racketeer Influenced and Corrupt Organization (RICO) statutes were used against a "violent gang" in California.

The federal RICO law was enacted in 1970 and codified as Chapter 96 of Title 18 of the U.S. Code. It was intended to combat traditional organized crime groups and Italian Mafia figures. Some suggest that the name RICO was a clever reference by the author of the law, G. Robert Blakey, to a character played by Edward G. Robinson in the classic gangster movie "Little Caesar."

The genius of the RICO statutes is that they work perfectly against organized criminal gangs. Any member of any criminal enterprise can be charged with RICO racketeering if he can be shown to have committed two of 27 federal or eight state charges within a 10-year period as part of the enterprise. A person can be charged even if that person did not directly commit the crime but only agreed to the commission or conspired with the perpetrators in any way.

Guilty verdicts result in sentences of 20 years per count and fines up to $25,000. In addition a pre-trial financial *restraining order can be obtained to seize all the defendant's assets and forfeitable property. This prevents the organization from liquidating the proceeds of its racketeering enterprise before a guilty verdict can be obtained. Even the private individuals victimized by the enterprise can file civil suits to recover damages.*

The very definition of a criminal gang begs prosecution under RICO. A gang is a group of three or more persons who have a common identifying sign, symbol or name and whose members individually or collectively engage in a pattern of criminal activity for the furtherance of the gang.

Gang members know that RICO can ruin their lives. The Mexican Mafia in particular understood the implications of the RICO act. They purposely avoided a formalized structure, hierarchy, a written constitution, or codified code of conduct to avoid the fate their mentors, the Italian Mafia, suffered under RICO prosecutions.

State conspiracy laws and the federal RICO act are the tools tailor-made to combat criminal gangs. In my opinion the highly touted gang injunctions are difficult and costly to establish. They are extremely manpower intensive and usually duplicate gang-limiting conditions already available through good probation and parole conditions. Some of them are unnecessarily restrictive and could result in negative case law decisions.

When physical and electronic surveillance tactics, good informant development and the cooperation of narcotics units, parole and probation agencies are used to target violent criminal gangs, prosecution under state conspiracy and the federal RICO are the way to go.

First, I would solicit a memo of understanding with as many law enforcement entities as possible in the affected jurisdictions. This memo would form a multi-jurisdictional gang task force targeting the gang as a criminal enterprise and enumerate the level of cooperation each entity was willing to commit. How many investigators? How much of the budget? Who would prosecute?

A RICO trial usually consists of two phases. First you must prove the criminal organization or enterprise exists. Secondly, you must prove that those charged in the indictment have each committed at least two acts of racketeering activity, one within the recent prescribed period and the second within 10 years. These are called "predicate acts" and they show a pattern of criminal acts as opposed to individual acts if they "have the same or similar purpose, results, participants, victims, or methods of commission, or otherwise are interrelated by distinguishing characteristics and are not isolated events."

The mere indictment of individuals under the RICO statutes usually results in many of the defendants pleading guilty to lesser charges. In the Mexican Mafia RICO of 1995, 22 defendants were originally indicted; all but 13 pled guilty. The trial resulted in 12 convictions and only one acquittal.

— Richard Valdemar

Implications for the Real World: Change the Mindset, Change the War

This book has implications for the theory of organizational resiliency, for future research and for practical use by law enforcement and government organizations. The findings and interpretations have direct implications for enforcement and government organizations attempting to dismantle the AF-DTO by targeting the core resiliency characteristics. By focusing law enforcement efforts on the resiliency characteristics (and two environmental factors) identified by the study, authorities can become more successful at dismantling the AF-DTO or similar organizations. Additionally, legitimate organizations, including corporations and businesses worldwide, may better their odds for survival during turmoil by applying some of the AF-DTO resiliency characteristics.

Dr. Paul R. Chabot

Theories to the "Battlefield"

Prior to this study of evil, organizational resiliency literature largely failed to address how organizational resiliency is manifested within a highly volatile criminal organization such as the AF-DTO. My research linked organizational resiliency to Weick's[129] theory of sensemaking, Weick et al.'s[130] theory of mindfulness, and Schwandt and Marquardt's[131] theory of organizational learning. These three constructs were identified in this study of evil as key components of the AF-DTO resiliency cycle, which is described in detail a bit later in this book.

Sutcliffe and Vogus[132] contend that it is critical to determine what exact attributes give rise to resilience. They also lament the paucity of research that attempts to determine these attributes, particularly at the organization level. The attributes identified in this book help to fill that research gap; they are the main contribution of this book.

Additionally, this book adds to the existing body of research conducted on similar studies of high-reliability organizations by Smart et al.[133] It also adds to Scott's[134] high-reliability theory, Hinrich's[135] high-performance work system, and Hamel et al.'s[136] four categories of organizational resilience, and these categories shed new light on Garmezy's[137] theory that resiliency cannot be guaranteed but simply facilitates the capacity to recover.

Weick[138] asked the question, "How can organizations be made more resilient?" This book identifies the characteristics that allow the AF-DTO to be more resilient, thereby answering Weick's question and incorporating more recent theories of mindfulness, sensemaking and high reliability. Sutcliffe and Vogus state, "Organizational resiliency is an essential corollary for positive organizational scholarship because it begins to articulate how organizations behave efficaciously and thrive amidst adverse conditions."[139] Weick,[140] whose theory was the basis for much of what I studied in graduate school, believes that organizations prepare themselves for failure, much like nuclear aircraft carriers do, and that these preparations alone are the main ingredient in the organizations' survival. Organizations are always preparing for the worst. The AF-DTO research found that, as demonstrated by the AF-DTO resiliency framework, the organization was constantly on guard for threats, so much so that it killed innocent people both inside and outside of the organization to simply send a message that the organization will not tolerate mishaps or failure.

While the AF-DTO prepared for failure by setting up contingency plans, which included multiple loads crossing border points at the same time to better the chance of at least a portion of the loads getting through, the organization's success was based on its fundamental ability to make sense of threats and implement methods for self-protection. This is what Lagadec described as *"an event that may be considered as an abrupt and brutal audit: at a moment's notice, everything that was left unprepared becomes a complex problem and every weakness comes rushing to the forefront."*[141]

I found that this occurred often, and the AF-DTO was able to counter the threats because of its ability to become aware of hostile occurrences. According to Wildavasky,[142] resilience is such a vital component of survival because it provides the ability to deal with unexpected threats after they become evident. The results fit well with Wildavsky's and Lagadec's statements and also with Weick et al.'s theory of mindfulness.

Mindfulness, according to Weick,[143] is the passkey into high-reliability organizing. Weick interchanges resilience with reliability. The resiliency characteristics identified through the data collection were the result of the organization's sensemaking, which occurred due to mindfulness of threats to the organization.

Mindfulness is the phase of the organizational resiliency cycle in which the organization becomes aware of threats based on its ability to identify with the five variables of improvisation, shown later in the revised conceptual framework. Sutcliffe and Vogus[144] share with Weick and others a belief that resiliency and mindfulness are connected. They theorize that organizational resiliency results from enhancing particular competencies, such as the processes that encourage mindfulness and enhanced capabilities to recombine and deploy resources in a new way.

The AF-DTO needed to reach the phase of mindfulness so that it could make sense of what was actually occurring. Fiol and O'Connor describe mindfulness as "a way of seeing the information gained through scanning, a way of evaluating that information, and a way of acting on it that contrast[s] with many of the assumptions of traditional approaches."[145] This description of mindfulness fits the AF-DTO framework and is a required component for an organization to move into the next phase in the resiliency cycle, which is sensemaking.

Weick's[146] later work on sensemaking has a strong connection with the AF-DTO knowledge-building process. The sensemaking described by Weick translates into how individuals actively attempt to understand the world around them. These findings significantly contribute to his work in this area, including his earlier work[147] in which he theorized that organizations are entities attempting to transform various forms of data into information that is understood for self-maintenance. Sensemaking develops a set of practices that assist in the understanding of acquired information. Weick's later work on sensemaking[148] directly connects sensemaking to resilience. The AF-DTO's process of sensemaking allows the DTO to accomplish what Weick theorizes about: that sensemaking allows the organization to examine threats, and this examination leads to the DTO's ability to learn and implement changes for survival.

Schwandt and Marquardt[149] rightfully believe that organizations which can adapt quickly and continuously will be able to survive; those that do not or cannot learn by adapting to the events will falter. The ability to adapt and reinvent is a key indicator of survival: "by increasing the speed and quality of their learning, they can succeed in a rapidly changing global marketplace."[150] The AF-DTO does just that. As seen in the framework developed for this book, the organization quickly becomes aware of faults, makes sense of them and then adapts, using any number of its core resiliency characteristics.

In order for the organization to reach sensemaking, it must first begin at a phase theorized by Rerup[151] as improvisation. Rerup believes that an organization must be awakened, and this occurs through the five phases shown in my attack plan. The findings of this research strongly mesh with Rerup's framework and theory. His framework was used to create the initial conceptual framework, while the final framework was based on new data from this study.

My research points to a resilience "cycle." The AF-DTO moves through all phases of this cycle and then returns to improvisation when there are new problems. Weick[152] believes that a resilient organization will maintain a commitment to resilience, will seek out what may go wrong and prepare plans and contingencies to work out catastrophic events.

At the sensemaking phase, the AF-DTO demonstrated its ability to learn from the negative stressors affecting its organization. Findings from the study show that organizational learning is an essential component of resilience. Monday and Myers theorized that organizations learn and become stronger even through the transition to becoming resilient, which is a gradual process: "[a resilient organization] thrives by positively adjusting to current adversity…it strengthens its capabilities to make future adjustments."[153] Carroll and Weick et al.[154] found that organizations must learn as much as possible from small precursor problems, transmit learning effectively across organizations, and improve processes based on proactive learning. The AF-DTO paid attention to the smallest of failures and learned from these mistakes, inputting new methods to circumvent future failures.

What is missing from the collective research on organization learning is a comparison with criminal organizations. That's why I changed things up a bit. A rotation of constructs was needed to facilitate an understanding of how the AF-DTO created characteristics to become resilient. It appears that organizational learning is simply an aptitude to allow the organization to implement its ability to create the characteristics needed to survive. Adaptation is one of the key findings in the organizational resiliency characteristics of the AF-DTO, further strengthening the notion that organizational learning is not the end result, but rather a tool used to create characteristics of resiliency. This contributes to existing theory by Beunza and Stark,[155] who believe that organizations have the ability to adjust to turbulent environments by bringing the environment within the organization. That is, the organization can get accustomed to the threat and train to be resilient against it. The AF-DTO resilience cycle provides a better understanding of their theory by showing that the AF-DTO environment is a key factor in the organization's resiliency, that the organization has—to some degree—brought the environment "into the organization," making the environment a factor in resiliency and controlling that environment. A blatant example is the supply of drugs to drug-users in the U.S., and the lawless society in Mexico.

Existing theories had not identified the entire core of AF-DTO resiliency characteristics. My research added a number of additional components to the conversation on organizational resiliency. This difference further strengthens the notion that criminal organizations like the AF-DTO operate on a much different level than legitimate corporations and that the unorthodox measures undertaken by the AF-DTO to prevent failure are not always written about in the same context.

Weick[156] believes that certain organizations survive in turbulent environments because they are always on guard, are always aware of their vulnerable surroundings, and therefore institute protective measures to ensure their existence. This is certainly true of the AF-DTO.

One of the AF-DTO's resiliency traits is leadership. Yukl[157] states,

When a group is under extreme pressure to perform a difficult task or to survive in a hostile environment, the role expectations for the leader are likely to change in a predictable manner...they look to the leader to show initiative in defining the problem, identifying a solution, directing the group's response to the crisis.

The AF-DTO has various leaders who are compartmentalized, and at the time of a crisis no one leader can make all of the necessary adjustments on behalf of the organization. What I found is that the compartmentalization of leadership components serves the primary purpose of isolating the internal organization leaders from one another for protection, but isolation also often forces decision making to be made within a variety of compartments, and at times decisions cannot be made by the leadership structures because organization members who are in fear of being killed for failure simply withhold information. Therefore, it is often these lower level employees who take matters into their own hands and carry out violence as a form of redemption from the mistakes for which they may be held accountable. This demonstrates a lack of information being presented to the leader for further direction. The AF-DTO lives by a simple rule: "Don't mess up or you will be killed."

Kendra and Wachtendorf described four dimensions of organizational reliance and believe the organizational resilience phenomenon is a "socially constituted adaptability to unpredictable ambient forces."[158] Their findings suggest that, in similar types of major events, a resilient organization must have leaders who are problem solvers. Although the AF-DTO relies on problem solving leaders, it also relies on members who are problem solvers.

Braverman[159] defined resilience as needing two components: (1) exposure to significant stressors or risks and (2) a demonstration of competence and successful adaptation. While adaptation is a component of evil's success, I also found that the exposure to significant stressors or risks was not a component trait of resiliency, but rather an occurrence that leads the AF-DTO to improvisation, the beginning point of the study's resiliency framework.

Another core resiliency trait is the AF-DTO's optimistic belief in itself and its ability to be successful. The notion of optimism being an organizational strength is supported by Wood and Bandura.[160] A group's shared belief in its own capabilities can have a great impact on the group. In the criminal culture of the DTO, shared optimism may be coerced through the threat of violence against those who resist the company mindset. Optimism and fear are used simultaneously. The AF-DTO can instill fear, but it also has two levels of optimism—one that is real (held by the leaders) and one that is false (held by much lower employees working out of fear and providing an impression of optimism).

This book's suggestions contribute to the work of brilliant thinkers like Weick and Quinn[161] who have theories on evolutionary and revolutionary change. It provides examples of change occurring in a revolutionary manner (immediately) due to imminent organizational threats and also examples of change occurring in an evolutionary manner (gradually) as the organization continually alters its operations based on its own growth and learning to better improve efficiency. The AF-DTO adapts (a key component of its resiliency characteristics) on an ongoing basis. For example, when the United States clamped down on methamphetamine made in the United States by Mexican DTOs, the AF-DTO lost significant amounts of money. However, over a period of two years, the AF-DTO was able to create identical methamphetamine production labs in Mexico, adapt these labs to the other DTO's current line of illegal drugs, and ship the drugs into the United States alongside their other narcotics.

The AF-DTO is essentially a business entity, but it is not constrained by the rules that apply to regular businesses. First, it operates in an environment over which law enforcement and legitimate government have very little control. Second, it has a vast consumer base that would be the envy of any legitimate business. Third, it can cheat its way to success, whereas legitimate corporations are bound by rules, red tape and societal guidelines. What's more, the AF-DTO will do whatever it takes to survive, including corruption, blackmail, murder and torture.

While some may look at organizational resilience in terms of dealing with the unexpected incidents, the AF-DTO's operational structure is more aligned with Perrow's[162] Normal Accident Theory which states that, when organizations are involved in dangerous works, failure is to be expected. The AF-DTO leadership expects some of their drug shipments to be confiscated; they expect some of their employees to be killed or arrested; they operate in an environment of danger where there will always be some failure. A contributing factor to Perrow's study is that, if applied to AF-DTO–style organizations, failure is not only expected; it is the primary cause for resiliency because it kicks off the improvisation process, which leads to creating resilience characteristics.

Weick and Sutcliffe[163] summarized the concept of resiliency with one question: "Does the organization possess the skills to make do?" In the context of the AF-DTO, thus far the answer is a resounding "yes." The skills that Weick and Sutcliffe refer to are the AF-DTO resiliency characteristics.

Mallak[164] theorized that resilience is the ability to thrive and survive in difficult conditions. I agree with this statement in the context of the AF-DTO's ability to bounce back from setbacks and failure. It brings into question the issue of "difficult conditions." The

AF-DTO operates in an environment that provides two key favorable conditions—a vast drug consumer base and a lack of government effectiveness. These two conditions help, rather than hinder, the organization. However, if either of these conditions were to cease, it would create a condition unfavorable to the organization's survival (i.e., a dried up consumer base or the implementation of an effective government in Mexico to better enforce the rule of law).

Hamel et al. described changes in organizational survival: "…continued success no longer hinges on momentum. Rather it rides on resilience—on the ability to dynamically reinvent business models and strategies as circumstances change."[165] Renewal was identified through this AF-DTO exploration as being the outcome that equals resilience. While the AF-DTO is not a traditional business, its business acumen is one of its core resiliency characteristics. What's different from the work of Hamel et al. is that the AF-DTO did not put great emphasis on working vigorously toward its future. Instead, the organization simply found ways to not fail, and this was largely accomplished through nontraditional concepts definitely not found within a legitimate business structure, including blackmail, torture, killing and extortion.

McCann's[166] four dimensions of organizational resiliency include the ability to absorb shocks and surprises, creatively explore alternatives, broadly access resources and execute transformational change. The AF-DTO does absorb shocks and surprises in the organizational learning construct and does create alternatives, as seen in the resiliency characteristics. It does broadly access resources (distilled in the resiliency characteristics), while executing transformational change (as shown through the AF-DTO's ability to adapt and renew itself). However, compared with legitimate businesses, the AF-DTO does so much more in the beginning stages (as indicated in this book's AF-DTO resiliency framework), prior to reaching the four dimensions described by McCann.

Behind the Line – Testimonial 12: "Gang Intelligence"

with International Gang Expert, Richard Valdemar

Webster's Dictionary defines intelligence as information concerning an enemy or possible enemy or an area. Another definition is the ability to learn or understand or to deal with new or trying situations. Surveillance is defined as close watch kept over someone or something. Here is a hint; one of the best ways to build usable gang intelligence to fight gangs is through surveillance.

SPI

When I joined the Intelligence Unit of the Los Angeles Sheriff's Department (LASD) it was called Special Investigations (SPI). Yes, spy. SPI once held files or real intelligence on criminal organizations, subversive extremists, motorcycle gangs, prison gangs, and dirty politicians. Los Angeles Sheriff Peter J. Pitches had been an FBI Agent before becoming the L.A. Sheriff. He worked under the FBI Director J. Edgar Hoover. Unlike most of today's sheriffs and chiefs of police, he actually understood the value of surveillance and intelligence.

Sheriff Pitches built up this intelligence unit and had a representative from the SPI unit brief him personally each week. The SPI Unit bypassed the normal bureaucratic department's rigid chain of command. In the LASD organizational chart of that day, SPI answered directly to the Sheriff.

After the Vietnam War spying became unpopular with the American culture. At least that's how the media painted the picture. Intelligence units and their valuable files fell under attack from the ACLU and other powerful subversive groups. They attacked these files supposedly to protect "Joe Citizen" from "Big Brother" and his domestic spies. The truth was that your average Joe Citizen's name never really appeared in any of these intelligence files, but lots of crooked politicians' names did.

Lawyers and plaintiffs won restrictive case law decisions against some police intelligence units. State and federal legislators, to protect their own backroom antics, also tried to limit the intelligence and surveillance abilities of the police. State and federal attorney generals' offices ordered restrictions limiting police wiretap and other intelligence gathering programs and mandated the purging of intelligence files.

Local police and sheriffs found maintaining large intelligence units increasingly more difficult. Many cities abdicated their criminal intelligence duties and relied instead on the bureaucratic federal agencies. Local Intelligence units like SPI were gutted or skeletonized.

In my opinion this loss in local police intelligence resulted in the explosive growth of organized criminal gangs on the streets. We were fighting gangs blindfolded by the lack of important intelligence. If those local intelligence units existed today, even international terrorist cells would be more quickly located and identified. The terrorists operating in small and medium cities would stand out to local units and the investigators who would have already been in place.

Utilize Intelligence

Whether you work in "Small Town" U.S.A. or "Mega Metropolis," intelligence is the key to how effectively you can direct your limited resources against gangs. There are many sources for this information; interviews, interrogations, informants, and search warrants are all ways to build your gang intelligence file. I suggest you utilize the best of your current information and set up regular surveillance operations. You should spy.

Static and Active Surveillance

Static surveillance is probably the easiest to use. Commit a couple of people to watch the gang hangouts. Photograph gang members and their vehicles. Look for a neighborhood home or other location that can be used as an observation post. I have used church bell towers, abandoned houses, "cherry picker" cranes, mobile homes, empty project apartments, and vehicles disguised as plumbing trucks and UPS vans. Be creative.

There are two schools of thought in the use of static surveillances; one theory says that this should be a passive monitoring of the group for intelligence gathering only, not as an opportunity to make arrests. Arresting any of the subjects might "burn" the surveillance and possibly give away the observation points, some say.

I prefer the second school of thought, active surveillance. Give the officers in the observation point (OP) a radio and assign a marked police unit to act on the information. If the surveillance team observes something of interest, they can radio to the marked unit to make the vehicle or pedestrian stop several blocks from the observation area. Arrests also produce good intelligence. With care this can be done without giving away the OP.

Electronic Surveillance

Can't afford to tie up three or four officers in a static surveillance? Electronic surveillance is another easy way to build intelligence files. Try a hidden time lapse camera. All you good deer hunters know what I mean. You can buy these digital cameras and set them up to snap photos every half-hour or so. Buy a fake hollow decorative garden rock and mount a camera in it. Set it up during the night and let it go. This can also be done from an unoccupied parked car, or a tree on the parkway. With just a little probable cause you can have a "pole camera" set up on a telephone pole across from gang central.

Electronic surveillance includes wire taps, or "Title III" operations in the federal jargon. There is one place that allows you to monitor gang members without having to write a lengthy wiretap warrant. Most state and federal prisons and county jails usually have systems in place that routinely monitor telephone calls of bad guys. Monitor the telephone calls coming from the gang unit or discipline row because that's where the best calls come from.

Mobile Covert Surveillance Team

If your department can afford the expense and manpower, I suggest a mobile covert seven-person surveillance team. A sergeant and six officers, each with a radio in an individual non-police-looking vehicle, are the basic components of the team.

Unlike what's often depicted in movies or on TV, one or two people cannot sustain a covert surveillance for any length of time. The optimum team would actually have 10 people: enough personnel to cover vacation relief and the ability to break a few officers from the team out for foot surveillance if that is required. Ten officers also provide a good number for their role as an entry team at most locations.

However, this seven-officer surveillance team should quickly produce results. I operated in a team like this for 20 years. When SPI investigators didn't have a target for us, gang parole units did, and homicide detectives also regularly utilized our team. Over the years we wound up arresting or having some part in the takedown of almost every major suspect in Los Angeles. This included most of the infamous leaders of the Crips and Bloods, the Mexican Mafia, Aryan Brotherhood, and most of the motorcycle gangs. Add to that the arrests of drug cartel leaders, and serial killers like Richard Ramirez.

The seven-officer team utilized all the previously mentioned tactics plus mobile covert and overt surveillances. Sometimes the most effective surveillance is an obvious one. My team operated in this overt style for several months while working the outgoing mayor of Compton, who was also a Blood gang member, before he was sentenced to prison.

The mobile surveillance team operates like a small Special Forces team. Its flexibility and ability to customize a response to suit the threat cannot be duplicated in any other team configuration. No detective unit, SWAT team, or special problems team compares to the covert surveillance team concept. The cost in manpower and budget is quickly offset by the damage this team can inflict on the targeted gangs.

Drug Trafficking Organized Crime groups and International Gangs are national and international threats to the very fabric of our society. It is time to utilize your best secret weapons, your 007 types, and your best electronic spying technology against them.

— Richard Valdemar

Setting our Sights on the Heart of Evil

We have now reached the phase in the book where you will be challenged with understanding the next stage needed to target the enemy. This phase demands attention to detail as we outline the framework of evil.

When I began looking at these evil organizations, I did take for granted certain vital factors necessary for resiliency after mindfulness is achieved. Mindfulness in the case of the AF-DTO simply allowed the organization to implement a number of organization-saving tactics to ensure its survival. Remember, mindfulness is really nothing more than the organization's ability to know what is going on within its environment of control. It is such an elementary concept—mindfulness—but without it, an organization will surely fail. Still, mindfulness is just one of several components that must flow from one step to the next, in a timely fashion, for true resilience to take shape. From the beginning, while I understood to some degree the type of organization I was up against, I needed to find a strong platform to examine the organization. It should be of no surprise that Weick et al.'s[167] work once again found a prominent and vitally important role in this process. Weick et al.[168] have created an impressive theoretical foundation for reliability and resiliency.

A review of countless reports and interviews found solid evidence of all components of the framework, but with some interesting additions and modifications. The revised framework I have titled "*AF-DTO Resiliency Cycle*" shows an organization operating within a continuum of both evolutionary and revolutionary change, based on environmental stressors that caused the organization to adapt to its environment and refine its ability to fight off failure.

Resiliency within the AF-DTO is like a ball—it does not have a beginning or an end. The organization's resilience is clearly based on the organization's ability to adapt and find ways to survive. The ongoing process of learning, both for the organization and for the individual leaders of the organization, does not cease. And in catastrophic events, the organization simply adjusts and, if need be, replaces leaders killed or imprisoned.

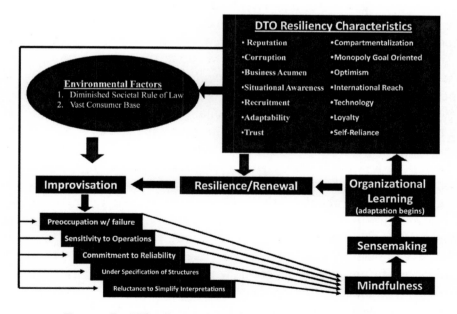

Figure 7: "The Drug Cartel Cycle" (by Dr. Chabot)

The simplest way to explain the resiliency cycle is to think back to when you were a child in a park playing with other children on a merry-go-round, where children run in circles pushing the merry-go-round while other children remain on it for the ride. All the while, children are jumping on and off as it continues to maintain rotations. This framework—the DTO Resiliency Cycle—is much like that merry-go-round. It includes improvisation, mindfulness, sensemaking, organizational learning and resilience. Through each rotation, a characteristic becomes evident at the organizational learning construct, and the characteristic becomes a part of the organizational memory. The characteristic then remains while waiting for further rotations and for others to join. All along, the resiliency framework is affected by two environmental facts: diminished societal rule of law and a vast consumer base. These two areas have been in existence prior to the birth of the AF-DTO and, combined, they have proven to be the lifeblood, allowing the organization to exist, prosper and develop resiliency characteristics.

A sustainable environment that's easily corruptible is vitally important for evil's survival. Evil feeds on the weak. This may be seen in the use of bribery or extortion to control susceptible (weak) cops, judges and politicians. Evil also needs an environment where those who get in the way can be freely killed and terrorized with little risk of being held responsible. The longer this type of environment is permitted, the stronger evil grows. It feeds and feeds, and soon another evil grows in the form of additional organizations. Soon, chaos emerges. Mexico has been unable to turn back the clock on corruption.

Uniquely, some of the resiliency characteristics relate directly to the inputs for mindfulness. According to Rerup,[169] improvisation—which leads to the five mindfulness inputs—is hard to maintain because it constantly requires attention. What this study proves is that improvisation is maintained by the organization's consistent cycling through the framework, using the resiliency characteristics to support the five inputs to mindfulness. For example, the DTO's resiliency characteristic of "preoccupation with failure" is enhanced by the resiliency characteristics of trust, loyalty recruitment, corruption and reputation. Next, the second input, "sensitivity to operations," is affected by the characteristic of situational awareness. The third input, "commitment to resilience," is supported by the organization's international reach, technology, monopoly goal-oriented structure and optimism. The fourth input, "under-specification of structures," is supported by the characteristic of compartmentalization. The final input, "reluctance to simplify interpretations," is supported by the self-reliance and business acumen characteristics. Collectively, the entire organization demonstrates constant ability to adapt. Therefore, the characteristic of adaptability is rightfully connected to all five mindfulness inputs.

Behind the Line – Testimonial 13: "Structure of Gangs"

with International Gang Expert, Richard Valdemar

Why do the otherwise productive anti-gang programs of New York, Chicago, Baltimore, and Philadelphia not work in Los Angeles? Why do these same cities seem overwhelmed by the flood of Southern California gang members?

Gangs act differently in different parts of the country. They are influenced by their environment and culture as they develop their own style, code of conduct, and structure. And when they migrate within the 50 States and internationally, they maintain some of that original structure. For gang programs to be effective, they must be built like "smart bombs" designed tactically to dismantle the structure and hierarchy of particular targets.

In New York and Chicago, gangs developed a clear corporate-style structure in the shape of an Egyptian pyramid. At the bottom are the street soldiers, topped by a hierarchy which is capped by a leadership and, finally, a president or king. For example, Larry Hoover is the King of the Folks Nation. Gangs that utilize this structure sometimes even have written constitutions and bylaws.

The Mexican Model

Not so in Los Angeles. Los Angeles street gangs evolved on the Hispanic or "Mexican Model." The street gangs here are much more democratic, with the ideal that every member has an equal vote. Within this structure are sub-groups or cliques, each with sometimes fiercely independent charismatic de-facto leaders. The L.A. street gang is really a coalition of cliques working as a unit, similar in structure to the cells of a terrorist organization such as al Qaeda.

Under this model, if you destroy a cell or clique or incarcerate a leader, another will just fill the power void. Since there are few lines of command and control, it becomes difficult to effectively impact the hierarchy. Each cell seems to act independently and yet supports the group in their common goals.

Ask an L.A. gang member who the leader of his gang is, and he will say, "I am!" The structure pyramid formed by Southern California gangs is like an Aztec pyramid. It has a broad base of foot soldiers and new inductees forming large semi-autonomous stones (cliques), narrowing toward the top. This narrowing occurs more because of member attrition through desertion, death, and prison than because of positional appointments.

Veteranos and OGs

At the top of this L.A. gang pyramid are the senior gang members. Although they are not granted the authority to command the gang to do anything, they are given informal figurehead and honorary titles. They are called "Veteranos" (veterans) in a Hispanic street gang and "Original Gangsters" or OGs in an African American gang.

They act like law enforcement senior officers. Although not given the pay, rank, and title of lieutenants or sergeants, they tend (especially on early mornings) to run the shift in the absence of official leadership. This is largely due to their experience, and not to official hierarchy. If a senior officer tells you, "You ought to make this notification" or "write this report," you would be foolish to disregard his or her advice. However, the officer probably would not try to order you to do it. The same is true of Veteranos and OGs.

Target the Left Arm

Despite all of the differences, there are structural similarities among East Coast, West Coast, and also Midwest gangs that can be exploited. All of these gangs have two "arms."

The right arm is the most familiar. It is the war-making militant fighting arm. It is made up of the gang members and

171

the structural hierarchy, of whatever type it might be. This is the arm that gang prevention and suppression programs usually target. But even if you successfully incarcerate and dismantle the members and structure of this militant right arm, new gang members will continue to replace them.

What many often forget is that gangs also have a left "arm." The left arm is the money-making arm of the street gang. Whether it is drugs, extortion, identity theft, murder or Gangsta Rap, the left arm is the source of money the gang needs to continue financing the war-making arm. This financial arm must be targeted to effectively dismantle the gang forever. The left arm must be tracked to the source of this income and completely cut off. Once this is done, the gang will be weakened and the right arm can be targeted more effectively.

In Los Angeles, even the gang members themselves have learned to target the Gangsta Rapper from a rival street gang. This is done not only to damage the rival gang's reputation and kill an enemy gang member, but also to dry up the gang's ability to finance continued warfare.

Gang units should work closely with narcotics detectives. This "left-right combination" is very important. But the most critical element in the fight against gang violence is good intelligence. In today's law enforcement agencies I see a low priority given to local criminal intelligence on the structure and leadership of the target gangs. This is often where budget cuts do even more damage. <u>Ask yourself, what general would dismantle his intelligence unit in the middle of a war?</u>

— *Richard Valdemar*

The Starfish and Spider Paradigm

Upon my arrival in Iraq, one of the highly recommended readings from the Special Operations Task Force commander, Lieutenant General Stanley Chrystal, was *The Starfish and the Spider* by Ori

Brafman and Rod Beckstrom. In short, the authors devise a clear explanation of why leaderless organizations are unstoppable. I agree, but let me explain. Evil organizations do a very good job of delegating responsibility and compartmentalizing their duties. When we would go after and eliminate senior al-Qaeda targets in Iraq, the overall organization remained intact. In fact, we have a term for this called "cutting grass." After hitting high level targets, others take their place. We must never stop going after these high level targets to slow down evil's march, but it will not eliminate their organizations.

Brafman and Beckstrom describe the spider organization as having one head. If you cut off that head, the organization dies. This is a centralized organization, and that is not how evil is structured at all! Rather, evil is structured like the starfish, a network of cells—the decentralized organization. The starfish is powerful because of the following:

- Starfish can sneak up on you because they mutate and grow so rapidly.

- They do not depend on a central organization for their existence.

- Power is spread throughout.

- It's impossible for "us" to firmly determine their overall strength in numbers.

- The cells can go in any number of directions—unlike a centralized organization that depends on its leader for guidance—and then move together, making the spider an easy target for the starfish to kill.

- Starfish organizations do not have a central base of money. Revenue comes in multiple forms, from multiple sources. In the case of al-Qaeda, for example, they are involved in human smuggling, drug trafficking (although some will debate this), extortion and kidnapping for ransom.

- The ideology within the starfish organization is the glue that holds it together.

Others have discussed mutations, or a combination of the starfish and the spider organizations. This should not be surprising. Evil is always trying to build a better mouse trap. We must not be distracted by those efforts. What we must do, as you will find later in this book, is make a sustained effort to inject chaos into the organization at every point possible. Never let evil get a footing. Put the enemy on the defensive constantly; otherwise, the cells will regroup and go on the offensive. This is why a battle against evil demands the utmost attention to detail and will. We must never rest and never take our victories for granted. We must pursue, pursue, pursue with absolute diligence and resolve, operating constantly at the speed of light.

Moving from Theory to the Battlefield

My intent all along has been to provide law enforcement, military, political leaders, and all able and willing citizens a better understanding of how highly resilient organizations operate and how to better use resources to target the core resiliency factors of the organization in an all-out effort to fully dismantle the organization. However, I also provide a window in which legitimate organizations are interested in creating or sustaining resiliency, with an understanding of characteristics that can be studied and applied to their organizations. My hope is that "good" organizations will build themselves into resilient organizations too, in order to beat back "evil." Obviously, those AF-DTO characteristics relating to criminal behavior are not appropriate for us "good guys;" however, others are appropriate, such as business acumen, situational awareness, recruitment, adaptability, compartmentalization, optimism, international reach, technology, loyalty and self-reliance. Each of these characteristics is constructed of multiple variables, as described earlier. The characteristics collectively can provide a strong framework for corporate resilience, marching forward either alone as one organization or collectively with many on a united front throughout the globe.

This study of evil has achieved two things: (1) today's evil organizations have been proven to be resilient organizations and (2) the core resiliency characteristics sustaining them have been identified. To further this effort, it would be prudent for the world governments to adopt a strategy to dismantle the sinister organizations by refocusing efforts on key resiliency characteristics, while also addressing the two key environmental factors—all of which help to sustain evil's presence.

Clearly, we can begin right now in our backyard with Mexico, and if this proves successful—as I know it will—similar efforts should be applied to the remaining Mexican DTOs operating in similar fashion along the other portions of the Mexican border. Next, the United States should compare the AF-DTO with U.S.–based organized crime (including the Mexican Mafia, Aryan Brotherhood, Nazi Low Riders and Black Guerilla Family) and use a similar strategy against these organizations.

Simultaneously, the U.S. government should look at the AF-DTO with regards to worldwide terrorist organizations and, if relationships are identified (and this is inferred from the research), should then use a similar strategy by focusing on resiliency characteristics. Later in the book, I will present my strategy to defeat al-Qaeda.

Lastly, the United States should focus on the final tier of domestic terrorist groups: organized street gangs like MS-13, White Fence, Bloods and Crips in an effort to dismantle the leadership and dry up the resources that feed their resiliency.

One fact that this book clearly demonstrates is that legitimate organizations targeting the AF-DTO must have superior technology to keep up with the AF-DTO's ability to obtain advanced technology. With cyclical federal and state funding, the inability to keep up constant pressure against the AF-DTO remains an ongoing issue. Leadership changes within our governments and other organizations can have a detrimental effect on the ability to sustain efforts against the AF-DTO. Also, the obvious red tape that exists within legitimate organizations targeting the AF-DTO is a clear hindrance to timely and sustained success.

Heyman and Campbell[170] point out a critical factor in the battle to dismantle DTOs: very little is truly known about them. Collecting information on a highly secretive and dangerous organization is obviously extremely challenging. Better real-time intelligence is needed, including more technology for wiretaps and, most importantly, the ability to use human intelligence (i.e., undercover agents, sources, etc.) to infiltrate the organization, as was done successfully in the United States against organized crime syndicates in Chicago with Al Capone and others.

Behind the Line – Testimonial 14:
"The Evolution of Chaos"

with DEA Director of International Operations, Michael S. Vigil, Ret.

In 1994 the Zapatista Liberation Army insurrection started in the town of San Cristobal, in the southern State of Chiapas, Mexico. The North American Free Trade Agreement (NAFTA) also went into effect in 1994. In March of that year, Donaldo Colosio, a PRI (Institutional Revolutionary Party) presidential candidate, was assassinated in Tijuana by a lone gunman. The following month, Jose Benitez, the chief of police in Tijuana was also executed very close to where Colosio was killed. Ernesto Zedillo was then nominated as the PRI (Institutional Revolutionary Party) candidate for the presidency by sheer luck. He didn't want the presidency, and he told one of his closest advisors, "Why did Colosio have to die at this point in time?" The comment was made as though he was speaking to Colosio. He was not prepared for the presidency, but he had no choice and had to accept it. He was named by outgoing Carlos Salinas de Gortari: the PRI was in a rush to support a candidate because of the impending elections. He wanted to show the pluralistic nature of the government by selecting Antonio Lozano Gracia as the Attorney General of the Republic. Since 1932, Lozano Gracia was the first National Action Party (PAN) candidate to ever hold a cabinet level post with the PRI.

As it turned out, the naming of Lozano Gracia was of great benefit to the DEA. I was in Guadalajara attending a management conference shortly after Lozano Gracia took over as Attorney General. My cell phone rang one evening and it was Lozano Gracia's Executive Secretary saying, "Mr. Vigil, the Attorney General of Mexico would like to talk to you." A few seconds later, Lozano Gracia was on the phone responding, "I know that you're a man who has the confidence of Mexico because of your efforts on behalf of the nation. Everyone speaks very highly of you." He added, "I want to meet with you because we're very concerned about the issue of drug trafficking." Lozano Gracia supported DEA operations and communicated with us on many sensitive issues. He was an exceptional Attorney General and a great humanitarian.

In June, 1993, I assisted the Mexican Attorney General's office in the construction of the National Institute for the Combating of Drugs (INCD). The Mexican Government wanted to create a new law enforcement component that would be incorruptible. So they got rid of a lot of agents, not because of corruption, but because they just wanted to start with new personnel who came from professional backgrounds and were not potentially tainted. I was the individual that many of the Mexican Federales always asked for assistance because of my high level contacts with the Mexican Government. Many competent and aggressive Federales lost their jobs and, of course, they called me for help. As a result, I went to the Mexican Federal Judicial Police Director General, Rudolpho Leon Aragon, and said "Rudolpho you need to hire all of these individuals because we work well with them." He replied, "Bring them," and soon re-hired them all. Within two years they were all commanders of many of the thirty-three states in Mexico. Guess who they reported to before they coordinated with their headquarters? They reported to me. We were able to do a lot of very, very significant things because of this loyalty.

In 1992 Mexico created CENDRO. I helped Jorge Tello-Peon construct the center that served as Mexico's National Intelligence Center. It provided Mexico with the ability to establish a nexus to many internal agencies, to include the security forces. It functioned very much like the U.S. Office of National Drug Control Policy (White House Drug Czar's Office) by creating Mexico's National Drug Strategy. It also served as a Command, Control, and Communication Center since it handled many of the national drug interdiction efforts. Additionally, it also functioned very much like the El Paso Intelligence Center (EPIC) handling both tactical and strategic intelligence.

Mexico continues to have issues that negatively impact the country; however, if we work together in a bi-national collaborative effort, we can have broader and more far reaching operational successes. The drug-trafficking organizations are very well entrenched. For example the one that used to be headed by Amado Carillo-Fuentes, the so-called "Lord of the Skies" was one of the most powerful cartels in the history of Mexico. His name was derived from pioneering the use of commercial aircraft, 727's, and French-made Caravels, to transport multi-ton quantities of cocaine from Colombia into Mexico. He, in my opinion, is one of the most dangerous and prolific traffickers that Mexico has ever spawned.

We were dealing with aircraft having speeds of approximately 500 nautical miles an hour and could outrun law enforcement aircraft. These aircraft were landing in the middle of the desert. Payloads were anywhere from eight to twelve metric tons of cocaine. On the way back to Colombia they were loaded with currency to pay for the drugs. The bulk currency sent to Colombia ranged anywhere from twenty to forty million dollars.

On one occasion a drug-trafficker's aircraft landed in the desert of Chihuahua. The traffickers had over seventy armed individuals providing security to the operation as evidenced by FLIR systems. They were able to offload the drugs and refuel the aircraft in less than eight minutes before it was airborne and headed due south.

Recently Mexico captured Osiel Cardenas Guillen, the head of the violent Gulf Cartel. Cardenas Guillen was captured after a massive gun battle with the Mexican army. The cartel leader had a security detail consisting of about seventy heavily armed individuals who also had sophisticated communications equipment. Prior to Cardenas Guillen, the cartel was headed by Juan Garcia Abrego who ruled with an iron fist. Both individuals are now serving time in U.S. prisons, which effectively remove them from their power base and the ability to give orders and commands to the organization. It is for this reason that foreign traffickers fear extradition to the United States. All drug traffickers have to realize that their power will be short lived before they are caught and sent to prison. The rule of law will eventually prevail and they will have to pay a significant price.

— Michael S. Vigil

Implications for the Future

A number of areas for future attention are warranted. The importance of brutality to the AF-DTO is perhaps understated. If such brutality were removed from the resiliency characteristics of the organization, would the AF-DTO remain a resilient organization? Brutality was the most prominent research finding, followed by corruption. If one could remove from the AF-DTO the characteristics not used by legitimate organizations, could the AF-DTO remain resilient? I don't think so.

As previously noted, DTOs and terrorist organizations have similarities.[171] A study examining similarities and differences between these two types of organizations is warranted and could lead to a better understanding of how to dismantle these types of organizations, as I will propose a little later in this book. Hoffman[172] wrote an article citing the resiliency strengths that businesses can learn from al-Qaeda in order to achieve a similar kind of resiliency. While I doubt that a crossover of strengths would be useful, it would be an important undertaking because those newly identified characteristics could help legitimate governments to better adapt.

Categories of Terror Groups

Separatist – to separate for purpose of independence, religious, political freedom
and domination, such as the *Liberation Tigers of Tamil Eelam*
(photo courtesy of U.S. Government)

Ethnocentric – align with their specific race against
all others, much like the *Klu Klux Klan*
(photo courtesy of U.S. Government)

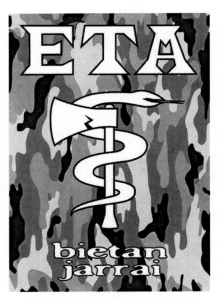

Nationalistic – for the purpose of breaking away from an existing nation to create one's own, to join with another for perceived "national" identity as seen with the *Euskadi Ta Askatasuna* organization, largely based in Spain
(photo courtesy of U.S. Government)

Revolutionary – exist to overthrow others (often capitalistic nations) and replacing it with their social or political structure, as seen with the
Communist Party of the Philippines
(photo courtesy of U.S. Government)

182

Political – fight simply based on their strong held political ideologies in order to change political policies and leadership, as seen within the *Kosovo Liberation Army* *(photo courtesy of U.S. Government)*

Religious – align with one religious belief, such as Islamic extremism, believing their views are infallible and not a negotiable subject, such as *Abu Sayyaf*, based in the Philippines *(photo courtesy of U.S. Government)*

Dr. Paul R. Chabot

Social – often referred to as single-issue or special-interest-terrorism, more home-grown and can involve animal right groups, environmentalists, among many other issues, as seen with the U.S. based *Weather Underground* of the 1960s and 70s
(photo courtesy of U.S. Government)

Domestic – home-grown entities operating against their own country for a variety of reasons often centered on politics and extreme social views, such as the *Earth Liberation Front* or the *Aryan Nation* – both based in the U.S.
(Anarchy logo typically used by radical groups, pictured here)
(photo courtesy of U.S. Government)

International or Transnational – organizations reach beyond their borders with worldwide cells in many countries, often concerned with events in a certain region or nation. *Hezbollah* is considered "international" with their focus on both Lebanon and Israel while *al Qaeda (logo pictured)* is seen as "transnational"
(photo courtesy of U.S. Government)

Sampling of Worldwide Terror Organizations

Al-Shabaab – an Islamic insurgent group fighting to overthrow the Somalia government – Its strength is estimated at 7,000 or more members
(photo courtesy of U.S. Government)

Islamic Resistance Movement *AKA "Hamas"* – a Palestinian Islamist political party with a strong military component with strong aggression towards Israel – Strength of more than 10,000 members
(photo courtesy of U.S. Government)

Harakat ul-Mujahidin – Islamic military group based largely in
Pakistan with members in the thousands
(photo courtesy of U.S. Government)

Hezbollah (Party of God) – a Shia military organization, and a
political party founded in Lebanon aimed at destroying Israel –
Membership ranges in the tens of thousands
(photo courtesy of U.S. Government)

Islamic Movement of Uzbekistan – a military organization based in Tajikistan – Purpose is to overthrow the local government and institute Sharia law – Membership is estimated below 1,000
(photo courtesy of U.S. Government)

Jaish-e-Mohammed (Army of Mohammed) – a mujahedeen entity with roots in Pakistan – goal is to separate Kashmir from India – Membership numbers are in the thousands
(photo courtesy of U.S. Government)

Kongra-Gel (formerly Kurdistan Workers' Party) – a Kurdish entity fighting Turkey from operations in Iraq, Syria and within Turkey for the creation of an independent Kurdistan – Membership is approximately 5,000
(photo courtesy of U.S. Government)

Moroccan Islamic Combatant Group (GICM) – a Sunni Islamist organization with ties to al Qaeda, based in North – Its reach extends to Europe and Canada – Membership numbers are evasive
(photo courtesy of U.S. Government)

189

al-Qaida – an Islamic militant organization with worldwide operations calling for a global Jihad on the Western world with tens of thousands of operatives in over 40 nations.
(photo courtesy of U.S. Government)

Revolutionary Armed Forces of Colombia (FARC) – a Marxist / Leninist revolutionary army based within Colombia – Membership is between 5,000 and 10,000
(photo courtesy of U.S. Government)

Chapter Nine

Organizational Resiliency

"Let every nation know, whether it wishes us well or ill, we shall pay
any price, bear any burden, meet any hardship, support any friend,
oppose any foe, to assure the survival and success of liberty."
— *John F. Kennedy*

As I have already pointed out, DTOs are resilient to extreme
internal and external factors that might otherwise dismantle their
core structure. This chapter identifies those organizational resiliency
characteristics. Understanding organizational resiliency within DTOs
is the first step in dismantling them. Yet, until this book, there has
been no research study that focused on organizational resiliency within
a high-level international drug trafficking organization. This void only
hamstrings efforts to dismantle high-level criminal organizations,
worldwide—when you know one, you know them all.

In this chapter, I will fill that gap by expanding the scope of
research applicable to organizational resiliency and DTOs. By
identifying the core resiliency characteristics of DTOs through both
evolutionary and revolutionary change and by analyzing the data from
both archival documents and interviews, we can understand the
process and the characteristics, the method and the madness of
DTOs—that is, understand what drives them and makes them so
resilient. By understanding the full scope of DTOs—their structure,
function, motivation, and operations—and more importantly, what
makes them so resilient to intense dismantling efforts by local, state
and federal governments and law enforcement personnel, we are in a
better position to take them down. We must turn the tide, chipping

away at DTO resilience, while in the process building our own set of resiliency characteristics to eradicate the evil that is a drug trafficking organization and other organized criminal syndicates.

To restate, after a decade of research, I found that DTOs have a number of specific characteristics - as well as two environmental factors – which contribute to their resiliency, and that all evil organizations share a near identical structure and process. The course of organizational resiliency within DTOs is cycled through several constructs in order to achieve their goals of sustainability and profitability—the latter of which is the very essence of DTOs that operate within a supportive environment. They are able to cycle themselves through a resiliency framework during times of significant stress, and thus maintain operability and elasticity when facing internal and external dismantling pressures. Horne, et al. said:

> *Resilience is an old and honored quality recognized throughout human history. Organizations are human enterprises and as such, the concept of resilience seems to be an appropriate standpoint from which to view the complexities of organizational change.*[173]

What is Organizational Resiliency?

There are various definitions of organizational resiliency. In a paper published by the Multidisciplinary Center for Earthquake Engineering Research, organizational resiliency is described as "the ability of a system to reduce the chances of shock, to absorb a shock if it occurs, and to recover quickly after a shock."[174] Organizational resiliency has also been described as "the ability of a system to resist the stresses of environmental loading based on the combination of the system pieces; their structural inter-linkages; and the way in which environments change, are transmitted, and spread throughout the whole organization."[175] Whatever the technical definition, it has become clear through my research and my experience that DTOs possess an ability to thrive in the face of intense efforts to dismantle them.

To put it another way, drug trafficking organizations are often described as snakes that grow a new head soon after they are dismembered. I've already introduced you to the term called "cutting grass"—wiping out the leadership of al-Qaeda, only to witness new heads arise. What is it that allows these organizations to thrive in a world where law enforcement agencies, military, and hired civilians are attempting to capture or kill their leaders while, simultaneously, other organizations are battling against them? How do these organizations become and remain so resilient?

This book examines this phenomenon. It determines what resiliency strengths allow evil to continue its existence while withstanding all kinds of pressures. My hope is that this information resonates with leaders of the world so that we may move quickly and effectively against terror and terror-like organizations, beyond drug cartels and al-Qaeda, to include street and prison gangs, which can be equally as resilient.[176]

As a side note, if you own—or someday hope to own—a company, there are lessons in this chapter as well. Evil does not have a monopoly over "resiliency." These organizations simply have mastered its technique, and you can as well. For once maybe we can take a positive lesson from what evil has perfected for the betterment of our legitimate organizations and institutions. Private industry, nonprofit organizations and volunteer groups can benefit from this knowledge by replicating resiliency factors used by evil organizations to ensure their survival.

Fact:	Evil continues to operate despite sudden and massive losses of personnel and equipment.
Fact:	Evil can reorganize, rebuild and continue with their operations.
Fact:	"Good" organizations are facing a higher number of unforgiving events that could doom them.[177] Even organizations that have enjoyed stable environments in the past are now facing uncertain technological, economic, political and cultural changes.[178]

Question: What makes a DTO different from organizations that attempt to survive but flounder and fall apart?

Answer, in part: Evil is often much better "structured" for survival than the rest of us. Evil seeks to be extremely reliable, a highly sought-after quality.[179]

Evil's Resiliency

Sinister resilient organizations share a number of closely related attributes. When you put these attributes together, a perfect resilient entity takes shape. Below is a striking list of these attributes practiced today by nearly all of the evil in the world.

1. Adaptability
2. Advanced technology and communications
3. Alliances with rival DTOs, U.S. street gangs and officials
4. Cash flow (unlimited)
5. Compartmentalization
6. Corruption of officials
7. Counterintelligence
8. Creativity in generating funds through new ventures
9. Dependence on violence to intimidate officials, community and rivals
10. Dependence on violence to manipulate the organization's membership
11. Fear of prosecution, being killed, or organizational extinction
12. Well-organized, hierarchal structure with few management layers
13. Flexibility
14. Geographic control
15. High degree of redundancy and duplication
16. Intelligence (timely)

17. Isolation of leaders
18. Membership recruitment
19. Monopoly over products or criminal methods (for example: drugs, cigarettes, guns, human smuggling)
20. Product protection
21. Protection of leaders
22. Relationships with partners (geographic or worldwide)
23. Fast replacement of leadership after loss of a leader
24. Fast response to adverse situations
25. Rules and protocol for members
26. Secrecy
27. Trust within their leadership circles.

These 27 broad themes are really the essential ingredients. Now, to make some sense of this, I created a core listing of the overarching resiliency characteristics. Let me say this was no easy task—a process of reviewing an overwhelming amount of information over multiple years. But in the end, I'm confident we have identified the very core, so here we go:

1. **Adaptability**

    Related component examples: creative sophistication; opportunism

2. **Business acumen (acting like a business)**

    Related component examples: ability to organize the operational structure; centralized leadership; aggressive growth; drug shipment/product control; leadership development

3. **Compartmentalization**

    Related component examples: leadership protection; decentralized components

4. **Corruption**

   Related component examples: bribery and blackmail of law enforcement /politicians / decision-makers

5. **International and/or reach outside of "base" location**

   Related component examples: stable flow of product/drugs; disregard for international boundaries; networking/partnerships with international criminal organizations/gangs

6. **Loyalty**

   Related component examples: internal discipline and obedience; control over personnel

7. **Monopoly goal orientation**

   Related component examples: control over product; killing of competitors; geographic control; infiltration of competitor trade lines; cooperation with adversaries of enemies

8. **Optimism**

   Related component examples: history of success; sense of entitlement; confidence

9. **Recruitment**

   Related component examples: quick replenishment of ranks; members have higher salaries than what can be earned from legitimate work; large organizational membership; "street smart" members

10. **Reputation:**

   Related component examples: brutality; attacks on law enforcement/government; revenge killings; witness/victim intimidation; creation of community of fear; branding themselves as an organization not to "mess with"

11. Self-reliance

Related component examples: financial independence; use of business facade for money laundering and investments; product and activity diversification (similar to how one may diversify stocks)

12. Situational awareness

Related component examples: intelligence collection and counterintelligence activity; reduced visibility when needed; deception tactics; infiltration of legitimate businesses; attention to minor details; diligence in all tasks performed

13. Technology

Related component examples: GPS, weapons, computers, communications equipment

14. Trust

Related component examples: not trusting outside entities or individuals; high family and/or organizational leadership trust

Together, these characteristics and components best represent the essence of evil's resiliency. A few very important items not listed above are in a category all their own. I call these "environmental factors." Basically, these are conditions that already exist in the territory now being controlled, thereby allowing sinister organizations to flourish. For example, drug trafficking organizations operating in Mexico live within a country that has "diminished rule of law." In short, corruption is rampant, good judges and cops are killed, and the media which often reports on drug cartel violence are themselves threatened and killed. When a region or country lacks the basics to enforce the rule of law, evil will—without a doubt—become entrenched into a system and grow into a strong oak tree.

A second environmental factor greatly aiding these drug cartels is the vast consumer base for illegal narcotics in the United States. The funding from such activity feeds evil, but of course, drugs are not their only source of revenue. They're also involved in weapons smuggling, kidnapping, human smuggling, black markets in music and movie compact discs, etc. By the way, drug legalization is not the answer to make cartels "go-away." Cartels exist to make money and have diversified their operations into other areas.

1. **Diminished societal rule of law:** The AF-DTO thrives in a country where the rule of law has been vastly diminished in some areas and is completely missing in others. Along with the practice of corruption, this allows the organization to continue with very little disruption from authorities. The diminished societal rule of law has enabled the organization to gain cult-like status in certain parts of Mexico.

2. **Vast consumer base:** The AF-DTO is dependent on U.S. drug users to ensure the organization's continued success and growth in the drug trade. With a vast consumer base, the AF-DTO will always have customers to sell to and make money from.

Together, these characteristics—accompanied by the environmental factors—sustain the organization during times of significant pressure, but also are in evidence during normal operational times when no such pressure exists. Although these are the particular characteristics highlighted here, it is important to remember that multiple strengths make up each of these highly refined resiliency characteristics and that slight variations are apparent in different evil organizations.

Resiliency is found in successful criminal organizations and is perhaps the most important arbiter to success. "Over the past several decades, Colombian narcotics trafficking organizations have transported greater quantities of cocaine and heroin into the United States."[180] This has occurred despite increased U.S. measures to counter their trafficking methods. The Colombian cartels adapt to these changes by altering their behavior and storing the changes in their memory, then create and select innovative ways to produce satisfactory results. This example demonstrates that resiliency is part of human nature and survival of the fittest, since drug cartels need their businesses to thrive in order to survive.

s *Dr. Paul R. Chabot*

Behind the Line – Testimonial 15: "One Step Forward Two Steps Back"

with DEA Director of International Operations, Michael S. Vigil, Ret.

Mexico's cooperation continues to be strengthened with the United States. It's no longer as Porfirio-Diaz once said, "Poor Mexico, so far from God and so close to the United States." So much has changed. Former President Vicente Fox restructured the Mexican Attorney General's office and did a good job in creating the Federal Investigative Agency (AFI). The agency is highly compartmentalized in order to prevent leaks of sensitive information. Only a few upper level managers are fully cognizant of the entire scope of active investigations and operations. The Mexican Government has also professionalized the ranks of its police by providing higher salaries and more benefits. Former President Fox brought the Mexican military into the counter-drug arena to have more of an impact on the drug traffickers that continue to cause major damage to the country. The Mexican Army, in previous years, had been relegated to nothing more than manual eradication of illicit crops. Today, the military is a dedicated force with units of soldiers who receive polygraph examinations and are tested for illegal drugs, and who undergo significant background testing. The Mexican military has really been a significant success story in terms of counter-drug efforts in Mexico and responsible for capturing many of the most significant traffickers operating in the country.

CISEN, which is their equivalent of the U.S. CIA, is the Center for National Security Investigations. In the past CISEN was used by the PRI to collect damaging information on oppositional party leaders. Now they are engaging heavily in counterdrug intelligence collection operations. CISEN has continued to make progress and evolve into a viable

200

intelligence agency. They have highly competent personnel and are working to develop a cooperative effort in sharing information, both internally and with other governments, such as the United States.

In contrast the Mexican military and the PGR still show some distress and need to work closer together. They are making progress, but are still not fully cooperating with one another. The trust is not one of organizations, but of personal friendships. For example, former Mexican Deputy Attorney, Jose Luis Santiago Vasconcelos, a personal friend of mine, was highly trusted by the Mexican military and he was the common thread between the agencies. Unfortunately, Jose Luis died in a tragic plane crash in Mexico City. Mexican and U.S. law enforcement lost one of its great leaders and allies. He was an exceptional person and will live on through his accomplishments and huge efforts against drug trafficking and organized crime.

President Fox, during his administration, started a new approach. When he took office he mandated that Mexico globalize their counterdrug efforts and work with other countries. He was a proponent of sharing information and working collaboratively.

I have also been an advocate of international cooperation; the key to any activity directed at large-scale trafficking in drugs is the sharing of information between countries. Mexico is moving in the right direction.

DEA and the United States, especially in the aftermath of 9-11, globalized its efforts in fighting drugs. The premise is that drug trafficking is a global problem and therefore requires a global solution. Unless we globalize, together, we basically minimize the operational impact, and our overall potential to combat evil.

Recently, we have seen some headway with our efforts in Mexico. We've been working closely with the Mexican authorities in terms of sharing information and identifying drug trafficking organizations to target in a collective effort.

Unfortunately, many are highly averse to sharing information with Mexico; this limits our ability to immobilize drug trafficking networks in a systematic and comprehensive manner. We can't afford to limit the impact in our fight – we cannot give up even one inch – we must fight on and build our international cooperative efforts.

The drug trade is a significant multi-billion dollar industry. You not only have the nexus to terrorism, but it poisons our youth and generates other crime and violence. Drug trafficking threatens the very fabric of nations and quickly spreads like a cancer into many countries lacking the infrastructure to combat this insidious plague. For example, Myanmar (Burma as it was once called) has the Wa which has literally become a government within the government. They engage in heroin production and distribution. They also manufacture a low grade of methamphetamine. The Wa has its own government and does not respect the borders with other countries such as Thailand. The political systems of many nations suffer as a result of the drug trade. Often, other countries simply refuse to get involved because they do not want to see "drugs" as a problem. It's an apparent "U.S. problem," but other countries are developing addiction problems as well; it's an ongoing problem for all nations with some seeing the drug trade as a necessary evil. We have lots of work yet to do.

— *Michael S. Vigil*

But, what is Resilience?

"And thus, like the wounded oyster, he mends his shell with a pearl."
— *Ralph Waldo Emerson*

Without question, a thorough understanding of resilience is required. By now, you have been exposed to what makes up an evil organization and you have often been told that evil is resilient. It is at this point in the book that you develop a deeper understanding by becoming a master of "resilient identification." In doing so, Webster[181] defines resilience *as "the capability of a strained body to recover its size and shape after deformation caused by compressive stress...an ability to recover from or adjust easily to misfortune or change."*

The worldwide literature on organizational resilience is fragmented.[182] Simply, in a short phrase, resilience is the ability to thrive and survive under difficult conditions.[183] It's about recovering from error.[184] It's the capacity to deal with incidents—whether expected or unexpected—once they have occurred.[185] In order to be resilient, an organization must be prepared for adversity. It must be able to learn, act and investigate without truly knowing what will be needed most in the future to avoid a disaster.[186] Organizational resilience is an essential corollary for positive organizational scholarship because it begins to articulate how organizations behave efficaciously and thrive amidst adverse conditions.[187] Another term for resilience is adaptability.[188]

Social researchers continue to refine their ideas about organizational resilience. Collins and Porras state that a firm must possess core values to become more resilient. Without these values, the firm will "expire."[189] Some authors connect and interchange the terms "hardiness" and "resilience,"[190] while others connect the concepts "radical change" and "adaptability."[191] Other researchers offer insights into the process of an organization becoming resilient: Organizational resilience results from enhancing particular competencies, such as the processes that encourage mindfulness and processes that enhance capabilities to recombine and deploy resources in a new way"[192]

The information I gathered suggests that the following abilities are largely responsible for organizational resiliency: (1) the ability to promote competence; (2) the ability to restore efficacy; and (3) the ability to encourage growth. The Resilience Alliance defines resilience as "(1) the amount of disturbance a system can absorb and still remain within the same state...(2) the degree to which the system is capable of self-organization...(3) the degree to which the system can build and increase the capacity for learning and adaptation."[193] Sutcliffe and Vogus conceptualize resiliency as the ability to restore and maintain efficacy.[194] Weick and Sutcliffe simplify the concept of resiliency in one question: "Do I have the skills to make do?"[195]

The Latin root "resile" refers to something that was once damaged or stretched, which will recoil or spring back to life or maintain its shape, weight or size. Grotherberg created the following definition based on her work on an international resiliency project:

Resilience is a universal capacity which allows a person, group or community to prevent, minimize, or overcome the damaging effects of adversity...resilience may be promoted not necessarily because of adversity, but indeed may be developed in anticipation of inevitable adversities. [196]

Braverman defines resilience as "a concept that incorporates two components: (1) exposure to significant stressors or risks, and (2) demonstration of competence and successful adaptation."[197] Greene defines resilience as "a universal capacity which allows a person, group, or community to prevent, minimize, or overcome damaging effects of adversities."[198]

Now that we know some of the definitions of the term "resilience," we should also understand what resilience can accomplish. Resilience provides insight into how organizations continue to achieve desirable outcomes amidst adversity, strain, and significant barriers to adaptation or development.[199] Resiliency is at the core of survival. It is what makes people pick themselves up and take the first step of a long climb back up a mountain. It is about being determined and focused to overcome adversity, to overcome significant challenges.[200]

Successful organizations maintain a keen instinct for survival in a world that allows only the strong to survive. Johnson and Kloman state, "We attempt to build resiliency into our existing systems so we can sustain. In preparing for disaster, we are essentially trying to manage our exposure to the unanticipated consequences that disasters pose. We attempt to build resiliency into our existing systems...so we can sustain the potential consequences."[201]

Hoffman, the vice president of external affairs and director of the RAND Corporation, stated, "*In terms of its organizational resilience and flexibility, its structure and communications, al-Qaeda is not unlike a successful, smart company.*"[202] He cites strengths attributed to al-Qaeda resilience as: (1) a clear message, (2) a firm purpose, (3) a charismatic leader, and (4) no fear of delegating. Al-Qaeda adopted a flatter, more linear organizational structure. Bin Laden was very good at issuing orders and making sure they were followed, while also making clear the goals and aims of the organization. Hoffman believes that a key indicator of al-Qaeda's success lies in the organization's ability "to recruit, to mobilize and to animate both actual and would-be fighters, supporters and sympathizers.... Despite the punishment dealt out to al-Qaeda over the past two years and more, it still remains a potent terrorist threat..."[203] Hoffman credits the organization's resilience to its ability to change direction slightly (comparing the movement to that of a shark in water) so that it can survive.

Organizational Resiliency Refined

By now, like the pieces of a puzzle coming together, you should begin to see the picture of a resilient organization. As that picture comes into focus, let's take into account a few important lessons from those who have invested their time on this very subject—laying the foundation from which resilience can grow. If you are asking yourself how to go about the process of creating a resilient organization to counter evil, that's the right question to ask. I recommend undertaking the suggestion of Hamel, et al.[204] who described four challenges that must be met before an organization becomes resilient. First, the organization must push away from its past and be willing to throw everything away for a new beginning. The company or organization must have the ability to see what needs changing and be willing to consider those needed changes. This challenge is referred to as the cognitive challenge. Second, the organization must create a menu of options to counteract failing strategies. This second challenge is known as the strategic challenge. Third, the organization must be willing to divert resources from what worked in the past to activities in the future by creating a broad menu of new ideas supported with the necessary talent, resources, etc. This challenge is known as the political challenge. The fourth and final challenge is the ideological challenge: the organization must think beyond its existing place in history and embrace a belief of near perfect execution and excellent operational abilities. Hamel claims that few organizations can master, or have mastered, these four challenges. The first and biggest obstacle that must be overcome is conquering denial, followed by becoming hopeful, and ending with spreading optimism throughout one's organization.

Becoming resilient, according to Hamel, is accomplished in three phases: revolution, renewal and resilience. Revolution is the creative destruction phase; it is innovative with respect to the rules of the organization. Renewal is the phase in which the organization must reinvent itself; this phase is also known as strategic renewal. It requires innovation with respect to one's traditional business model.[205] These two phases lead to the third phase—resilience. When an organization has reached the resilience phase, it is capable of continuous reconstruction, requiring innovation while keeping in mind the organization's behaviors and values that favor perpetuation over innovation. According to Hamel, "Any company that can make sense of its environment, generate strategic options, and realign its resources faster than its rivals will enjoy a decisive advantage. This is the essence of resilience."[206]

Quarantelli[207] described the disaster research conducted by the U.S. Military between 1950 and 1965. In particular, he detailed studies conducted at the National Opinion Research Center, which were commissioned by the Chemical Corps of Medical Laboratories at the Army Chemical Center in Maryland. Researchers at the National Opinion Research Center examined a 1948 incident in Donora, Pennsylvania, in which a local population became ill from toxic fumes and 25 people were killed. This retrospective study examined wartime conduct of a populace by analyzing how the populace responded to natural and industrial tragedies. The same group conducted a study of survivors of plane crashes to determine the psychological reactions and actions of individuals and local populations in a calamity. The purpose of the study was to develop methods for deterring panic and minimizing emotional and/or psychological failures.

What you see in the beginning phase of creating your resilient organization is the courage to start from scratch, to have the willingness to toss everything on the table and walk through a door you have never entered before. The process of building a better mouse trap has its roots in one desire: to simply do something better. From the little known research on resilience, we have identified in this book that the concept of building a better organization to fight evil should be at the front of your cerebral cortex. You see, you are not alone. Others all around the world have been trying to build something better, for good and evil purposes. Hitler advanced his beliefs and organizational structures and was constantly on guard to destroy his enemies quicker and more efficiently. The Allies also learned, adapted and grew in their efforts in World War II to counter the spread of evil. It was an evolution of both human and organizational resilience.

A level of connectivity is required for resilient organizations. A shared sense of organizational purpose/mission and interactive planning consistently appear as critical success factors in the continued resilience of organizations.[208] In relation to public safety organizations, this connectivity is vital. "The organization will need to rapidly know its challenges, the competencies it has or needs to meet these challenges, and the information about how it has adapted to changing conditions."[209] Horne states that in order for this level of connectivity to occur, "organizations will need to be very cohesive entities."[210]

Resiliency appears to emerge after some type of crisis, and crises can be defined by many types of events. Warren Walker of the RAND Institute states that crises are rare events. He explains, "Each crisis is different from other crises. Among the variables that define a crisis are its type (e.g., flood, explosion, war and airplane-crash), location, affected population, and relevant support organizations."[211] Lagadec[212] describes organizations in crisis as having three stages that can cause the organization serious harm. The first two stages can be overcome by implementing various forms of emergency procedures that have been practiced and become a part of the organization's memory. However, the third stage is so severe that the emergency procedures become obsolete. According to Lagadec, "the specialized emergency function is no longer enough to bring the situation back."[213] Ellis'[214] study of one of the world's most reliable urban transport systems found that reliability was partially due to an organization's resiliency to various forms of actions that could subdue the system for normal operations. For example, if an organization is left alone to interpret its meaning, it would be able to limit its reach to the tipping point of no return.[215] The ability to interpret meaning is an essential component of this book's discussion surrounding mindfulness, which is a component of the conceptual framework, which will be discussed in more detail later and in this book's appendix.

Chapter Ten

Organizational Resilience for the "Good Guys"

"I am not afraid...I was born to do this"
— Joan of Arc

W hat can our legitimate organizations do to counter evil?
Simple—become resilient as well. History provides fascinating
examples of what our "good guys and gals" must apply to their
organizations if we are to have a fighting chance defeating the enemy.
Let's start this conversation with one of the most prolific events in
American history—the attacks on September 11, 2001. In "Strength of
a City: A Disaster Research Perspective on the World Trade Center
Attack," Kathleen Tierney observed:

> *The September 11 attacks and their aftermath are a living
> laboratory for those wishing to better understand how
> individuals, groups, and organizations respond under extreme
> disaster conditions. Along with other major disaster events,
> 9/11 revealed much about institutional responses and
> collective behavior in crises, underscoring what is already
> known about the social processes that characterize such
> events, while at the same time highlighting aspects of disasters
> that the literature has yet to explore fully.[216]*

Interesting information has emerged from reports written after
9/11. One such report looked at resiliency factors that could be
implemented in private industry and the banking business based on

what was learned from the attacks at the World Trade Center. This study concluded that four key practices were necessary for U.S. financial system security.

First, the organization must identify all of its critical activities. Second, the organization must determine the appropriate resumption and recovery objective (how long do they expect to be out of commission before up and running again). Third, the organization must have sufficient out-of-region resources that can help with the recovery and resumption objectives. Fourth, the organization must test the recovery and resumption arrangements. Combined, these activities should ensure the business's resilience during turmoil or attack.[217] Carly, et al. provided research showing that massive transformation is unstoppable and that resilient organizations contain the necessary components for reorganization and renewal.[218] However, according to high-level personnel in the Fire Department of New York, training was the most important factor in their resilience.[219]

Researchers from Washington University studied the effects on an emergency response unit and found four factors relating to their resilience: (1) firefighters chose that line of work; (2) the personnel had training; (3) workers were rotated and given considerable amounts of debriefing; and (4) the department received high amounts of public support.[220] McCann states, "resiliency helps the organization manage disruptive change," and argues that organizational resiliency and organizational agility are two different things: "Agility helps the organization manage rapid change, while resiliency helps the organization manage disruptive change."[221] If this is the case and agility can be related to hardiness and sustainability, then McCann would see hardiness and sustainability as unrelated to resiliency. But not all researchers agree. Some combine the characteristics of hardiness, sustainability and agility into resiliency, like ingredients in baking a cake. McCann identifies four dimensions of resiliency: absorbing shocks and surprises; creating and exploring alternatives (planning for crisis and making hard choices for renewal); broadly accessing resources (using talents and resources both outside and inside the organization); and executing transformational change (redesigning itself to support a new self-concept).[222]

Bell states, "Organizational resilience has taken on a new urgency since the tragic events of September 11. The ability to respond quickly, decisively and effectively to unforeseen and unpredictable forces is now an enterprise imperative."[223] His five core concepts include (1) leadership, (2) culture, (3) people, (4) systems and (5) settings. Similar to other researchers, Bell believes that leadership is "key;" particularly for organizations that have no choice but to continue to operate.

In our quest to understand resilience in evil and how to create our own resilient organization, we have reached this section of the book—creating a resilient organization. I encourage you to reread this section again, but also refer to the first appendix in this book. It walks you through some of the profound research providing guidance and assurance needed in both creating a resilient organization and in understanding the makeup of evil ones.

Robb[224] addressed complex adaptive systems (which he also refers to as learning systems) that have the ability to change with the environments. These learning systems are made up of two subsystems. First is the performance system; the goal is to perform the existing objectives and tasks in the interest of surviving in the immediacy. The second is the adaptive system, which is a long-term process aimed at performing and meeting future goals. "Successful adaptive/learning systems are characterized by robustness in both subsystems and by strong linkages between them."[225] Robb theorizes that these two subsystems are linked together through a foundation of architecture, skills and culture, as depicted in *Figure 8*.

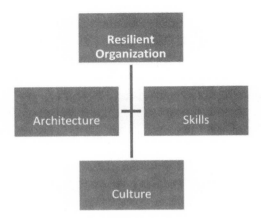

Figure 8. Resilient Organization Components[226]

With the performance and adaptation systems functioning side-by-side, each system concentrates on what it knows best to ensure short- and long-term survival. The performance system focuses concurrently on various levels such as customer needs, efficient business processes, and measuring goals and performance for teams and individuals. These goals are simply short-term processes that must be updated, improved, changed, deleted and so forth to remain competitive. In the long-term, there is also a need for the adaptation system and its sole purpose of bringing new life into the organization through new ideas, solutions, etc. The skills for each system are illustrated below.

Performance Skills

- Task performance and operational execution
- Performance management: focusing behaviors and goals within a narrow range
- Problem solving
- Rational, analytical, linear thought
- Convergent thinking: closure and focus
- Focus on the concrete and specific
- Action

Adaptation Skills

- Visioning
- Diversity and individuality in generating a wide range of possible viewpoints, goals, perceptions and behaviors
- Exploration of environmental change and its implications for organizational focus, structure and potential diversification (external focus)
- Creativity, experimentation
- Emotional competency
- Divergent thinking: opening up options, resisting early closure
- Focus on the system, its organizing principles, structures, values, assumptions
- Self-reflection, humility

Skills Needed for Performance and Adaptation[227]

Resilient organizations not only have rules and procedures to keep them strong, but they also promote a culture in which members see themselves as "living communities with an economic/task responsibility."[228] Much like the skills listed in the earlier figure, a resilient culture is set within a styled set of characteristics, as shown below.

Performance Culture

- Production oriented
- Perfection
- Error detection and correction
- Evaluative
- Tends toward unsafe, unemotional, protective concealment
- Task oriented
- Alignment of people

- Tends toward exclusivity
- Conformance of standards
- Planning and control: plan your work and work your plan
- Compliance oriented
- Tendency toward dependency relationships

Adaptation Culture

- Innovation oriented
- Experimentation and learning
- Appreciating, wondering, creating, speculating, trying
- Accepting; not judgmental
- Safe: to speak up, to be authentic
- Relationships, meaning, and play orientation
- Diversity and individuality
- Inclusive
- Questioning standards
- Emergence: letting things unfold and develop
- Commitment oriented
- Adult, responsible relationships: mutual autonomy and interdependence

Culture for Performance and Adaptation[229]

The above-listed frameworks proposed by Robb set the stage for his Resilient Organization Framework. After he developed the framework, he designed and administered a survey to various organizations. The study was conducted on a minimal sample and produced limited findings.

Sutcliffe and Vogus[230] proposed the framework in *Figure 9* for understanding the factors that lead to resilience and the factors that lead to failure.

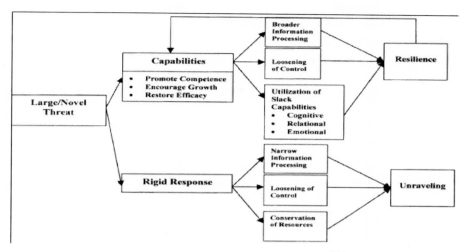

Figure 9. Resilience Framework[231]

Sutcliffe and Vogus[232] hypothesized that organizational resilience occurs when individuals who are the most likely to have the needed immediate information and knowledge are able to make decisions for the group because they are authorized to do so. Organizational resilience depends upon individual teaching, the development of specialized information and personal experience. From this theorized process, a sense of accomplishment and capability grows within the individuals, who are better prepared to act on behalf of the organization. Despite these actions, resilience cannot be guaranteed; rather, resilience simply facilitates the ability to recover.[233]

McCann[234] suggests six dimensions of organizational resiliency: being able to absorb shocks and surprises, creatively exploring alternatives, broadly accessing resources, and executing transformational change, or else rethinking its purpose and identity, and when necessary, recreating itself to support its new self-concept.

Bruneau et al.[235] described four dimensions of resilience: (1) robustness, (2) redundancy, (3) resourcefulness and (4) rigidity. Kendra and Wachtendorf used these four dimensions to study organizational resilience. They redefined the organizational resiliency phenomenon as "socially constituted adaptability to unpredictable ambient forces."[236] Their findings suggest that, in similar types of major disasters, resilient organizations must have leaders who are problem solvers and facilitate employees to deploy rapidly adaptive strategies. They credited training as being one of the most important foundational items in creating a resilient organization. Creative thinking, flexibility and the ability to improvise in newly emergent circumstances were equally important factors.

Bigley and Roberts[237] studied the Incident Command System (ICS) model and found that, if followed, it will create organizational reliability (*see Figure 10*). They researched a fire department's use of the ICS model and described three factors specific to, and evolving from, an environment that enables an organization's ability to cope with catastrophes.

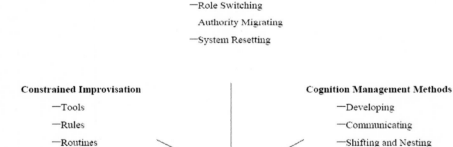

ICS Factors Leading to Organizational Reliability in
Complex and Volatile Task Environments

Structuring Mechanisms

—Structure Elaborating

—Role Switching

Authority Migrating

—System Resetting

Constrained Improvisation

—Tools

—Rules

—Routines

Cognition Management Methods

—Developing

—Communicating

—Shifting and Nesting

Organizational Reliability

Figure 10. ICS Factors Believed to Lead to Reliability[238]

According to Bigley and Roberts,[239] an ICS is a highly structured process. *Figure 11* shows their conceptualization of the process. Note that there is a resemblance to how the AF-DTO organization is structured.

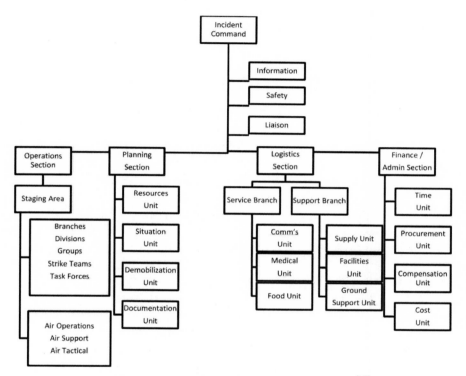

Figure 11. Incident Command Structure[240]

Martin[241] used variables from business model constructs to form a model for resiliency. Martin applied these variables and theorized that an organization which follows this model will become resilient. Martin's assumptions on organizational resiliency stem from his model's resiliency investment variables. He posits that a resilient organization must have leadership, individual strategies and an ability to be proactive. Martin's model is shown in *Figure 12*. The sections in bold are areas added to the existing business model variables. The existing business model variables are found on the left of the arrows.

Key Business Element / **Resiliency Investment**

↓

Business Strategy → **Resiliency Goals**

Corporate Policies → **Governance and Compliance**

Organization and Personnel → **Organization Command and Control**

Clients and Key Service Relationships → **Reliability Strategies**

Processes → **Continuity and Resumption**

Information → **Management and Protection**

Technology → **Redundancy and Recovery**

Facilities and Infrastructure → **Safety, Security, and Dependability**

Figure 12. Model for Business Resiliency[242]

Horne and Orr[243] examined behaviors that create resilient organizations and found that "Resilience is a fundamental quality of individuals, groups, organizations and systems as a whole to respond productively to significant change that disrupts the expected pattern of events, without engaging in an extended period of regressive behavior."[244] *These researchers were an example of the very few who argued that a collection of resilient people within an organization does not equal a resilient organization.* They believed that having too many of these types of people may actually work against the process of resilience because the overbearing nature of their personalities will override the shared vision of the others. The Horne and Orr model for organizational resilience contains seven behaviors:

1. **Community:** The organization's leadership must always remember that their employees must feel a sense of purpose and shared vision and have an understanding of goals.

2. **Competence:** The organization must be able to change to adapt to changes in the environment.

3. **Connections:** Relationships between groups, people and the system must be flexible under pressure: "The connections allow us to establish, maintain and sustain linkage and alignment throughout the entire organization."[245]

4. **Commitment:** All parts of the organization must be able to work together during uncertain times with goodwill and trust, thereby creating "functional trust among members of the organization."[246]

5. **Communication:** The organization must share relevant information, make sense of that information and understand what works and what fails in creating a plan together.

6. **Coordination:** Small and large change efforts occurring within the organization must be timed and linked together to reach the preferred outcome.

7. **Consideration:** The organization must be mindful of its employees. All of the changes may cause overload, and the organization should plan accordingly.

Rerup[247] examined an organization's ability to remain resilient while experiencing an unexpected incident by exploring the concept of anticipation. Rerup defines resiliency as "the ability to predict the future in order to prevent failures" and improvisation as "the ability to recombine chunks of past experience into new patterns of action."[248] He found that an organization that wants to prevent unexpected events from happening must create anticipatory skills. Further, if an organization wants to remain resilient while handling an unexpected event, it must construct both improvisational and anticipatory skills. *Figure 13* provides a framework for understanding how organizations improvise.

Rerup[249] explored two sources of organizational resilience: (1) the ability to forecast the future in order to prepare for its outcomes and (2) improvisation, which is the ability to chunk together past experiences into new patterns of action. He posits that improvisation is relative to resilience because it is not possible to know in advance all the dangers that could potentially depose one's organization. If an organization wants to remain resilient when faced with unexpected events, it must cultivate both improvisational and anticipatory skills. His study examined NASA's Fifth Mission, the mission to the moon that resulted in no loss of life and created resilience through improvisational and anticipatory skills.

Question	Characteristic
When do people in organizations improvise?	People improvise when they can no longer «maintain» and act by following existing routines (Cyert & March, 1963: 121). Improvisation is more common than we expect because every time a routine is performed it unfolds in a slightly different way (March & Olsen, 1989: 39). Improvisation is the mean used to reenact the new routine because «in an unknowable, unpredictable world, ongoing readjustment is a constant» (Weick, Sutcliffe & Obstfeld, 1999: 88).
What is improvisation?	Improvisation is an adaptative activity that involves «reworking precomposed material and designs in relation to unanticipated ideas conceived, shaped, and transformed under the special conditions of performance, thereby adding unique features of every creation» (Berliner, 1994: 241). By experimenting with preplanned material, agents recombine subsequences of routines (precomposed material) whereby they «stand some chance of discovering complicated and interesting combinations of [actions] that none of [them] previously imagined» (March, 1976: 78).
How do people improvise?	Improvisation is similar to Schumpeter's (1950) concept of «creative destruction» and takes two things: experience and creativity. People improvise by «exploiting» recombinations of bits and pieces of experience (subsequences of actions) and by «exploring» creatively new ways in which to use their past experience (March, 1991). Improvisation can be done in total isolation, but it is usually a social or joint act.
Why do people improvise?	Improvisation is a matter of survival: either people improvise or they 'die'. Improvisation is key because in a dynamic environment their expertise is futile unless it is put to use in creative ways that match situational demands.
What is the function of improvisation?	Improvisation is an explorative sequence of action that facilitates innovation, generates safety, and provides for organizational resilience. Improvisation keeps people and activities going and prevents the collapse of action.
What is the outcome of improvisation?	The outcome of improvisation is survival and learning by doing understood as creation or upgrading of knowledge, skills and competency. Improvisation is a skill that fades if it is not exercised on a regular basis.

Figure 13. Understanding Improvisation in Organizations[250]

Another example of improvisation and resilience can be found in the detailed findings in the "Family Service of Morris County Office of Morristown Study," dated September 11, 2001. While a high number of New York City Firefighters (FDNY) had been examined for post-traumatic stress disorder, only 14 percent met the diagnostic criteria for this disorder. The study concluded that the low rate was a result of the firefighters' resilience. McKinsey[251] conducted an in-depth study on how the 9/11 events affected the FDNY, carrying out more than 100 interviews with FDNY personnel who had responded to the 9/11 incident and listening to more than 60 hours of communication tapes. In total, he spent more than 1,000 hours working with FDNY personnel to finalize the report. His findings are as follows:

- **Leadership** established good command and control during the first minutes of the incident. However, some units responded directly into the towers and failed to report to the staging areas. Therefore, senior management could not properly track its personnel.

- **Confusion** was initially observed between the World Trade Center One (WTC1) and World Trade Center Two (WTC2). However, the responding units entered in a controlled and orderly way.

- **Communication** problems hindered the leadership's ability to communicate.

- **Personnel** inside of WTC1 did not hear orders to evacuate when WTC2 collapsed.

- **Interagency coordination** was minimal.

- **Resource management** was complex; they had too many resources to manage and lead.

The investigative report made recommendations for improvements. The findings can be construed as "measures to increase resiliency" and are as follows:

- Increase operational preparedness:

  - Expand use of incident command system;
  - Further develop the agency's operation center;
  - Create incident management teams;
  - Deploy a flexible recall schedule;
  - Seek formal mutual aid agreements from other agencies;
  - Modify and enforce staging protocol; and
  - Expand hazmat capabilities and reevaluate other special operation capabilities.

- Improve planning and management:

  - Enhance the department planning and operation process;
  - Expand and reorganize the operational planning unit;
  - Improve communications and technology capability;
  - Revamp the communication and technology management process;
  - Immediately address urgent needs; and
  - Improve ability to disseminate immediate information.

Whether these new procedures can be tested in a real-life incident as volatile as 9/11 remains unknown at this time. The suggestions listed by McKinsey are one approach to improving an organization's ability to endure and operate in horrific conditions. It is important to understand that FDNY continued to operate during the 9/11 incident and was without sufficient command, control, workforce and equipment.[252] Kendra and Wachtendorf[253] also studied the resiliency effects of the FDNY after the attacks of September 11, 2001. They found that the key resilience attribute was that the emergency management organization had not been destroyed. The FDNY continued its operations as an organization, doing what its members knew how to do—respond to emergency calls and provide service to the public.

Freeman, Hirschhorn, and Maltz[254] studied the September 11, 2001 attack's effects on a company based in one of the World Trade Center towers: Sandler, O'Neill and Partners, a firm that lost 30 percent of its workforce in the collapse and was expected to close its business. However, within one year the firm was fully operational and doing better than before the attack. The study largely credited the firm's moral purpose to bounce back. The study also credited the ability to secure help (additional money was donated from around the world to help damaged businesses). Freeman, et al.[255] referred to a "pool of opportunity," since death and destruction created voids and opened new leadership opportunities that were filled without guilt because of the connection to moral purpose. The firm was able to operate and do better than expected in spite of catastrophic and very painful loss.

Woods[256] describes a system's resilience as having the following criteria: (1) a buffering capacity, which enables an organization to absorb or adapt to change within a major breakdown; (2) flexibility, which provides the resolve to restructure due to outside pressures; (3) margin, which is the closeness of the organization's operational distance to another kind of performance boundary; and (4) tolerance, which helps the structure to withstand pressures. Woods refers to the process of managing resilience as "resilience engineering." He theorized that managing an organization's resilience should involve assessing the threats to organizational decision making, monitoring any drift toward failure boundaries, and monitoring the organization's ability to keep an eye on risks. This type of resilience engineering should seek to develop and manage practices to measure sources of resilience. Resilience engineering, according to Woods, can be used to assist organizations to develop tools to support sacrifice decisions across production/safety tradeoffs in order to help ensure survival.

Behind the Line – Testimonial 16: "Failed and Fruitful Tactics"

with International Gang Expert, Richard Valdemar

Gang Task Forces

Federal gang task forces formed by the feds and participating jurisdictions to target local street gangs can be a good thing. They can be a good thing if the power, leadership and decision making is pushed down to the lowest level, not up to a bureaucratic czar.

During the time I was part of the FBI's Los Angeles Metropolitan Violent Gang Task Force, we prosecuted three RICO (Racketeer Influenced and Corrupt Organizations Act) cases (1995, 1997 and 1999) against the Mexican Mafia prison gang. The First RICO was the most successful; the last one was the least successful.

In the first and most successful RICO, leadership was largely spearheaded by the Los Angeles County Sheriff's Department and the LAPD. In the less successful RICOs, the L.A. FBI took over major control. This does not mean that the FBI agents were not good gang cops; they were just not as totally familiar with the gangs as the 'locals' (as they liked to call us). Also, every decision had to be made or approved in D.C. This often became a frustration and a major investigation inhibition. This was especially irritating when MS-13 leader, Nelson Commandari, slipped through the task force's fingers during some of this FBI indecision.

Gang Programs Run by Ex-Gang Members

I don't know how many times this failed policy has to fail again (using your taxpayer dollars) before elected officials finally realize that it is a complete waste of your money. Anti-gang programs should be run by people who understand the problems of your community but have avoided drug, crime, and gang involvement. Any teacher, preacher, lawyer, cop, psychologist, gang crime victim, good mother or good father would be more effective in gang prevention than a dozen 'ex-gang members.' And there are many such good citizen community programs, but they are rarely given government financial assistance.

Gang Injunctions

In my opinion, gang injunctions are too manpower and man-hour intensive. They do not produce the anti-gang results that one good gang wiretap or probation and parole sweep might produce. They might be somewhat effective in some small communities with nascent gang problems but, in urban metropolitan areas with multiple established gangs, they are not so effective.

I fear that gang injunctions eventually produce bad case law and greater legal restrictions against law enforcement. The gang non-association restriction against fellow gang members and the banning of members from their own neighborhoods are two examples. If gang members cannot hang out in their own neighborhoods, they will move into rival turfs or, even worse, into your community. And restrictions against siblings, mothers and children, fathers and sons, and other relatives from 'associating,' seem to me to be totally unreasonable. The appellate courts are going to rule against gang injunctions sooner or later.

Saturation Patrol

After a particularly heinous gang crime, many jurisdictions intensify patrol and saturate the gang turf with gang units and suppressive patrol. This rarely produces any lasting results against gangs and almost never results in any significant crime cases, solve rates or court filings.

So why do we do it? It is for 'show' only. It looks like the police are doing something about the gang problem on the 5 o'clock news, even when they don't have a clue. We even establish gang enforcement teams (GET) who run from community to community 'putting out fires.' This is a very inefficient use of invaluable police manpower just for show.

A better use of police manpower and man-hours would be to simply assign a second officer to every one-man car in the gang areas and to train them in anti-gang tactics. Two-officer patrol units will make more and better stops than one-man units can safely do. They will more safely contact groups of young men (like gang members, for example), and they will make more arrests that will result in more filings and convictions than the temporary gang suppression knee-jerk tactic. Two-man patrol and gang units are a more long-term remedy and not just for show.

Improved Communications among Officers

Strengthen the communication between patrol, gang and narco units. This will attack the gang problem from multiple directions. Tactically this is called a flanking maneuver. The major targets of each of these police divisions are often the same people. However, their individual knowledge of the dangers and weaknesses of these targets are very rarely shared with other police units. They often see themselves as competitors. Force them to share intelligence.

We-Tip and Secret Witness

Make it easy for citizens to talk to cops, in any language. Establish an anonymous witness call-in system. Encourage children and their parents to report crimes and identify criminals. Make it a priority to protect and serve crime victims and witnesses first. Develop incentives for police informants in and out of custody.

Immigration Enforcement

Do not ignore the illegal immigrants in your community. Enforce immigration laws. Today many illegals are also gang members and often involved with international drug cartels. Like 'Typhoid Mary' they are at the same time the victims and the carriers of deadly infectious diseases. The organizations involved in trafficking in drugs also traffic in human slavery, false documents, extortion and vendettas. To ignore this and pretend to fight gangs is foolish. Unfortunately, many of you are prohibited from inquiring into a subject's immigration status by policy or by local law.

Educating the Community

It is important to educate the media about the true nature of gangs and to let them meet the gang victims (usually from the same ethnic background as the gang members). The media has been spoon-fed with the liberal stereotypical version of gangs because law enforcement has historically answered 'no comment' to their questions.

When you educate the media (as liberal as they might be), the community will be enlightened by the more truthful news coverage they produce. An enlightened public will call the politicians to answer for their failures, and they will make better decisions as citizens and as jurors.

— Richard Valdemar

We Better Get it Right

This section is important for one simple reason—we must know when we are looking at resiliency and when we are not. For example, McCann makes a clear distinction between an agile organization, which can adapt to change, and a resilient organization, which can manage disruptive change. Disruptive change can lead to organizational failure. "*While organizational agility is certainly essential, so is organizational resiliency. Rapid change requires agility; disruptive change requires resiliency.*"[257] Meyer's study of a hospital strike found that rigid job descriptions and centralization were negatively associated with resilience.[258] What does this mean in our fight against evil? Everything—and it begins with the simple need to truly know our enemy—its strengths and weaknesses. It is most important to know—does the organization qualify as a resilient organization? The golden point to pick up here is simple—if our "good guys" are attempting to create resilient structures of their own to go up against evil, they better have it right; they better understand that a process is truly behind this and failure to accept this fact will lead to humiliating defeat. We must get it right. We must not cut corners. We need the right people in the right places, making the right decisions based on these facts. I argue it may be better to know your enemy than to know yourself. If you know your enemy so well, you can teach others, and those "others" had better be the leaders who will craft our organizations to go after the enemy.

Because organizational resiliency is not a mainstream topic in governments around the world and because disagreement exists among some on what "resiliency" means, moving forward will be difficult. Personally, I see the lack of literature and resources in the area of organizational resilience as rather astonishing, considering how vital it is for survival. So where does this pit you—the risk-taker—in the global and eternal battle against evil? All too often in life, humans are afraid to do what is different; we often look for the safe passage, the door that has already been walked through. We are creatures of habit. In today's society, risk-takers are far too few because the consequence of failure is so evident in our cultures. We must allow people to take risks and to fail. In the words of General George Patton, "sometimes you lose a few battles in a war." Every time we step outside of our safety zone, we take risks; those risks and those risk-takers must be found and elevated to positions of leadership in our battles. You see, the lack of training on the topics in this book is enough to scare away the mundane bureaucrat, who may lead teams made up of great people. Unfortunately, these people and their mission are held back because of leadership failures. Should we not give zero comfort to the inept, one-dimensional bureaucrat, who is afraid of risk and change, just because the subject of resiliency is rarely talked about in our battles against evil? Oust these cowards at every chance and elevate the brave, the courageous, and the risk-takers. Give them the authority to challenge the relatively unknown despite our worldwide blackout on the understanding of evil. Yes, bringing resilience forward in your organization requires you to have the leadership capabilities to create revolutionary change, which brings me to the next point. You need to be the resilient leader when making these changes; it won't be easy.

Be a Resilient Leader for Your Resilient Organization

And so, we reached an understanding of resilience needed as a leader against evil, a core quality of the human psyche since birth. (We are built for survival; we contain an inner understanding that has allowed humans to become the predominant beings on earth.) When humans who embrace their resilient inner being lead organizations, it sets up the ideal resilient organization. Think of it like a chess game: the leader of the evil organization is pitted against you in the game. He demonstrates resilience by his survivability as the organization's leader. At the same time, you demonstrate your resilience by leading through the typical government hoops (which, by the way, should be sidelined in our battles), congressional hearings, media reports, etc. that challenge you as you build your resilient organization.

Stumpher defined resilience as a pattern of psychological activity that builds up a belief for the purpose of being strong in the face of harsh circumstances. He explained, *"[Resilience is] the goal-directed behavior of coping and rebounding...of accompanying emotions and cognitions. It is a dynamic phenomenon, influenced by both the internal characteristics of the individual, and various external life contexts, circumstances, and opportunities."*[259] He posited that people do not have resilience, but create it in certain circumstances. Ashmos and Huber[260] suggested a connection between organizational and individual resilience through the interaction between subsystems and systems. Organizations are social systems. The capabilities of organizations and their ability to be resilient are determined by their strength of blending together various characteristics that create the resilient organization.

However, as Weick[261] revealed, just because an organization has resilient members (i.e., individuals), it does not necessarily mean that the organization is resilient. It's time to "get your game on" and bring resilient leadership into the fold of a newly created resilient organization if you want to have a fighting chance against global terror.

Communities against Evil

A true aim of our efforts in fighting evil goes beyond just "fighting evil." It also goes beyond our efforts to create resilient organizations and leaders to target evil. In fact, I believe our true effort must be accompanied by an exciting concept—creating resilient communities. It's simple: you, I, we, cannot be everywhere at once. We must depend on "the good" within people of communities to fight alongside us, to take the risks, to grow and bring light into darkness. This should be our ultimate goal, and we can learn a lot from the good work that churches perform in communities, as a starting point. Many of these communities are on the verge of anarchy. They may have leaderless governments; they may have virtually no finances, no infrastructure, but if they have hope, they can build a resilient community—coming back from the brink of extinction.

Kumagai[262] conducted a case study entitled "Developing a Resilient City." In the study, he examined an earthquake disaster in the city of Kobe, Japan. Nothing can prevent destruction from such a catastrophe, but what he found was that a community can bounce back from a devastating blow. His findings pointed to four key areas that ensured this city's survival and can do the same for others. First, educate your citizenry and empower them to take charge when necessary. Second, build strong structures that are capable of handling such ferocious earthquakes. Third, maintain institutional preparedness; that is, maintain a clear flow of information among government agencies, businesses and citizens. Kumagai hints that this process should be acculturated into everyday life so that the process becomes the norm. Fourth, change policies when needed and don't let bureaucracy bog down the decision-making process, especially when in the middle of a catastrophic event.

Behind the Line – Testimonial 17: "Learn our Lessons"

with DEA Director of International Operations, Michael S. Vigil, Ret.

Harm came to America on September 11, 2001—tragic loss of innocent people, who simply woke up, went to work or boarded a plane, only to be viciously attacked. While the world views this as terrorism, I find it troubling that Americans don't also view the violence and deaths associated with drug trafficking in the same manner. Thousands of people die every single year throughout the world due to the harm brought on by illegal drugs – far more than those killed on that fateful day in September of 2001.

Around the globe, criminal drug trafficking networks spread poison and death. Drug trafficking also generates violence and massive crime in many countries. We have entire portions of nations controlled by drug-trafficking organizations, like the Armed Revolutionary Forces of Colombia (FARC): they believe that the "ends justify the means." The FARC continues to grow – in over a generation they have moved into a lucrative business of manufacturing and distributing cocaine to support their operations. Today, without a doubt, they are a full-blown international drug trafficking organization.

Former Colombian President Pastrana wanted to win the Nobel Peace Award so badly that he was willing to negotiate with the FARC, which continued its decades long efforts to overthrow the Colombian government. As part of the peace negotiations, Pastrana gave the FARC a 'despeje' or protected zone in southern Colombia, free of any intervention or interference from the police or military. At the end of his presidency, he realized that he had made a mistake because the FARC had no intention of following the agreements set forth in the peace treaty. Pastrana eventually sent in the military and police, but by this time the FARC had taken advantage of the peace negotiations and had established large cocaine laboratories and built large communication towers to coordinate its drug activities with other FARC units.

The FARC initially began their involvement in the drug trade by protecting clandestine laboratories and airstrips for drug traffickers. Now they are a worldwide drug trafficking organization and are involved in all facets of the international drug trade. The FARC has never been serious in entering into peace negotiations with the government and are fully dedicated to overthrowing it and establishing a communist regime. The FARC will continue to hamper the Colombian government and they control several areas throughout the country. They also engage in political assassinations and kidnappings, collect "war taxes" from wealthy ranchers and landowners.

Violence is well and alive in Mexico today. This is due in part to the creation in 1994 of the Human Rights Commission, which was created because of pressure from the U.S. to create an institution to "to protect human rights." We all believe in human rights, it's critical to any working democracy; however, any commission that oversees this process has to be balanced and objective.

When it was created, it initially operated in an overzealous manner – to the point that when arrested drug traffickers claimed torture by the Mexican authorities, they were fired or put in jail. This served to "declaw" the Mexican security forces and made them less hesitant to carry out their responsibilities. This had significant negative ramifications for Mexican authorities – the drug traffickers were playing the system very well. In my opinion, this situation gave the drug traffickers momentum and the impression that they could now enact violence on Mexican security forces.

The relationship between the Mexican drug trafficking organizations and the Colombians is also at issue here. The alliance between Mexican and Colombian drug traffickers has also created a foundation for increased violence in Mexico. The violence of Colombia's underworld brewed a lesson for others – and in a short time, these underworld leaders were tutoring the Mexican trafficking organizations on how to inflict identical damage in their homeland. That is the reason we see the high level of violence in Mexico – they learned very well from their counterparts in Colombia.

During the infamous reign of Colombia's well known drug cartel leader, Pablo Escobar, it grew increasingly proficient at intimidating the government by murdering police, political leaders, including Ministers of Justice. Escobar was so powerful, when he surrendered to the Colombian government to avoid extradition to the U.S., he built his own prison on the outskirts of Medellin and called it "La Catedral." He also hired the prison guards and ran his drug empire from within the prison. He also had individuals brought to the prison who were killed and buried in the field where Escobar and his henchman played soccer. Escobar later escaped and was eventually killed in a Medellin suburb in a shootout with police.

Issues today on both sides of the border are vital to national security – and it's much more significant than just an illegal alien problem. Mexico is very concerned about the bulk currency entering into their country from the U.S. They are also focused on weapons, and highly dangerous military devices such as fragmentation grenades. Mexico has the same problems on its southern border as we face on the southwest border.

Overall border management around the world is important. A lot of nations have no border control which allows for drug traffickers and insurgents to cross freely. Pakistan's border with Afghanistan is a good example. Insurgent forces and drug traffickers are able to move without any control and this creates instability, particularly in Afghanistan. In Pakistan, the Northwest Frontier Province is a lawless area with virtually no government control. In this region, weapons, like AK 47s are openly made and marketed on the streets without serial *numbers. For just $30 you can buy an AK 47 in these open- air markets; you can also purchase opium and hashish. The stores that sell these drugs are identified by the sheepskins hanging on top of the doorways.*

Furthermore, corruption plays a significant role in not being able to implement effective border control and management. The Afghanistan economy critically needs to generate revenue from the duties levied on imported goods but endemic corruption impedes and erodes this process. Bribes are part of life in that country and will have a long term impact on the countries security and institutional development.

When you conduct a comprehensive evaluation of Mexican drug traffickers, almost every major drug trafficker comes from Sinaloa, Mexico. The region is highly agricultural and for some it was definitely more lucrative to grow illicit cash crops such as opium poppies and marijuana. Additionally, the initial drug traffickers were more than willing to tutor and mentor young kids who wanted the better things in life.

The drug trade became a way of life with many families and it was passed on from generation to generation. They formed alliances with one another through marriages and sometimes out of necessity. On occasion, they fought for control of geographic areas; this is the current situation in many parts of Mexico. Unfortunately, this spills over indiscriminately and affects innocent people. Many of the lower ranking members of the Mexican cartels are uneducated and brutal men who think nothing of butchering humans; it suits their purpose.

The U.S., each year, provides millions of dollars for equipment and training to foreign governments; but all of that can be circumvented if a civil service type system is not developed in tandem to address and eliminate corruption. The issue of corruption can negate all the resources and capacity building we provide in good faith. In Afghanistan, for example, a police General makes about $600 dollars per year. This is inadequate

234

to support a large family and therefore they accept bribes to survive. Secondly, the job of an Afghan policeman can be short lived since he can be removed by an incoming superior who wants to put a friend or political ally into his position. This sends a clear message; take all the money you can before you lose your job. It is not a good situation.

Simply, it's the corruption that overrides everything else – it will undermine our very best efforts. We must resolve this key issue if real progress is to be made. Look around the globe; wherever corruption exists, terrorism and organized crime will erupt from their blood-stained soil.

Finally – the U.S. provides a poor example to the rest of world. How do we tell other nations to "say no to drugs and drug production," when we have States in America, like California, that continue to allow the hoax of medical marijuana. Marijuana is both grown and sold, openly, without prosecution. We need to get our own house in order! One way to do that is to stop the smoke and mirrors of medical marijuana.

— Michael S. Vigil

Chapter Eleven

In the Cross Hairs: Learning from Past Battles

"If you know the enemy and know yourself, you need not fear the result of a hundred battles. If you know yourself but not the enemy, for every victory gained you will also suffer a defeat. If you know neither the enemy nor yourself, you will succumb in every battle."
— Sun Tzu, Art of War

Colombian DTOs have been in existence longer than the AF-DTO (Arellano-Felix Drug Trafficking Organization). In fact, the AF-DTO has depended on Colombian DTOs (Drug Trafficking Organizations) for drugs and replicated much of the operational structure of their counterparts in Colombia. Therefore, an understanding of Colombian DTOs, through the review of archival documents, is an important factor in understanding the historical success of the AF-DTO. According to Kenney,[263] the Colombian DTOs are some of the most resilient in the world. He states, "While a number of government officials and researchers have long recognized the flexibility and resilience of Colombian trafficking enterprises, there have been no attempts to develop a systemic, learning-based explanation for how these criminal organizations respond to state counter-narcotics efforts."[264] His research revealed that Colombian DTOs alter their behavior in response to previous experience and new information. They then store this knowledge in procedures and routines, including the collective memory of participants, and select and retain innovations that create positive results. In short, DTOs learn, and in doing so, they become more effective, while making it more difficult for the government to shut them down. Kenney credits organizational learning as the reason why the drug industry persists in Colombia, despite various successes against them by both the U.S. and Colombian governments. Kenney details the types of learning, both tactical and strategic, that benefit the Colombian DTOs. Tactical routines may involve changing communication rules, processing practices and transportation routes, and developing new procedures for drug distribution. Strategic routines involve more long-term thinking, such as diversifying into new products and markets and restructuring organizational units and decision making hierarchies. Kenney provides a practical example: Colombian narcotics organizations learn when participants gather, interpret, and apply information to collective behavior through organizational practices and procedures.[265]

Colombian DTOs move through additional phases of organizational learning that involve acquiring information (counter surveillance), recording and storing information through organizational memories, interpreting knowledge and experience, and applying knowledge and experience. Kenney also notes that despite the success of some Columbian DTOs, others fail to learn and are destroyed. The resilient ones remain because "they continue to possess the knowledge, skills, and experience necessary to outwit their many licit and illicit competitors."[266]

Kenney helps us to better understand the dynamics of resilience within a successful DTO by pointing out that a system within a system is at play. This subsystem is called "information." Information includes counter-drug intelligence, drug intelligence, strategic intelligence, operational intelligence, and tactical intelligence. Kenney provides the following insights into why it is difficult to gather the needed information required to fight DTOs. First, it's very hard to infiltrate these organizations to gain information. DTOs' practices and activities are designed to minimize their exposure to authorities. Second, the structural features of DTOs make them difficult for undercover agents to infiltrate the upper level of leadership; usually only family members are at the top of DTOs. Third, they have compartmentalized structures that work as discrete cells that rarely interact with other parts of the organization. Fourth, legitimate authorizations are bound by rules and laws of gathering evidence and taking action, but DTOs are not constrained by formal rules or laws and can bend and break rules to best suit their needs.

When we think about drug trafficking, we often think of cocaine, Colombia, and the resilience of Colombian DTOs that have operated for decades. "In spite of significant government efforts to identify, disrupt, and dismantle these transnational enterprises, today the Colombian narcotics industry produces more cocaine and heroin than ever before."[267] But we don't have to look that far to find large, resilient DTOs; we simply need to look across our southern border into Mexico.

According to Kenney, authorities have begun to use innovative measures, but with limited luck. Law enforcement will pay informants for information. These informants are often criminals, but it is still an important way to get needed information. However, informants with intimate knowledge of the leadership within DTOs are limited. The DTOs trust only those within their inner circles. What's more, informants sometimes deliberately provide false information to authorities to obtain quick cash. Thus, success is limited when it comes to obtaining physical evidence, but it is enhanced greatly when using electronic surveillance at the tactical and operational levels. This type of surveillance includes eavesdropping technologies such as telephone taps, telephone transmitters, simple transmitters, laser interceptors, satellite relays, and radio telemetry. Another successful tool is the pen register, which traps and traces devices to record phone numbers. For law enforcement to be successful in using these tools, they must be quick: "counter-drug intelligence is time-sensitive."[268]

On the flip side, DTOs also use intelligence in order to "allocate resources, exploit market opportunities, and improve their drug production, transportation, and distribution technologies."[269] They go as far as collecting information about the latest interdiction and enforcement strategies. To do this, they employ their own undercover operations, surveillance, and research. According to Kenney, they use various sources, including government documents, court records, media reports, and literature on military and police operations.

Also, to the hindrance of U.S. efforts, criminals benefit from the U.S. Freedom of Information Act (FOIA). It enables them to retrieve detailed information about investigations and operations. This is done to reduce exposure to counter-narcotic efforts by learning how authorities operate.[270] Law enforcement must follow the law when conducting business, but criminals don't have to, which allows them to efficiently gather information. DTOs are not worried about violating someone's civil rights or failing to show probable cause for a search or detention.

Kenney's[271] 2003 article, "Intelligence Games: Comparing the Intelligence Capabilities of Law Enforcement Agencies and Drug Trafficking Enterprises," reveals some interesting insights into factors that could lead to dismantling DTOs. First, intelligence is critical to drug enforcement. In order to create efficient programs to attack the DTOs, law enforcement needs to properly allocate resources and evaluate results, and the decision makers need timely and accurate information. To destroy processing labs, intercept drug shipments, apprehend alleged traffickers, and confiscate illegal proceeds, law enforcers require knowledge about specific criminal enterprises and their methods of operation.[272] The intelligence must be timely, dependable, and accurate.

Constantine outlines the following key thoughts regarding how to dismantle these organizations: (1) be patient, because it will not happen overnight; (2) go after the top leadership; (3) obtain greater assistance from U.S. and Mexican authorities; (4) find ways around the DTOs' encrypted technology and surveillance systems; (5) fight corruption; (6) understand how the DTOs operate and live; (7) learn from experiences with Columbian cartels—both U.S. and Mexican experienced fighting the Columbian cartels—as well as the experiences of Mexican DTOs imitating and collaborating with the Columbian cartels.[273]

Those who cannot remember the past are condemned to repeat it.
— George Santayana

Behind the Line

Sergeant Anthony Vega and I worked together in a police-patrol capacity over a decade ago. He has risen through the ranks of his local department and has been involved in some amazing cases; one is highlighted below, and in his own words.

Behind the Line – Testimonial 18: "Infiltrating Evil"

with Narcotics Sergeant, Anthony Vega

In September of 2008, Vega's team found themselves in the middle of an intensive investigation directed at the La Familia Drug Trafficking Organization; an 18-month long investigation spanned across the United States and directly connected to over 20 States and bordering countries.

In 2008, La Familia was, for the most part, undetected and nowhere near being a primary focus of media attention. While other cartel groups such as the Gulf Cartel and Los Zetas attracted the attention of Mexico and U.S. authorities, La Familia had remained minimally visible, but as this case continued to grow and layers of those involved were uncovered, La Familia grew into a massive presence in our investigation.

La Familia, based in the state of Michoacán, Mexico, was unlike any other drug trafficking cartel our investigators had come across. They possessed their own religion based on a Robin Hood type ideology, obtaining profit for the success of those residing in their state. La Familia had multiple cell groups and the group we targeted would prove to be cautious and overconfident in their ability to transport narcotics not only into the United States from Mexico, but throughout the western region of the U.S.

Identifying La Familia safe houses, in July, 2009, investigators obtained trafficking information regarding a shipment of narcotics destined to an un-incorporated area of Riverside, California. The information received regarding the specific safe house to be used in the transaction was vague. This left us scrambling to multiple locations searching for suspicious activity which is consistent with a drug shipment arrival. As investigators monitored approximately four separate locations, a glimpse of suspicious activity began at the location in the unincorporated area of Riverside.

The location of the suspects was a challenge. They were located in a tight knitted residential neighborhood deep within a cul-de-sac. This made surveillance difficult. Investigators used multiple tactics to ensure the operation was not compromised. They had to be vigilant in their surveillance assignments; street level criminals such as nickel and dime bag drug dealers, gang members and thieves all remained on the lookout for the presence of law enforcement. In this particular scenario, the investigators committed to stay in one spot for several hours so not to raise suspicion of both street level criminals. However, the Cartel members were also on the lookout for anything out of the ordinary.

A few hours into the surveillance, we observed indicators leading our investigators to believe we selected the right location, and it soon became crystal clear the Cartel members were preparing for the arrival of narcotics. Late in the afternoon, several vehicles began to arrive at the duplex. Shortly thereafter, vehicles began to pull out from behind the property and hit the street to scan the neighborhood for anything that might look out of place. In particular they were looking for one of two things: 1.) either a rival drug trafficking organization or 2.) law enforcement on a stakeout.

Our team never flinched or let their nerves get the best of them as the Cartel spent nearly 30 minutes searching. As Cartel co-conspirators peered into our vehicles, investigators continued to remain hidden at times by crawling into trunks and almost completely under the seats of surveillance vehicles. We were successful in our efforts to remain unseen, which was apparent as the subjects visibly relaxed. Suddenly, a male subject walked out to the street while on the cellular phone. It was obvious to us all, something was about to happen.

A black Honda Civic arrived and off-loaded several packages, immediately left the area and continued to make drug deliveries to multiple Southern California locations. Packages of narcotics remained in the duplex, subjects stayed watchful for anything threatening. Minutes later, a White Toyota 4-Runner arrived with an Arizona license plate. A male drove the 4-Runner as a female sat in the passenger seat. They would later be identified as Rosa Galindo and her son Ramon. Ramon positioned the truck in the driveway, next to the front door of the residence. Packages were seen being wrapped with clothing and placed onto the back seat of the 4 Runner. When the vehicle was loaded and they quickly fled the area.

Ramon drove directly to a nearby gas station and parked next to a gas pump. He walked straight into the gas station and stood at the window watching for undercover vehicles for approximately 10 minutes. Rosa sat in the vehicle trying to identify signs that they were being followed. Eventually Ramon filled his tank and began his journey back to Arizona. Several counter surveillance maneuvers were standard for these Cartel associates; however, a good undercover team can remain undetected. Using common counter surveillance techniques, such as running red lights, speeding and sudden lane changes, we were translucent. We had prepared every possible scenario and were ready for anything they threw at us.

After a 50-mile mobile surveillance through residential neighborhoods, city streets, decollate roads, and rural highways, they exited the interstate freeway to refuel. It was then that the decision was made to take enforcement action. After refueling, Rosa and Ramon swapped seats, and exited the gas station with Rosa now driving the vehicle. As Rosa began to get back on the highway, we conducted a traffic stop and seized approximately 10 pounds of methamphetamine, concealed in ceramic lawn decorations. After taking Rosa and Ramon into custody, it was determined the ceramics figurines containing narcotics had been a lucrative method for the organization to cross hundreds of pounds into the U.S. over the past 10 years.

— *Anthony Vega*

Chapter Twelve

Fusion Centers: The Offensive End of Counterterrorism

"You must be the change you wish to see in the world."
— Mahatama Gandhi

Drug trafficking organizations (DTOs) are both adaptive and resilient. They are aware of challenges, and make sense of their environments. DTO leaders learn from their failures, adjust to difficulties and use or create resiliency characteristics to sustain themselves. I describe this flexible behavior as a resiliency cycle.

This chapter provides a strategy with which to tackle the DTOs. What this strategy proposes is to simultaneously attack each of the DTOs resiliency characteristics, using the asset best suited for that mission, with the goal of shrinking the DTO—much like applying pressure to all sides of a balloon. Results need to be measured and evaluated so goals can be reassessed and refocused. Then the process of attacking the resiliency characteristics needs to begin again, further shrinking the organization. This process repeats itself over and over, much like peeling back layers of an onion. Eventually, the DTO will become shrunken and damaged, and thus vulnerable to organizational failure.

This strategy can be effectively employed against DTOs and other sophisticated criminal and terrorist organizations worldwide. Gangs, pirates, and organized crime cells can be impacted severely and even neutralized following this protocol which targets resiliency characteristics.

This is a precise, focused strategy requiring leadership, resources, patience and repetition.

The Bottom Line

- This strategy, to be successful, requires visibility and "buy-in" from *relevant* government leaders. Hence, this strategy needs a high-level "torch carrier" to rally executive level government officials to stand behind it and promote it. For success to be achieved, the full spectrum of resources must be identified and employed. Progress against DTO resiliency characteristics must then be *tracked* for evaluation and adjustments as the process is repeated. The end goal, after repeated assaults against the points of greatest resilience, is the dismantling of the organization's ability to function.

- Note that this strategy provides a framework for measuring success against DTOs, and all evil for that matter, by applying and evaluating government resources (and their outcomes) aligned against DTO resiliency characteristics. Authorities will be able to clearly articulate how DTOs are being fought and dismantled. We can begin our full-fledged fight here and now.

To date, a comprehensive strategy to defeat DTOs and evil worldwide has not been developed, in my very strong opinion. What I have created here is a framework that provides a detailed description of DTO resiliency characteristics and how to best attack these attributes. The only sure way to dismantle these organizations is with government resources aligned against the identified resiliency characteristics. The framework also provides government with the opportunity to measure its success against each of the characteristics, in order to facilitate reassessment and realignment of resources while also having a reporting structure.

Global DTOs exhibit specific characteristics which are endemic to the region in which they operate. These characteristics, or traits, have been influenced and shaped by regional political, cultural, economic, and geographic factors. Thus, this strategy is adjusted accordingly, in order to maintain global application.

It is important to note that significant government effort already exists which targets a number of these characteristics. This study would serve to better organize these efforts, while exposing new targets and weaknesses for exploitation and attack.

Evil's Resilience Prevails

The U.S., Mexico, and Columbia have all made strides in combating DTOs. Yet, despite their combined efforts to dismantle these organizations, DTOs continue to operate by learning from their failures and setbacks. Acknowledging the ability of DTOs to not only adapt and survive, but to proliferate, as well, will provide greater insight and understanding for those of us who fight these organizations. Acknowledging the organization's ability to persist can best be framed by describing DTOs as *resilient organizations*. From this standpoint, we can move forward and enact a plan that calls for applying strategies against each of the identified resiliency characteristics. In short, the organization can be better fought by separating each of its strengths and tearing them down one by one, using the entire breadth and depth of both government and community resources.

Before this process can begin, we must first identify the DTO resiliency characteristics. The following is the model I have developed depicting organizational resiliency within the DTO organization.

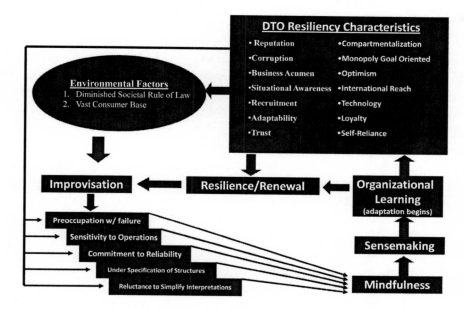

Figure 14: The DTO Resiliency Cycle (by Dr. Chabot)

As mentioned earlier, the conceptual framework above is much like a push type merry-go-round, where children jump on and off as it continues to maintain its rotations. The framework includes improvisation, the five constructs, mindfulness, sensemaking, organizational learning and resilience. Through each rotation, a characteristic becomes evident in the organizational learning construct, and the characteristic becomes part of the organizational memory.

Throughout, the resiliency framework is affected by the two environmental factors: diminished societal rule of law and vast consumer base (for drug consumption). These have proven to be two important factors for the survivability of DTOs. Historically, organizations fail if they are no longer able to obtain/maintain legitimacy and the support of the populace. The diminished rule of law (and in many cases, complete absence of rule of law) in Mexico allows the DTOs to thrive and grow in that country.

Evil's Resiliency Cycle

In the model (Figure 14, previously), you will notice that the resiliency characteristics relate back to the inputs for mindfulness. Improvisation, which leads to the five mindfulness inputs, is hard to maintain because it constantly requires attention. What this strategy shows is that improvisation is maintained as the DTOs consistently cycle through this framework, using the resiliency characteristics to support the five inputs to mindfulness. For example, the DTO resiliency characteristic "preoccupation with failure" is enhanced by the resiliency characteristics of trust, loyalty, recruitment, corruption and reputation. The second input, "sensitivity to operations," is affected by the characteristic of situational awareness. The third input, "commitment to resilience," is supported by the organization's technology, monopoly goal-oriented structure, and optimism. The fourth input, "under-specification of structures," is supported by the characteristic of compartmentalization. The final input, "reluctance to simplify interpretations," is supported by the self-reliance and business acumen characteristics. Collectively, the entire organization demonstrates a constant ability to adapt; therefore, the characteristic of adaptability is rightfully connected to all five mindfulness inputs.

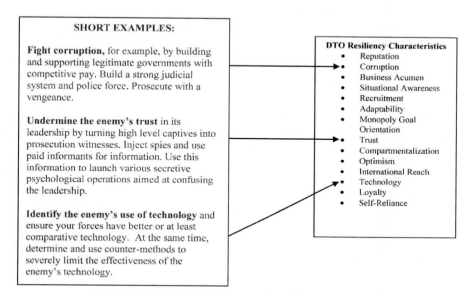

Attack the Enemy's Resiliency Characteristics

SHORT EXAMPLES:

Fight corruption, for example, by building and supporting legitimate governments with competitive pay. Build a strong judicial system and police force. Prosecute with a vengeance.

Undermine the enemy's trust in its leadership by turning high level captives into prosecution witnesses. Inject spies and use paid informants for information. Use this information to launch various secretive psychological operations aimed at confusing the leadership.

Identify the enemy's use of technology and ensure your forces have better or at least comparative technology. At the same time, determine and use counter-methods to severely limit the effectiveness of the enemy's technology.

DTO Resiliency Characteristics
- Reputation
- Corruption
- Business Acumen
- Situational Awareness
- Recruitment
- Adaptability
- Monopoly Goal Orientation
- Trust
- Compartmentalization
- Optimism
- International Reach
- Technology
- Loyalty
- Self-Reliance

Figure 15: example of attacking enemy's resiliency characteristics (by Dr. Chabot)

By attacking and removing DTO resiliency characteristics, governments can have greater and more sustained success against an enemy proven to be adaptive to change. In looking at the following information, please keep in mind that this was a snapshot in time; the information was devised at a point in history – and in your efforts to better understand how evil operates, I have taken this snapshot and broken down all of the related frames that made the organization so strong at its peak.

Adaptability

The AF-DTO is (I will keep present tense throughout – although today, the organization is largely underground and a fraction of what it was) quickly able to adapt to circumstances that threaten its existence. The business of drug trafficking requires the organization to find reliable workers and reliable trafficking routes to supply the organization's lifeblood of money in an ever-changing environment. Two subcategories assisting in the DTO's adaptability are the organizational ability to use creative and sophisticated tools— underground tunnels, intelligence, technology—and opportunistic efforts to simply find ways to succeed in highly difficult situations.

Business acumen

While the organization is made up of highly volatile individuals, these individuals operate the organization as a professional business. The stakeholders of the organization are primarily concerned with making money—the single, focused measure of success. Therefore, they create and follow the organizational structure, hierarchy, rules, policies, training, etc. that are necessary for running the organization effectively. The organization is led by a centralized leadership that demands corporate growth. To meet this demand, the leaders establish rules and train their personnel to be highly effective. The organization does not tolerate slippage in its ability to make money and uses adaptive ability to find other ways to supplement lower-than-expected cash flow, which involves branching out to other ventures—trafficking of other types of drugs, human smuggling and kidnapping for ransom.

Compartmentalization

The organization protects itself by separating out its component operations and allowing relevant information to be known only by those with a "need to know." The AF-DTO has so many compartments that losing one or two of them to law enforcement will not greatly affect the organization's ability to survive. Additionally, any compartment that is compromised by law enforcement will not be able to share much information about other compartments of the organization. Within this compartmentalization exists another layer for the leadership personnel, all of whom are separated from one another; and only a select few know where everyone is at all times. The decentralized leadership structure allows the compartments to operate independently from one another so that one does not have to rely on the other for operational success.

Corruption

The organization's lifeblood is its ability to corrupt individuals and entire components of government. It accomplishes this through the use of bribery, blackmail, fear of torture, brutality and death.

Diminished societal rule of law

The AF-DTO thrives in a country where the rule of law has been diminished in some areas and is completely missing in others. This allows the organization to continue with very little disruption from authorities. The diminished societal rule of law has enabled the organization to gain cult-like status in certain parts of Mexico. This cultural glorification then feeds back into the loop of diminished societal rule of law.

International reach

The AF-DTO has built a network, well beyond its own borders, with other criminal organizations based in the United States, Latin America and Asia. These relationships are needed to ensure availability of drugs and of personnel to protect and sell the product. The AF-DTO has a total disregard for international boundaries, which further facilitates its ability to ignore the rule of law in other nations.

Loyalty

The organization demands loyalty from its members. Loyalty is ensured by strictly disciplining employees for failure and by forcing them to participate in brutal and inhumane acts on those who fail. Fear is a definite subcomponent of this characteristic.

Monopoly Goal Orientation:

The AF-DTO is not constrained by governmental policies disallowing its dominance. The organization does not allow other DTOs to exist within its territory and kills competitors, including DTO members located outside of the AF-DTO's understood region of control. The AF-DTO only allies with rivals if, at that moment, the alliance is in the AF-DTO's best interest. The tactics used to ensure monopoly are severe.

Optimism

The organization's leaders believe strongly in what they do and believe that they have what it takes to perform. They do not settle for mediocrity, always striving for near perfection. The organization's long history of success helps to feed its leaders' belief that the organization is not susceptible to organizational failure. They have been so successful for so long that they have developed a sense of entitlement, not only to the work that they do, but also to the geographic regions and governments they subvert. From this sense of entitlement, the leaders have gained a strong sense of confidence, which in turn further feeds their winner mentality.

Organizational learning

The organization is constantly learning from both success and failure. The refinement of its activities and operations is vital to its growth and survival. A subcomponent of organizational learning is the AF-DTO's continued efforts to mentor its members regarding changes to improve the organization. The organizational learning is often immediate, as in the case of drug loads lost or arrests of members.

Recruitment

The AF-DTO largely employs individuals with proven records of loyalty and the ability to carry out violence when needed. The organization is able to recruit by using its reputation for violence, those who would otherwise be unwilling to join or accommodate the organization's needs. The AF-DTO's vast cash flow allows it to pay its members higher wages than legitimate employers found in Mexico. The organization also recruits college graduates and individuals with specialty skills in business, banking, real estate and so forth to manage the organization's assets. However, the organization's brutality comes in part from the recruitment of violent individuals with "street smarts" who have had a tough upbringing and are clearly able to handle the violence needed to excel in the organization. Because of these advantages, the AF-DTO has built a large and diverse organization.

Reputation

The strongest indicator of the organization's resiliency is its ruthless reputation for using fear and violence to get whatever it needs. Members kill and torture at will and with near impunity. Their victims include police officers, district attorneys, politicians, military personnel, witnesses, family members of those who crossed the organization, reporters, rival DTO members, innocent women and children, etc. The organization's reach is international. It has created a community of fear and branded itself as an organization that will stop at nothing to get what it wants. This reputation is often all that is needed to ensure compliance from those who otherwise would be unwilling participants.

Self-reliance

The organization has a proven history of being able to go underground and stay unnoticed for a period of time during highly turbulent times (such as the AF-DTO killing of a prominent priest). The organization has wealth spread throughout many countries and within many industries, including legitimate businesses. It is financially independent and has an intricate network of money laundering operations that have proven vital to the organization's ability to move drug proceeds into other ventures. Equally important is the organization's ability to involve itself in other illegal activity (e.g., kidnapping for ransom, selling counterfeit documents, and trafficking of other drugs, such as methamphetamine). The organization has become so large and has used its illegal funds to create so many legitimate businesses that, ironically, it could sustain itself without ever having to traffic narcotics again.

Situational awareness

The AF-DTO uses its vast networks and resources to gather intelligence on its adversaries, including law enforcement and government, as well as rival organizations and individuals. This

253

intelligence, along with counterintelligence operations (infiltrating law enforcement, government and rival organizations) provides the organization with a true understanding of the "battlefield" in nearly real time. The organization reacts to threats based on the information it obtains. The organization's situational awareness is further assisted through the use of deception and diligent attention to the smallest of details that could go wrong. The organization is constantly vigilant in its operations and acts accordingly to both threats and opportunities.

Technology

Advanced communications systems (scanners, police radios, phone systems, etc.) are vital to the organization's success. The organization purchases the latest and most sophisticated equipment from all available sources. Purchases include upgraded vehicles with armor and other protective and deceptive features, as well as bulletproof vests and other protective armor. Skilled core members are experts in the understanding and implementation of these technologies. On average, the AF-DTO possesses better technology and equipment than its adversaries. This is a huge disadvantage and one that needs to be swiftly addressed and corrected.

Trust

Organizational leaders are related to one another through blood, a critical factor that creates a high level of trust among the leadership. The organization rarely allows a non-family member to have organizational control. The AF-DTO leadership has not been infiltrated by any leaders who were not related by blood. None have shared information with authorities. The leadership does not completely trust its lower level members, often having these members tortured and killed for simply being under suspicion of assisting adversaries or law enforcement.

Vast consumer base

The AF-DTO is dependent on U.S. drug users to ensure the organization's continued success and growth in the drug trade. With a vast consumer base, the AF-DTO will always have customers to sell to and make money from. But it's not only drugs we need to worry about. They also engage in smuggling weapons, human trafficking and more. We must not fall prey to legalizing drugs in hopes of doing away with cartels. Remember, these are resilient organizations that exist to make money by any means necessary, which is why they have their hands involved in so many "traditional" organized crime ventures.

Peeling Away the Layers

Applying pressure on each of these characteristics is much like pushing on a balloon from all angles. Over time, the shrinking of the organization will mean that the threat to governments is more manageable. This effort can also be compared to "peeling away" the layers of an onion as it gets smaller through each rotation of government attack on DTO resiliency characteristics.

Organization resiliency prevents organization dismantlement. The organization is able to learn from failure and apply methods to counter or limit its vulnerabilities. Organizational resiliency is not an end state but rather an evolutionary, and at times, revolutionary cycle that allows an organization to better itself based on its ability to apply new learning to its way of conducting business. Organizational resiliency is not in itself an applied technique, but is a result of an organization demonstrating its ability to fight back (learn, adapt) to prevent catastrophic failure.

Organizational resiliency is achieved only through a number of phases, as described in the DTO resiliency framework (i.e., cycle). DTOs have become resilient against various efforts to destroy them (although a number of government actions have severely impacted DTOs), and the organization's leadership has learned from each of these efforts how to adapt and how to implement necessary change in order to survive. The role that organizational resiliency plays within the DTO network can be best understood by examining episodes of organizational hardship and the actions taken by DTOs in response to these hardships in order to survive even when extreme conditions present a likelihood of failure.

Here is a diagram showing the resiliency within al-Qaeda. You will notice an identical process the organization goes through to research "resiliency." The environmental conditions have changed just slightly, which has also slightly affected a few of the resiliency characteristics described above for drug cartels. In essence, there is virtually no difference.

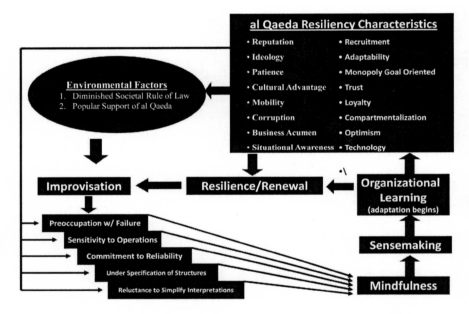

Figure 16: The al-Qaeda Resiliency Cycle (by Dr. Chabot)

Next Steps

Governments must align resources against these resiliency characteristics, including the environmental factors of "diminished societal rule of law," and "popular support of DTOs," (in progress to some extent), and regularly measure each effort, using performance measures for each of the characteristics. If your assets are correctly aligned against the enemy's resiliency characteristics, the enemy will diminish in scope and capability over time. You must have in place methods for measuring your successes or failures. For example, you may choose to measure how many propaganda pieces the DTO has released, or measure their finances/fundraising (drug trafficking proceeds, extortion contributions, human smuggling payments etc.) and personnel recruitment numbers by examining your allied or internal intelligence reporting. You must have a premier intelligence gathering/collection program in place or all of your efforts will fail.

Measure Results
Is the Enemy and its Effectiveness Shrinking?

THE ONION – DISMANTLE DTOs

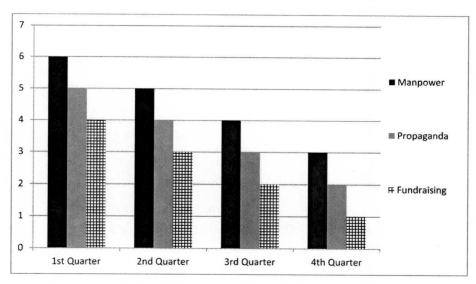

Figure 17: Example of measuring results against the enemy
(by Dr. Chabot)

This continuous measurement will allow the government and law enforcement to adjust to the changing behavior of DTOs as the DTOs adapt to new pressures. It will also allow government to provide specific and measurable updates on progress. Each cycle is like peeling away the layers of an onion. With each cycle, the DTO becomes smaller and less of a threat.

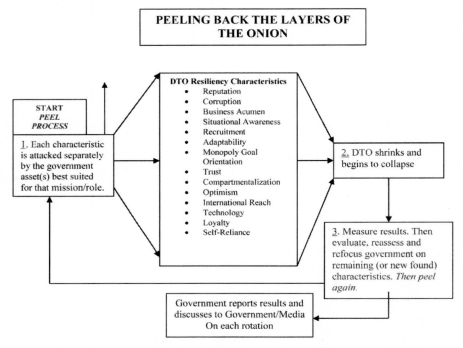

Figure 18. "Defeat Evil Strategy Cycle" (by Dr. Chabot)

Employing this strategy will allow governments to fight using their wits while expending fewer resources. The information gleaned from the application of this strategy may be applied globally in regions where terror networks and DTOs run and hide. Results must be measured and used to gauge government's effectiveness. Evaluation (completed annually, at a minimum) of these results should lead to a reassessment of activities, followed by refocusing on the remaining resiliency characteristics. During the reassessment phase and at each interval in the cycle, success/findings reports should be made available to both government leaders and the media. The DTO network will shrink further with every focused round of attacks on its resiliency characteristics.

As described in Figure 18 (Peeling Back the Layers of the Onion), dismantling or marginalizing resilient networks is the focus of this book. You should now have a good understanding of how critical resiliency is to the strength and adaptability of evil around the world. This new understanding, coupled with the knowledge of how to systematically reduce the enemy's center of gravity and its ability to rebound, provides the optimum setting for a strike.

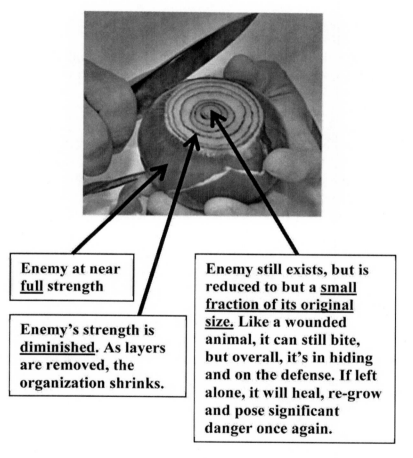

Enemy at near **full** strength

Enemy's strength is **diminished**. As layers are removed, the organization shrinks.

Enemy still exists, but is reduced to but a **small fraction of its original size.** Like a wounded animal, it can still bite, but overall, it's in hiding and on the defense. If left alone, it will heal, re-grow and pose significant danger once again.

Figure 19: "Peeling the Onion" example (by Dr. Chabot)

The attack plan calls for an all-out assault on the organization's vital components and nothing else. Think of it this way—if you are a police officer or soldier faced with an enemy determined to kill you, you have one of two choices: kill the enemy or run. Isn't that right? As we discussed earlier, running away is simply giving up. Giving up is something we just won't tolerate. This leaves you with just one obvious choice—taking out the enemy. In taking out the enemy, you don't shoot to wound; you shoot to kill. In the police academy or military academy, the instructors never teach you to shoot to wound, and neither will I.

Killing the enemy requires not random shots in the dark, but rather precise aim and delivery based on training and intuition, trusting your tactics and your inner self—all you have learned about how to fight for survival and put the target down. As you fight for survival, your rounds should be aimed at the vital organs. It's not a mere human you are up against, but rather the "starfish" described earlier. The starfish is headless, so a headshot will not take out your target! You must focus on every aspect of that organization that allows it to breathe, to grow, to adapt—its vital organs. In the case of evil, the organs are the resiliency characteristics. As previously described in the "onion model," you will fire at these characteristics, examine the target, adjust, fire another volley, then examine the target, adjust and fire again. This process repeats itself in slow motion, over and over and over. As the target loses energy and mass, it begins to shrink and sink into itself like a black hole, in slow motion. You must keep your eye on the target—never tiring, never giving an inch and never letting your guard down. You must be as ruthless in your attack on this organization as it is to its victims. Turning your back just slightly in an early victory lap can allow evil to grow in the shadows like a monster in a horror movie, lying on the ground after what appears to be its end only to rise again. Does the movie *Friday the 13th* or *Halloween* ring a bell? Let life imitate art for a moment—there really is no difference.

In 2008, al-Qaeda in Iraq was decimated by roughly 90 percent, but in a few short years, we are again hearing of a resurgence of the enemy. Why? Did we take our eye off the enemy? Did the enemy sense an American weakness? Could America's presidential announcement of withdrawal of troops in the near future have given new hope to the al-Qaeda organization?

I cannot overstate how important it is that the mistakes of the past must never be repeated. The surge in Iraq worked, and continued to work, for a number of reasons. Two prominent reasons involve American's patience following the outstanding execution of a battle plan that understands the enemy. As I lay out the plan against evil in this book, you too will understand the enemies before us. You will see that they are virtually identical in their organizational structures—structures that were perfected through each organization's ability to fight failure.

In laying the groundwork for the attack, you must know not only your enemy but also yourself, and very well at that. What are your strengths? Your weaknesses? How do you change weaknesses into strengths? Standing up against evil demands a critical self-analysis and strong leadership in maximizing your assets, as well as plugging your holes, and stocking your shelves. An army cannot move across a land without a solid supply line of resources such as food, gas, weapons and good intelligence.

As we lay out the strategy in this chapter, return to the earlier figure of the onion. Block one states that *"Each characteristic is attacked separately by the government asset(s)."* The characteristics in this model are 15 resiliency characteristics in the center block and the remaining environmental factors.

For the sake of argument, let's say you identified all of your assets and are ready to wage war. You compartmentalize these assets to work simultaneously against the enemies' strengths, each working as a team and focused precisely on one objective. All along, each team is sharing information, sharing intelligence in a fusion center, tracking evil as it morphs. There is no such thing as "at the end of the work day." Our operations do not stop. They roll on 24/7/365 (24 hours a day, 7 days a week, 365 days a year)—just like a police dispatch center.

The fight is on. Your teams are in place, your targets selected. For brevity, I have chosen just three of these 15 to discuss for now. But before I begin, I want you to think about what you would do in this situation. As I draw upon my experience and research, there will be other enemies, pushing us to grow, adapt and learn to become better and more efficient and effective than yesterday.

I have chosen to begin by describing in detail a brief on a three-prong attack: (1) reputation, (2) recruitment, and (3) loyalty. Let's look at the first characteristic of "reputation." DTOs have refined their reputations in Mexico for the purpose of instilling the fear of them or inspiring worship of them. To attack this characteristic, I will examine my organization to find out what asset or assets I have to diminish the DTO's reputation.

(1) Reputation: You launch a massive media campaign (TV, radio, leaflet drops, etc.) going after the enemy by describing their killing of children and women. Find victims who have survived their attacks and cloak their identities in commercials telling their stories. Go after the hearts and minds of the citizens and assure them that the good will prevail over evil. You may also choose to use various psychological operations, reporting information you intend for the enemy to hear, which will cause them to alter their methods of operations enough for you to exploit the story with the public. As you break down the organization's "reputation," other items are affected, including the recruitment of future soldiers who will see the organization as less organized and more confused.

(2) Recruitment: An organization must recruit or die. It must replace those killed or captured. In reversing an organization's recruitment ability, I recommend focusing on drying up the organization's financial resources. These recruits don't work for free, and I learned in Iraq that if you take away the source of money, evil shrinks fast. Al-Qaeda for example, shrunk by nearly 90 percent in 2008 due to attacks on its financial base, which included going after foreign sources of money and illegal acquisition of money from extortion and other illicit operations. We must also increase the protection of borders if new members are crossing over from other nations. Other unique and non-unique ideas will work, such as looking at U.S.

based youth antidrug campaigns that focus on kids, to help take away the appeal of "membership," embarrassing the enemy at every angle. Take away the "sexiness" and "coolness" of membership.

(3) Loyalty: Ah, yes, "loyalty." A term often referenced with gangs and organized crime syndicates. Attacking loyalty is yet another opportunity to allow your creativity to flow. Here are a few suggestions to consider in attacking this highly important characteristic. As you learned from the previous example, "it's all about the money." Go after the money with money—offer large rewards for members who "rat" on their organizations, and replicate the U.S.-based Secret Service system for witness protection by finding new identities for those who come forward. Although few will take this offer, you have begun to chip away at the core characteristic. At the same time, hit high-level targets with extreme frequency. The higher levels of these organizations will often have members with the highest levels of loyalty, because they are family, close friends or long-time colleagues. Leak reports about the organization's weaknesses and reports about their senior members to cause leadership to question their members' loyalty. Strongly let out the word about how the organization kills its own members. Use the media—show pictures!

What is being done here is actually very simple. You are attacking the resiliency concepts by applying common sense to identify, for example, what is the exact opposite of the resiliency concept you are targeting. As seen above with the concept of "loyalty," you simply want to either find or create resources that will make the organization suspect "disloyalty." You are turning the tables. You are identifying their strengths and turning them into weaknesses.

In a real operation, such action should be handled in an intelligence fusion center operating 24/7/365. Its structure is a combination of law enforcement, military and civilians, all of whom have passed through an extensive background investigation. This fusion center is connected via secret lines of communication to embedded smaller cells throughout the territory of the enemy. In these cells are personnel who can immediately access and take action against the enemy.

Full autonomy must be given to the fusion center, which is led by a very small board of directors, of equal representation from all groups in the fight. Together this board, and this board only, selects their leader, the "Director." The board does not approve or disapprove of the Director's daily operations—that form of bureaucracy would simply destroy our very efforts. Rather, the board acts to protect the director so that he/she can act quickly on intelligence and, when needed, to replace that leader if results are not produced.

A full-time component of the operation is constantly measuring success and failure. This is a process that never stops (a component of our resiliency)—learning from our failures quickly, while also fine-tuning operations against the enemy. As progress is made over time, the board will report any "success" to the media because we must win the hearts and minds not only of the civilians in evil's backyard but also of the politicians who are funding our efforts.

After all of these operations move forward, it's time to again reexamine the organization's strength to see how the enemy has adapted to our efforts—looking again at all the resiliency characteristics—and, if needed, realign our resources or develop new specific strategies for operations that are having no impact on the enemy.

As you attack the resiliency characteristics simultaneously, the organization will shrink. But you won't know this, and you won't be able to prove it to the doubters in the world, unless you scientifically measure for results using both qualitative and quantitative methods that have passed the most stringent academic standards. The data allow for the creation of a quarterly or annual report that becomes a key piece of information when reevaluating efforts in the fight. This must be a living process—ongoing, every day, always collecting and measuring our efforts. We must know when we fail and when we succeed, and do so at the speed of light.

Must Keep in Mind

Weakening the environmental factors that support the DTOs is critical for government's success and for a community's stability. Shoring up the rule of law and weakening civilian popular support will stifle the DTOs' ability to breathe and grow. Likewise, when a number of the resiliency characteristics are diminished, this will help to strengthen societal rule of law and weaken DTOs' popular support. Measuring improvement in the rule of law and diminished popular support of DTOs is a worthy indicator of government's performance in attacking DTOs' resiliency characteristics.

Each DTO resiliency characteristic is made up of components. When government leaders strategize to attack each characteristic, the components must be the focus. The characteristics are simply overall headings, so each component must be considered individually.

Organizational Failure

At the end of the day, what we want for evil is "organizational failure." Marion[274] describes three types of organizational failure: failure in startup organizations; failure attributable to major technological shock or similar catastrophic changes; and failure of mature organizations, upon which the author focuses her writing. The literature does not consider public organizations, especially those that have no choice but to continue to operate, as is the case with many public safety agencies and organizations worldwide. Failure for these types would be catastrophic, not only to the organization itself, but also to those they are charged with serving and protecting. However, Fortune[275] describes how most organizations that fail or make major mistakes do not keep a record of those mistakes, and the failings continue over time because the organizations fail to learn from their mistakes. Wildavsky[276] theorizes that organizational learning occurs through small-scale trial and error. From this small-scale trial and error comes a form of organizational learning that most theorists recognize. Human beings "...cannot behave with perfect rationality, [but] intelligently designed organizations can do so by compensating for human fragility. In doing so, organizations behave more rationally and effectively than individual human beings."[277]

When a DTO makes a mistake, such as losing some or all of a shipment of narcotics, it learns from that mistake. Schwandt and Marquardt[278] posit that organizations that are able to adapt quickly and continuously will be able to survive. The ability to adapt and reinvent is a key indicator of survival. And "by increasing the speed and quality of their learning, they can succeed in a rapidly changing global marketplace."[279] Comfort[280] conducted a study in her book, *Shared Risk: Complex Systems in Seismic Response*, in which she describes four conditions that affect the emergence of response systems under threat. Comfort included terrorist organizations in this theory and suggests that it also applies to DTOs, which are often characterized as terrorist organizations. These four conditions are:

1. Articulation of commonly understood meanings between a system and its members;
2. Sufficient trust among leaders, organizations and citizens to enable members to accept direction;
3. Sufficient resonance between the emerging system and its environment to gain support for action; and
4. Sufficient resources to sustain collective action under varying conditions.[281]

Comfort stresses the importance of trust in overcoming uncertainty. She describes various types of systems, such as emergent adaptive systems, operative adaptive systems and auto-adaptive systems. When describing the terrorist events of 9/11, she posited that the flight from Boston which flew into the World Trade Center was not an adaptive system because sensemaking collapsed. The flight from Newark, on the other hand, illustrated an emergent adaptive system; the passengers knew their fate and crashed the plane into an open field. She described an operative adaptive system as federal agencies responded to the attacks with rapid mobilization. These are valuable descriptors of organizational types that may help further our understanding of resiliency within DTOs. Devising and testing measures of fragility and resilience in organizational systems will contribute significantly to our ability to maintain self-organizing, auto-adaptive emergency response systems.[282]

You see, what our strategy boils down to is not simply going onto the battlefield with just the best weapons, but also with the best understanding of what we are up against. The "fog of war" refers to the confusion present on the battlefield. In order to maintain objectivity and clarity within the theater, it is critical that we have done our homework, that we know the enemy, and that we have the confidence in our battle plan to bring it to fruition. The patience I mentioned much earlier makes its presence known here. Patience, accompanied by the confidence in the way ahead, accomplishes much.

Where do we go from here now that we have the power of knowledge on our side and understand what to look for? Execution of the battle plan and fighting for every single inch of ground!

As we wage war, the one main difference between taking out a human target and targeting an organization is one word highlighted above—patience. The enemy has perfected this characteristic in many parts of the world. They are known to study their target for weeks or months on end before taking any action at all. Often, those being recruited into the organization go through months of testing and surveillance before they are brought into the fold. While we should never sit idly by as the enemy strikes out against the innocent, our victory requires patience when results are not immediate.

One of my favorite movies is *Any Given Sunday,* a football story centered on a hard-edged coach who wants victory. During a football half-time pep talk to his team in the locker room, the coach—played by Al Pacino—sums up a point we all must instill into ourselves. As people, we must fight for every single inch. It's so important. Here is the edited quote from the movie:

Dr. Paul R. Chabot

I don't know what to say, really.
Three minutes to the biggest battle of our professional lives
...all comes down to today.
Either we heal as a team or we are going to crumble,
inch by inch, play by play, till we're finished.
We are in hell right now, gentlemen, believe me.
And, we can stay here
and get the stuff kicked out of us
or
we can fight our way back into the light.
We can climb out of hell
one inch, at a time.

You know, when you get old in life, things get taken from you.
That's part of life.
But, you only learn that when you start losing stuff.
You find out that life is just a game of inches.
So is football.
Because in either game—life or football—the margin
for error is so small.
I mean, one half step, too late or too early, you don't quite make it.
One half second too slow or too fast, and you don't quite catch it.
The inches we need are everywhere around us.
They are in every break of the game, every minute, every second.

On this team, we fight for that inch.
On this team, we tear ourselves and everyone around us
to pieces for that inch.
We claw with our fingernails for that inch.
'Cause we know, when we add up all those inches, that's going to
make the difference
between winning and losing, between living and dying.

268

I'll tell you this: in any fight,
it is the guy who is willing to die who is going to win that inch.
And I know, if I am going to have any life anymore,
it is because I am still willing to fight and die for that inch
because that is what living is.
The six inches in front of your face.

Now, I can't make you do it.
You gotta look at the guy next to you.
Look into his eyes.
Now, I think you are going to see a guy who will go that inch with you.
You are going to see a guy who will sacrifice himself for this team
because he knows, when it comes down to it,
you are going to do the same thing for him.

That's a team, gentlemen.
And either we heal now, as a team, or we will die as individuals.

That's all it is.
Now, what are you going to do?

Evil continues to spread around our globe while the brave continue to fight in spite of doubting governments and the fearful innocent. We fight, and continue to fight, for every inch—making the enemy small, smaller and finally smallest—through each rotation of attack. By now, I hope you understand why this book focuses on the enemy's resiliency characteristics—it is the resiliency characteristics that allow evil to thrive. By understanding what elements constitute evil, we are better prepared to press forward, as a team, and fight!

Behind the Line – Testimonial 19:
"Gangs Abandon Honor for Unholy Alliance"

with International Gang Expert, Richard Valdemar

No Vale Nada La Vida, La Vida no Vale Nada
(There is no value in life, life is worth nothing)
Comienza Siempre Llorando, Y Así Llorando Se Acaba
(It begins always in crying, and like that in crying it ends)
Por Eso Es Que En Este Mundo, La Vida no Vale Nada
(That is why in this world, life is worth nothing)
— Camino De Guanajuato (The Road to Guanajuato)

Que bonitos son los hombres que se matan pecho a pecho
(How beautiful are the men who kill each other chest to chest).
Con su pistola en la mano defendiendo su derecho
(Each with their pistol in hand defending his own rights).
— El Corrido del Teniente y de Gonzales (The Ballad of
the Lieutenant and Gonzalez)

I'm very proud of my grandfathers who fought for the revolution in Mexico under Pancho Villa, "el Jefe del Norte." When I was a young teenager, I would accompany my beloved grandmother to the movie theater that featured Spanish-language movies. We watched popular Mexican movie stars such as Pedro Infante, Luis Aguilar and Cantinflas in movies about the Mexican Charros, the Ranchito and the Mexican Revolution.

The movies often included Mexican folk ballads (corridos) about the difficult and often violent life of the people of Mexico after the Revolution. These were highly emotional songs filled with pride and the honor of real hombres both peon and Caballero. The songs of the Mariachis and a few drinks take me back to this period and the great honor I felt for my people—people of great moral character.

There was even honor among former thieves, as General Villa himself was once a bandit. During this time, men faced each other on the battlefield or in tiny cantinas armed with pistols or machetes and knowing the next contest might be their last. Any man who harmed women or children was a coward worthy of hanging.

In 1967, while riding with a Quan Canh Vietnamese military policeman through the narrow streets of Nha Trang, Vietnam, the Q.C. questioned my ethnic background, saying I looked more like a Vietnamese than an American. On the dirt street, I drew a crude map of the U.S., and then drew Mexico's outline beneath it. He shook his head to show he still did not understand.

A few minutes later, he suddenly tapped me hard and smiled. He motioned with his hand a large 'X' across his chest saying, 'You same same.' He then used his hands to mimic the brim of a huge hat. He then said, 'You same same...Cu cur Ru cu cu...paloma!' as he belted out the words from a famous Mexican folk song ('Cucurrucucu Paloma').

He then directed me to the little movie theater in town where my old Mexican movie heroes were still receiving top billing. It was strange to see them with Vietnamese subtitles, but the Vietnamese people loved Mexican movies and Mexican corridos too. They admired these Mexican charro knights on horseback.

This proud noble warrior culture was fostered also from our Native American heritage. Almost everyone from the American Southwest has some Native American blood in his genealogy. The Mexican people are largely mestizo (a mix of Spanish and Indian). Native American and Indigenous Mexican tribes held great esteem for warriors who fought not just with skill, but also with honor and courage. A warrior was judged by the greatness of the warriors he met in combat. Some warriors struck their enemy with a "coup stick" in battle and counted coup rather than killing rival warriors.

Like the Sicilian Mafia and other ethnic gangs before them, Hispanic gangs developed and transferred this warrior mentality into their criminal gang culture. They developed unwritten codes of conduct and rules of engagement. The greatest glory was given to gang members who fought equal or bigger rivals in a "fair" fight.

"Rat Packing" an opponent showed no bravery or honor at all. "Mano-a-mano" (Spanish for "hand to hand") was the accepted true test of a warrior. In the 1940's Zoot Suit era combat devolved into bottles, bumper jacks, tire irons and switchblade knives. Popular Cholo culture credits the White Fence gang with the escalation to the first drive-by shooting in the 1950s.

However, the church was still neutral and sacred, no gang member would attack another while he was with his mother or other family members, and non-gang members from the gang barrios were usually fairly safe. This code of conduct was most strongly enforced in juvenile halls, jails, and prisons. Child molesters, rapists, and abusers of the elderly were in mortal danger from the gang inmates, as sure of swift retribution as any traitor or snitch.

The Mexican Mafia prison gang was influenced by several warrior codes of conduct. "Jap" Mike Kudo, a Japanese-American who was a member of a Hispanic gang and the book of the Five Rings.

Sun-Tzu's "The Art of War" was required reading. Almost all Hispanic prisoners study the history of the ancient warrior tribes of Mexico and often even learn their Nahuatl language.

In 1992, the Mexican Mafia altered the traditional Hispanic gang code of conduct and put out the edict to all Sureño (Southern California) gang members that there could be no more "drive-by-shootings," to prevent the killing of innocent victims.

A gang member's children, parents, and other family members were not to be retaliated against for the violations of the code committed by the gang member. Even the brutal Aryan Brotherhood held to this standard and was split when some members ordered the murder of member Steve Barn's elderly father. Even the "Dogs of War" protected the innocent.

There are 'gangs' today that pride themselves in wanton savagery with a 'no quarter asked, no quarter given' philosophy. They attempt to justify pitiless barbarian acts and torture in the name of twisted fanatical cult religions or occult worship. They slaughter and rape innocent men, women, and children and dismember their bodies to prove their virility. They're uncivilized monsters, soulless fiends and cowards.

I'm talking about the fanatical Muslim terrorists and the demented Drug Trafficking Organizations (DTO) or cartels. Today, these two groups are attempting to form an unholy trinity by recruiting and uniting with American street gangs. In Anthony Kimery's "Unholy Trinity" in the August, 2009 issue of Homeland Security Today, the author documents some of the incidents in Latin America showing this connection between al-Qaeda and Hezbollah and the DTOs.

Kimery writes, "the evolving alliance between jihadists, narco-cartels, and street gangs personify the three greatest cross-border threats faced by the United States: terrorism, narcotics, and crime. Just because their alliance may not entirely make sense from an American perspective, does not mean that it is beyond the realm of possibility—or probability. All indications are that the threads are coming together."

In a conversation I recently had with former Mexican Mafia member Ramon 'Mundo' Mendoza about this unholy trinity, he remarked, 'Any gang alliances with Muslim fanatics and Mexican cartel thugs should be abhorrent to any self-

respecting gang member. What barrio warrior joins with Satan worshipers (like worshipers of Santa Muerte) and baby killers, and thinks that makes him a man?' Mundo added, 'In my day these are the kind of cowards that the Mexican Mafia would have killed in prison.'

The lure of filthy lucre is too great. Gang members betray the ancient warrior's code of conduct for new tires and fancy rims, or a dime bag of dope. Honor is replaced by 'bling.'

And instead of earning his street "creds," a Cholo will tattoo fake ones on his face. His loyalty to his own barrio is replaced by loyalty to far-off Sinaloa, Mexico. Instead of imitating the great Aztec warrior chief Montezuma, he now will imitate the cowardly terrorist Osama bin Laden.

My Latino brothers, these Muslim fanatic hordes are the same ones your Spanish ancestor "El Cid" drove back into Africa. And do you really think that these Mexican drug thugs are what you could call noble warriors and macho men? Or are they just pitiless punks with guns?

— *Richard Valdemar*

Chapter Thirteen

Call to Action

"We have before us an ordeal of the most grievous kind. We have before us many, many long months of struggle and of suffering. You ask, 'What is our policy?' I will say; 'it is to wage war, by sea, land and air, with all our might and with all the strength that God can give us: to wage war against a monstrous tyranny, never surpassed in the dark lamentable catalogue of human crime. That is our policy.' You ask, 'What is our aim?' I can answer with one word: 'Victory—victory at all costs, victory in spite of all terror, victory however long and hard the road may be; for without victory there is no survival'."
— Winston Churchill

Behind the Line

I first met Ron Brooks while serving under General Barry McCaffrey at the White House Drug Czar's Office. Ron was the go-to-guy for the General on law enforcement matters. After learning of Ron's background, it was no surprise why. Ron Brooks is the President of the National Narcotics Officers' Association's Coalition, which represents 44 state narcotics officers' associations with a combined membership of more than 65,000 police officers throughout the United States of America. Mr. Brooks is a veteran police officer and spent most of his 30-year law enforcement career working in drug enforcement. In 2005, he retired from state service as assistant chief with the California Department of Justice, Bureau of Narcotics Enforcement, and went on to become the director of the Northern California High Intensity Drug Trafficking Area Program.

Behind the Line – Testimonial 20: "Drug Trafficking is Terrorism"

with Ron Brooks, President, U.S. National Narcotics Officers Association

On September 11, 2001, almost 3,000 Americans were murdered by terrorists from foreign lands. The intensity, magnitude and sheer evil of that single attack were a wake-up call to the world. Ironically, the events of 9/11 overshadowed a different kind of attack—chemical attacks that occur each day in cities and towns in the form of death-dealing illegal drug trafficking.

We must live with—and prepare for—the threat of foreign terrorism. Still, I believe that drug trafficking and abuse are the most significant continuing threats to our domestic security. We are engaged in a mortal battle with illegal drug trafficking organizations, drug funded gang activity, and violent drug-related crime.

Illegal drug overdoses kills tens of thousands annually. The impact on the U.S. economy is estimated to be more than $180 billion each year. But those stark numbers don't paint the complete picture. The unrelenting attack by international drug cartels, American street gangs, meth cookers and neighborhood drug traffickers is a tragedy that touches every family in America. How can we quantify the lives ruined, opportunities lost and heartache caused by drug abuse?

Since September 11, 2001, the focus of U.S. federal assistance to state and local public safety agencies has shifted to protecting the homeland from terrorist activities and equipping first responders. Of course, it is important to fund preparedness and response capacity, but that shift has come at the expense of the drug enforcement mission. That shift has not only affected America's communities, but has impacted aspects of the Global War on Terror.

By shifting state and local law enforcement assistance resources to homeland security, we must not lose our focus on drug enforcement and drug prevention. Protecting our homeland must mean protecting citizens from drug traffickers and violent drug gangs at home. To save the perimeter but lose the heartland would be a hollow victory.

Since September 11th, no child on U.S. soil has been injured or killed in a foreign-organized terrorist attack. But almost every child, regardless of race, gender or economic background, will be asked by friends or acquaintances to try dangerous illegal drugs. Each child will struggle with a choice that has the real potential to ruin their life, a choice that—wrongly made—will cause them to sacrifice their health, mental state, education and family.

Stumbling into the world of drugs will likely force them to be estranged from family, friends and faith, far too often robbing them of life itself. Unfortunately, many of our nation's young people will make that life-altering choice this year—a choice with devastating results.

Task Forces Work

Drug traffickers and drug facilitators are not bound by the borders of one State, any more than they are bound by the borders of one nation. Criminal mobility is why multijurisdictional task forces are critical in battling this threat to our personal, community and national security. A joint approach is critical in targeting drug trafficking organizations.

Multijurisdictional task forces are the lifeblood of state and local drug law enforcement; they help reduce the impact of drug and firearm traffickers, gangs such as MS-13, pharmaceutical diversion, and organized crime in America's communities by

277

linking organizations with information, leveraged assets and a real-time advantage for law enforcement.

Since September 11th, there has been ongoing criticism that federal law enforcement, the intelligence community and the Department of Defense did not adequately share information to reduce the risk of terrorism. That is certainly not the case in drug enforcement. Multijurisdictional drug task forces, federal, state, and local drug investigators are collocated and working cooperatively in cities, towns and rural communities throughout the country. Agencies across the nation have established trusted relationships, make excellent use of the Regional Information Sharing Systems (RISS) and the High Intensity Drug Trafficking Area Program (HIDTA), Intelligence Centers (ISCs), and are de-conflicting tactical operations and sharing case information in accordance with the National Criminal Intelligence Sharing Plan.

With regard to HIDTA, that information sharing would not occur without the cooperation that comes when agencies have the resources and ability to be housed together with a unified command structure working to address a common regional strategy that is funded federally but administered by balanced executive boards that equitably represent the interests of all participating agencies. Our information sharing and investigative cooperation is enhanced even more because our guidelines and executive boards mandate that cooperation.

Drug trafficking is an interstate and international problem which necessarily calls for federal involvement. The best way for the federal government to assist state and local law enforcement is through multijurisdictional drug task forces, which take full advantage of state and local ground level intelligence and expertise, but which contribute to federal investigations of regional, national, and international drug trafficking organizations.

A national, integrated threat demands a national, integrated response with state and locals leading the way, but with the federal government providing meaningful support. HIDTAs provide agency-neutral environments with balanced management led by an executive board with equal federal, state, and local participation. This neutrality and balanced system of governance fosters information sharing, tactical and subject deconfliction, and local and regional intelligence analysis that most state and local agencies simply don't have the resources or training to perform themselves and that federal agencies are inadequately focused and equipped to perform.

Drugs Fuel Violent Crime

Violence, intimidation, and disinformation are the primary tools of drug traffickers. Drug criminals use force and intimidation to control turf, ensure the swift payment of drug debts and deter those who might cooperate with law enforcement. A U.S. Bureau of Justice Statistical study of state prison inmates found that criminals who were under the influence of drugs while committing their crime accounted for 27% of all murders and 40% of robberies, a dramatic example of the link between drug use and violent crime. For this reason, drug law enforcement is critical to reducing violent crime and saving lives.

If we agree that drug abuse in America is a national problem—with enormous potential impact on every state, community and family—and one that requires a coordinated international, national, state and local law enforcement response; if we agree that drug abuse poses a significant threat to the security of our nation on many levels; if we agree that drug profits fuel terrorism and weaken our ability to respond to terrorist threats; and if we agree that drug trafficking and drug abuse present a palpable risk to our families, then we should all reach the same conclusion: A coordinated strategy that includes all levels of government, including federal resources for targeted and effective multijurisdictional drug enforcement activities, must be a top priority of the federal government.

From a personal point of view, my civilian friends often ask me about the physical and emotional toll that 33 years of facing the danger of ruthless drug dealers has taken on me. The truth is that, as a police officer, you learn quickly to live with constant danger.

What keeps me up at night is the death, fear, economic despair and ruined lives I see as a result of drug addiction and drug-fueled violent crime. It is hard to watch generations of families succumb to the downward spiral of drug use, abuse and addiction. It is heartbreaking to carry children out of meth houses reeking of poisonous gas.

Drug enforcement officers are driven in their commitment to fight the scourge of drug abuse by recurring images of innocent children languishing in dirty diapers, living in deplorable and dangerous conditions and suffering from malnutrition and drug addicted parents, who often abuse them and who are unable to care for them. We are driven to face the danger of drug enforcement by witnessing impressionable young lives ruined when they are lured into a culture of crime by adults promising quick money. We see kids become dealers for adults or lookouts that facilitate the drug sales operations of adults.

— Ron Brooks

Thursday, September 30, 2010, Falcon Lake, Texas/Mexico border.[283] David and Tiffany Hartley sped across the water on Jet Skis. They were heading back to the U.S. side of Falcon Lake along the Rio Grande after a photo expedition to Tamaulipas. While they had heard of pirates in the area, they never could have expected what was about to happen.

Three speedboats chased them down and opened fire. David was shot in the head and sank into the water. Tiffany, fearing for her life, made the agonizing decision to seek safety. She would find it, but she would never see her husband again.

Twelve days later, Rolando Flores, the Mexican commander in charge of the investigation, was found dead, his head sent to Mexican military officials in a suitcase, presumably by drug cartels to ward off any heat.

The business of smuggling illegal narcotics into the U.S. has for many years claimed the lives of innocent victims and supported drug-related terror by the DTOs, including kidnapping, torture and killings. No longer can we say that the threat is on its way. It's here, knocking on our door, having real consequences, touching our lives.

The DTOs will continue their rampages unless the American and Mexican governments identify the core resiliency factors of these organizations and destroy them one by one to bring about organizational failure.

In 2004, the Federal Government spent nearly 19 billion dollars on the drug war,[284] with a large percentage of this money funding various enforcement initiatives. Collectively, Federal Government agencies worked together to establish a priority list of targets, known as the Consolidated Priority Organization Target (CPOT) list. Despite this effort and the U.S. government's decades-long effort to dismantle DTOs, these organizations continue trafficking illegal narcotics into and throughout the United States. The DTOs refuse to die. But in reality, things would also be so much worse if we had done nothing all these years.

In 2011, the leadership structure of the AF-DTO remained operational (but nowhere near its peak days) despite the arrests of numerous key leaders.[285] Its continued operational status demonstrates that the organization continues to replace its membership, find leaders ready to take the helm, and ensure survival. Again, this is an organization that refuses to die.

This book introduces key indicators of organizational resilience and demonstrates the process through which the evil remains resilient. The process begins with improvisation and continues on to the five variables of preoccupation with failure, sensitivity to operations, commitment to reliability, under-specification of structures and reluctance to simplify interpretations.

These five variables lead to situational awareness, whereby the organization makes sense of threats and adapts to them. Due to the nature of the business, evil is in a constant state of alert and must continue to cycle itself through the resiliency framework.

The information laid out in this book will aid domestic and international law enforcement and military in attacking not only high-level DTOs, but also other, similarly structured evil organizations, such as prison gangs (which control domestic street terrorism activities within the United States and abroad through the use of over 100,000 U.S.-based, low-level gang members), as well as worldwide terrorist organizations like al-Qaeda (which continue to grow and threaten democracy and challenge weakened governments), the growing threat of pirates on the high-seas, and organized crime syndicates lurking in the shadows. This has shown to be extremely beneficial when combating sinister entities.

Legitimate businesses and corporations can adopt a number of evil's resiliency characteristics (as long as they do not cross criminal, moral and ethical boundaries) for their own use, to move their organizations toward a model of resiliency. As such, organizational resiliency must find its place at the forefront in our conversations as we battle to improve the world we live in. Working together to better understand what creates resiliency in a variety of contexts is essential in our efforts to dismantle evil organizations and in helping to assure the success and longevity of legitimate organizations and institutions on whom we depend for democracy—the protection of the people from the dangers of an ever growing serpent.

It is time to fight, time to pray—time to pray and fight. The doubters of the world must choose a side, for neutrality is nothing less than cowardly. Evil thrives in the shadows you create by turning your back on those on the front lines. You, the coward, have become part of the larger problem, giving confidence and safe haven to evil.

You, I, we—together we should fight this evil until the end for humanity, so that our children may live in a better world than that which is offered to them today. I ask two simple questions: If not now, when? If not us, who? The weight of the free world rests on the shoulders of each of us. We must never negotiate with evil. We must take our sword and thrust it into evil's heart.

Our strategy to fight evil is bold, yet simple. However, global resolve is weak. We must identify our allies, forge strong bonds and wage war together. Many nations will sit on the sidelines and watch. Those countries who show up on the battlefield—win or lose—will take home the glory, knowing they did their job in facing down the enemy, knowing that only God can truly eliminate evil altogether. But until that day comes, we must fight every day so that the children of this world have the opportunity to live without the fear we see spreading into every corner of the globe. Time is running out for global action; indecision is no longer an option.

Each of us has a moral purpose in life. Along our pathway, waiting for us, are temptations and fear. When you picked up my book, you made a decision to learn about an enemy. Now that you are at the end of my book, you should demand an answer to this one question, "What can I do to help?" Ask God to provide you with His guidance. We're in this eternal battle against evil. Where are you needed most in this fight and what can you contribute? It could be on the battlefield carrying a sword, charging the enemy, or it could be in a classroom teaching children the basic value of life and moral principles.

All children are born innocent. This is a fact we must never forget. Sadly, many are given so little choice at a young age that they drift into worlds of chaos. Parents are the single most important aspect of a child's life. Parents must bear the full responsibility for the future of their young. The pressures facing youth globally largely decide the outcome of each one's future. Drugs and alcohol play a large part in this problem, as well as gangs and poverty. What we fight for is something greater than ourselves. It is for the future generations, those who have not yet taken their first breath. Evil cannot exist without an army of people to fill its ranks. Although today's evil empires are filled with humans from all walks of life who at one time, as children, were innocent. How did we lose them? Simple: when a society's morals and values degrade, the resurgence of evil's temptations rise. You can see it globally through the tearing of the moral fabric—

including efforts to legalize drugs and prostitution and the glamorization of actors, performers and politicians who advocate the very things we, as parents, tell our children not to do. How do we raise healthy children when these systemic problems are prevalent in our communities? Cutting off the supply to evil begins at home, in our neighborhoods, schools and workplaces. If we do not act, those whom you care about most may soon become victims, lying in the countless graveyards being filled by the hand of the devil.

It is foolish for humans to think we can ultimately defeat evil on our own. We can no-more defeat evil than we can eliminate crime off our streets. Our best hope is to be the *resistance*; to build courageous coalitions with a unified strategy to push back as hard as we can against every dark shadow on the globe—to make evil as small as possible, tearing apart its resiliency characteristics in order to limit its reach and its ability to inflict chaos into our world.

Only God can *truly* defeat evil. Until that day comes, we as humans have a duty to stand-up and do all we can to protect our families, each other and all of humanity from the tyranny of the dark side. Battles ahead will be won and lost – many of our comrades will fall – that is to be expected; it's the price we must pay for having the courage and the duty to never give up, no matter the fear, no matter the consequence, no matter the odds. Where will you line up in this battle? Wherever He places you, is where He needs you most. If we choose to accept this mission, His mission, we together—all the people, all nationalities—become *one team, with one fight* as we surge ahead in our *eternal battle against evil.*

"May the Lord keep watch between you and me when we are away from each other."
— Genesis 31:49

Behind the Line

Commander Matthew Mowad is a true man of the Bible who understands the necessity of serving in uniform for a greater good. Commander Mowad completed his undergraduate studies at Biola University and graduate studies in Global Leadership at the University of San Diego. He has served 17 years in the U.S. Navy as a Surface Warfare Officer and a Naval Aviator and is currently the Vice Chair and an Associate/Assistant Professor of Naval Science at both the University of Southern California (USC) and the University of California, Los Angeles (UCLA). Commander Mowad and I served in Iraq together on General McChrystal's staff. Commander Mowad specialized in joint special operations intelligence and mission planning, for which he was awarded the Bronze Star Medal. He is a long time member and group leader for Officers' Christian Fellowship.

Behind the Line – Testimonial 21: "We Have a Duty"

with Commander Matthew Mowad

From the creation of man, God has provided a clear distinction between good and evil. For mankind, He established the governments and laws to protect us as well as the authority to serve justice in order that we may live free from the influence of those who choose to let their sinful nature inflict harm on others. Followers of Christ must understand their responsibilities in supporting God's will for justice and the fight against evil.

God wants us to be free from the influences of evil and harmful behavior.

In the Old Testament God continually commanded the Israelites to conquer their neighboring enemies. He knew that, even though His chosen people were trying to live godly lives, they would often be overcome with temptation and turn away from holiness. In order to succeed as a society and for good to overcome evil, they had to obey God and remove evil from their presence.

God recognizes the authority of government & law enforcement and commands us to do the same.

"Let everyone be subject to the governing authorities, for there is no authority except that which God has established. The authorities that exist have been established by God. Consequently, whoever rebels against the authority is rebelling against what God has instituted, and those who do so will bring judgment on themselves. For rulers hold no terror for those who do right, but for those who do wrong. Do you want to be free from fear of the one in authority? Then do what is right and you will be commended. For the one in authority is God's servant for your good. **But if you do wrong, be afraid, for rulers do not bear the sword for no reason. They are God's servants, agents of wrath to bring punishment on the wrongdoer.**" (Romans 13:1-4)

"Settle matters quickly with your adversary who is taking you to court. Do it while you are still together on the way or your adversary may hand you over to the judge and the judge may hand you over to the officer, and you may be thrown into prison. Truly I tell you, you will not get out until you have paid the last penny." (Matthew 5:25-26)

God wants us to enforce justice and is displeased when we do nothing.

"So justice is driven back, and righteousness stands at a distance; truth has stumbled in the streets, honesty cannot enter. Truth is nowhere to be found, and whoever shuns evil becomes a prey. **The Lord looked and was displeased that there was no justice. He saw that there was no one, he was appalled that there was no one to intervene.**" (Isaiah 59:14-16a)

God wants us to enforce justice without corruption. Often misunderstood, the following passage is explaining Jesus' *anger with the merchants in the temple area. He was not upset at them for conducting business in the temple area. He was upset because of their criminal activity in cheating and stealing from others.*

"Jesus entered the temple courts and drove out all who were buying and selling there. He overturned the tables of the money changers and the benches of those selling doves. 'It is written,' he said to them, My house will be called a house of prayer, but you are making it 'a den of robbers." (Matthew 21:12-14)

Note in the following passage that when men came before John the Baptist to be baptized and they asked how they should behave, he did not tell the soldier to stop being a soldier, he told him to be a soldier of integrity.

"Even tax collectors came to be baptized. 'Teacher,' they asked, 'what should we do? 'Don't collect any more than you are required to,' he told them. Then some soldiers asked him, 'And what should we do?' He replied, 'Don't extort money and don't accuse people falsely—be content with your pay." (Luke 3:12-13)

God wants us to persevere and be persistent in our fight against injustice. He does not want us to give up.

"Then Jesus told his disciples a parable to show them that they should always pray and not give up. He said: 'In a certain town there was a judge who neither feared God nor cared what people thought. And there was a widow in that town who kept coming to him with the plea, 'Grant me justice against my adversary.' For some time he refused. But finally he said to himself, 'Even though I don't fear God or care what people think, yet because this widow keeps bothering me, I will see that she gets justice, so that she won't eventually come and attack me!' And the Lord said, 'Listen to what the unjust judge says. And will not God bring about justice for his chosen ones, who cry out to him day and night? Will he keep putting them off? I tell you, he will see that they get justice, and quickly." (Luke 18:1-8a)

Dr. Paul R. Chabot

The second greatest commandment of God is that we love our neighbor as ourselves (Matthew 22:36-40). How can we even consider that we are being faithful to God if we are not loving and protecting our neighbors, our fellow citizens and mankind? By his or her faith, a Christian has even more of an obligation to serve in the fight for justice. Either by missionary work, political means, law enforcement, legal justice or military action, a Christian should be the first to volunteer their service to those in need. A Christian's entire life should be one focused on service and sacrifice for others so "that they may see your good deeds and praise your Father in heaven" (Matthew 5:16). If we are not doing everything possible to protect others' well-being, moral development and freedoms – we are not loving our neighbors as ourselves and we are not living in the will of God. **"Greater love has no one than this, that he lay down his life for his friends" (John 15:13).**

— *Commander Matthew Mowad*

Appendix One

Terrorist Organizations of the World

As Identified by the U.S. Department of State and their partner
organizations
(not a complete listing)

AFGHANISTAN

Al Qaeda
MISSION: A Caliphate throughout the globe – Overthrowing Western governments by working with Islamic extremists
OPERATIONAL LOCATIONS: Global
AFFILIATIONS: Many Sunni Islamic extremist groups

ALGERIA

Armed Islamic Group
MISSION: To overthrow the secular Algerian regime and substitute it with an Islamic state
OPERATIONAL LOCATIONS: Algeria
AFFILIATIONS: Algerian expatriates and followers around the globe

The Salafist Group for Call and Combat
MISSION: Overthrow the Algerian government. Implement Islamic theocracy
OPERATIONAL LOCATIONS: Algeria
AFFILIATIONS: Armed Islamic Group networks in Europe and extremists in Africa sympathetic to al Qaeda

CAMBODIA

The Party of Democratic Kampuchea
MISSION: Overthrow the Cambodian government
OPERATIONAL LOCATIONS: Cambodia

Dr. Paul R. Chabot

AFFILIATIONS: None
Note: This organization conducted a campaign of genocide, killing more than 1 million in the late 1970s

CHILE

Manuel Rodriguez Patriotic Front
MISSION: Carry out operations of the Chilean Communist Party as its armed wing
OPERATIONAL LOCATIONS: Chile, United States
AFFILIATIONS: None

COLOMBIA

National Liberation Army (ELN)—Colombia
MISSION: Substitute the existing government with a Marxist regime
OPERATIONAL LOCATIONS: Colombia and Venezuela border regions
AFFILIATIONS: Cuba government
Note: A Marxist insurgent organization largely inspired by Fidel Castro

Revolutionary Armed Forces of Colombia
MISSION: Replace existing government with a Marxist system
OPERATIONAL LOCATIONS: Colombia, Venezuela, Panama, and Ecuador
AFFILIATIONS: None
Note: Created as the military wing of the Colombian Communist Party

EGYPT

Al-Jihad a.k.a. Egyptian Islamic Jihad, Jihad Group, Islamic Jihad
MISSION: Overthrow the Egyptian regime and substitute it with an Islamic state; attack U.S. and Israeli interests in Egypt and overseas
OPERATIONAL LOCATIONS: Egypt, Yemen, Afghanistan, Pakistan, Sudan, Lebanon, U.K.
AFFILIATIONS: *al Qaeda*

Al-Gama'a al-Islamiyya
MISSION: Overthrow the Egyptian administration and substitute it with an Islamic state; attacking U.S. and Israeli interests
OPERATIONAL LOCATIONS: Egypt, Sudan, United Kingdom, Afghanistan, Austria, and Yemen
AFFILIATIONS: Unknown

GEORGIA

Zviadists
MISSION: Takeover Gamsakhurdia's successor Eduard Shevardnadze's rule
OPERATIONAL LOCATIONS: Georgia and Russia
AFFILIATIONS: Unknown

GREECE

Revolutionary Nuclei
MISSION: Fight against U.S, NATO EU agendas
OPERATIONAL LOCATIONS: Greece
AFFILIATIONS: Unknown

Revolutionary Organization
MISSION: Removal of U.S. bases, elimination of Turkish military presence and severing of Greece's relations to NATO and the E.U.
OPERATIONAL LOCATIONS: Greece
AFFILIATIONS: Unknown

Revolutionary People's Struggle
MISSION: To fight back against what they refer to as, "imperialist domination, exploitation, and oppression"
OPERATIONAL LOCATIONS: Greece
AFFILIATIONS: Unknown

HONDURAS

Morzanist Patriotic Front
MISSION: Halt U.S. involvement in Honduran affairs
OPERATIONAL LOCATIONS: Honduras
AFFILIATIONS: Unknown

IRAQ

Abu Nidal Organization
MISSION: Establishment of a Palestinian State
OPERATIONAL LOCATIONS: Iraq, Lebanon, Middle East, Asia, and Europe
AFFILIATIONS: Unknown
Note: Has carried out attacks in over fifteen countries, killing or injuring nearly 1,000

Mujahedin-e Khalq Organization
MISSION: Defeat Western values

OPERATIONAL LOCATIONS: Iran, Iraq
AFFILIATIONS: Entities within Iraq

Palestine Liberation Front

MISSION: Creation of a Palestinian state
OPERATIONAL LOCATIONS: Iraq
AFFILIATIONS: Receives support from within Iraq and Libya

ISRAEL

Kach and Kahane Chai

MISSION: To upend the Israeli government
OPERATIONAL LOCATIONS: Israel
AFFILIATIONS: Receives support from sympathizers in the United States and Europe

JAPAN

Aum Supreme Truth

MISSION: To remove the Japanese government from power – to do the same to governments around the globe
OPERATIONAL LOCATIONS: Japan and Russia
AFFILIATIONS: None
Note: Responsible for the 1995 subway attack in Japan, killing 12 and injuring thousands

Chukaku-Ha

MISSION: Defeat Japan's government and Western influence in Japan
OPERATIONAL LOCATIONS: Japan
AFFILIATIONS: None

Japanese Red Army

MISSION: To overthrow the Japanese government; world anarchy
OPERATIONAL LOCATIONS: Regions around Asia and Lebanon
AFFILIATIONS: Relationships with Palestinian terrorist groups

LEBANON

'Asbat al-Ansar

MISSION: Destroy Lebanese government
OPERATIONAL LOCATIONS: Lebanon
AFFILIATIONS: al Qaeda

Hezbollah

MISSION: Destruction of Israel
OPERATIONAL LOCATIONS: Lebanon, Europe, Africa, South America, North America, Asia
AFFILIATIONS: Iran and Syria governments

NORTHERN IRELAND

Real IRA

MISSION: Elimination of British presence
OPERATIONAL LOCATIONS: Northern Ireland, Irish Republic, U.K.
AFFILIATIONS: Unknown

OCCUPIED REGIONS OF THE WORLD

Al-Aqsa Martyrs Brigade

MISSION: Creation of a Palestinian state. Removal of Israeli military and Israeli citizens from the West Bank, Gaza Strip, and Jerusalem
OPERATIONAL LOCATIONS: West Bank, Israel and the Gaza Strip
AFFILIATIONS: Unknown

The Palestine Islamic Jihad

MISSION: Creation of Islamic Palestinian state; destruction of Israel through "holy war"
OPERATIONAL LOCATIONS: Israel, Jordan, Lebanon, Syria
AFFILIATIONS: Iranian and Syrian governments

PAKISTAN

Harakat ul-Mujahidin

MISSION: Unite Kashmir with Pakistan
OPERATIONAL LOCATIONS: Pakistan, Afghanistan, Kashmir
AFFILIATIONS: al Qaeda

Jaish-e-Mohammed

MISSION: Unite Kashmir with Pakistan
OPERATIONAL LOCATIONS: Kashmir, Afghanistan
AFFILIATIONS: al Qaeda, and ties to Afghan Arabs and the Taliban

PERU

Sendero Luminoso

MISSION: Destroy the local government and replace with communism
OPERATIONAL LOCATIONS: Peru
AFFILIATIONS: None

PHILIPPINES

Abu Sayyaf Group

MISSION: Creation of Islamic state
OPERATIONAL LOCATIONS: Philippines, Manila, Malaysia
AFFILIATIONS: Islamic extremists in the Middle East and Asia. Ties to *Mujahidin* in Afghanistan

New People's Army

MISSION: Overthrow the government of the Philippines
OPERATIONAL LOCATIONS: Cells in Manila and other urban centers
AFFILIATIONS: none

RWANDA

Army for the Liberation of Rwanda

MISSION: Overthrow Rwanda's government; complete the genocide begun in 1994.
OPERATIONAL LOCATIONS: Mostly Democratic Republic of the Congo and Rwanda, but a few may operate in Burundi
AFFILIATIONS: unknown
Note: Carried out the genocide of 500,000

SIERRA LEONE

Revolutionary United Front

MISSION: Overthrow the Sierra Leone government; take control of diamond-producing regions
OPERATION LOCATIONS: Sierra Leone, Liberia, Guinea
AFFILIATIONS: Libya, Gambia, and Burkina

SPAIN

Basque Fatherland and Liberty

MISSION: Creation of Marxist rule in various local regions
OPERATIONAL LOCATIONS: Spain and France
AFFILIATIONS: unknown

SRI LANKA

Liberation Tigers of Tamil Eelam
MISSION: Creation of an independent Tamil state
OPERATIONAL LOCATIONS: Sri Lanka
AFFILIATIONS: unknown

SYRIA

Popular Front for the Liberation of Palestine
MISSION: Oppose current negotiations with Israel
OPERATIONAL LOCATIONS: Syria, Lebanon, Israel, and the occupied territories
AFFILIATIONS: Syria

Popular Front for the Liberation of Palestine-General Command
MISSION: Oppose Arafat's PLO
OPERATIONAL LOCATIONS: Europe, Middle East, Lebanon, Israel, West Bank, and Gaza Strip
AFFILIATIONS: Syria and Iranian government

TURKEY

Revolutionary People's Liberation Party
MISSION: Uphold Marxist ideology and demonstrate its anti-U.S. and anti-NATO stance
OPERATIONAL LOCATIONS: Turkey
AFFILIATIONS: Unknown

UNITED STATES

Jamaat ul-Fuqra
MISSION: Cleanse Islam through forcefulness
OPERATIONAL LOCATIONS: North America, Pakistan
AFFILIATIONS: None
Note: Responsible for assassinations and fire bombings in U.S. during the 1980s

UZBEKISTAN

Islamic Movement of Uzbekistan
MISSION: Establish an Islamic state
OPERATIONAL LOCATIONS: Afghanistan and Tajikistan
AFFILIATIONS: Islamic extremist organizations in Asia

Appendix Two

Additional "Resiliency" Research and More

Organizational Resiliency Research

S utcliffe and Vogus believe that researchers should pay more attention to resilience because current theory fails to fully take into account the totality of what a resilient organization means. *"A resilience perspective would also promote a new way of seeing by arguing that organizations are more efficacious than some deterministic perspectives in organization theory allow."*[286] The resilience perspective is significant in order to accurately theorize organizational adaptation in environments that are consistently hostile. Resilience is a vital component of survival because it provides the ability *"to cope with unanticipated dangers after they become manifest."*[287]

Smith describes organizational resilience in the context of being concerned with crisis prevention. There are two main areas of work in crisis prevention. The first is concerned with the development of a crisis preparation culture. The bulk of this work concerns the development of cultural types and pathologies within organizations. The second area is concerned with the ethical aspects of corporate behavior and the creation of resilience as a consequence of suspect ethical behavior.[288] If Smith is correct in his assumption that organizational resilience is largely concerned with crisis prevention, then we must also take into account Mallak, et al.'s[289] study of tools to help plan for a crisis. He states that four tools are needed to help prepare for a crisis: (1) risk analysis, (2) contingency plans, (3) logic charts, and (4) tabletop exercises. Risk analysis is simply identifying what can possibly go wrong. Contingency plans are backup plans in case things go wrong. Logic charts require following prescribed new procedures. They "provide an overview of principal emergency response events and recovery operations."[290] Lastly, coordinating the tabletop exercise involves assembling the employees and creating scenarios in advance—a form of role-playing (i.e., certain people have various specific roles during a crisis, much like a fire drill in a school house).

Grove[291] believes that developing organizational resilience will allow an organization to adapt quickly to events—both planned and unplanned—while ensuring that operational performance maintains its equilibrium. Grove's dissertation is a qualitative study focused on senior management's ability to build organizational resilience after a significant downsizing.

Goble, Fields and Cocchiara[292] devised a strategy modeled after IBM's approach to business to help institute organizational resilience within information technology businesses. They proposed six layers to evaluate operational resiliency: (1) strategy, (2) organizational, (3) processes, (4) data/applications, (5) technology and (6) facilities/security. They hypothesized that resiliency begins with strategies that help organizations examine vulnerabilities and risks: "a resiliency plan must be viewed as a continuum within an overall business strategy."[293] Without such a plan in place, the rest of the resiliency layers would fail. Innovation appears to be an important factor, as does the ability to change and adapt. Goble, et al. explained, "achieving organizational resiliency should go beyond typical organizational issues and may include the creation of virtual, flexible and distributed workplaces to enable collaboration among employees, suppliers and customers anywhere, anytime."[294] From this layered plan, the main building blocks for resiliency were devised: recovery is the ability to bounce back quickly; hardening is the fortification of infrastructure to make the organization less vulnerable to disaster; and redundancy is the duplication of efforts.

Horne's article, "The Coming Age of Organizational Resilience,"[295] focuses predominately on private industry. However, Horne provides six core resiliency concepts deserving of attention by public safety organizations:

1. **Communication** of goals, directions and patterns that relate to changes in markets, finances, operations, mission or vision throughout the entire organization.

2. **Coordination** of large and small change efforts throughout the organization to present a "whole goal" picture of the workforce.

3. **Commitment** by all sectors of the organization to work together during periods of organizational uncertainty (with a sense of trying) to maintain trust and goodwill.

4. **Consideration** by organizational leadership that change surrounds and creeps into people's lives to such a degree that people may perceive even small shifts in organizational activity as overload.

5. **Connections** for communication and interaction within the organization that is focused, functional and flexible enough to adapt to rapidly changing needs and conditions.

6. **Community** perspective that is rooted in converging areas of self-interest by organizational members with regard to training/learning, compensation, work standards, culture and work environment, and future vision[296]

These six concepts convey the key actions and attributes necessary for organizational survival. Leadership and culture are two focus areas. Yukl states, *When a group is under extreme pressure to perform a difficult task or to survive in a hostile environment, the role expectations for the leader are likely to change in a predictable manner...they look to the leader to show initiative in defining the problem, identifying a solution, [and] directing the group's response to the crisis.*[297]

Kumpfer[298] proposes six key constructs with a view to organizing the research literature about factors that contribute to resilience:

- **Stressors or challenges** that disrupt equilibrium and the perceived degree of stress;

- **Environmental contexts** such as family, culture, community, school and peers;

- **Person-environment transaction** including perception, reframing, changing environments and active coping;

- **Internal resilience factors** including cognitive, emotional, spiritual, physical and behavioral;

- **Resilience processes,** which are stress-coping processes that allow the individual to bounce back; and

- **Positive outcomes.**

Resilience within Humans

For the purpose of this book, the emphasis is on the organization, not the individual. However, it is important to uncover individual resilience factors in order to create a full understanding of organizational resilience. Researchers Sutcliffe and Vogus pointed out that *The bulk of what we know about resilience grew out of research on vulnerable children in psychopathology and developmental psychology.*[299] Werner and Smith looked exclusively at resilience within children.[300] There is significant literature on youth resilience. The factors applying to children who overcome difficulties may be similar to those of adults and also of organizations. After all, organizations are made up of people, and those who are able to direct organizations during catastrophic events may share similar characteristics. Braverman states, *In recent years, there has been tremendous interest in understanding why some children grow up to be healthy and well-functioning adults despite having to overcome various forms of adversity in their lives.*[301] He defines resilience as "the phenomenon of successful development under high-risk conditions,"[302] and he provides examples of the following six factors: risk factors, competence, resilience, vulnerability factors, protective factors and developmental assets. He states: "[Resilience] is a concept that incorporates two components: (a) exposure to significant stressors or risks, and (b) demonstration of competence and successful adaptation."[303]

299

Hind states, "To understand fully the resilience of an individual, it is important to consider the interaction between the individual and the environment. This can be broadened to a consideration of organizational culture and the concept of a resilient organization."[304]   Hind describes the resilience audit,[305] which was created so that people could detail self-perceptions, their unit, and organization. The results of the audit are formed to show items of weaknesses that affect the overall operational capability of the organization. The audit is an attempt to bridge the connection between the individual and the organization.

How does resiliency take shape and translate into action? According to Diana Coutu, resilient individuals possess three characteristics: "a deep belief, often buttressed by strongly held value that life is meaningful, and an uncanny ability to improvise."[306] Bouncing back from hardship is possible with just one or two of these categories, according to Coutu, but to be *truly* resilient, all three are needed. She adds, *These characteristics hold true for resilient organizations.* If this is true for *organizations*, as the author states, then a study about what factors lead to these three characteristics could specifically examine each one of the characteristics to further this hypothesis. However, there is a challenge regarding how one defines "organizational resiliency" because it has been defined differently by researchers around the globe. Some researchers define resiliency as "organizational hardiness,"[307] while others refer to it as "organizational sustainability"[308] or "high organizational reliability."[309]

Although individual and organizational resilience exist in literature, distinctions and similarities can be found. In Weick's work on sensemaking, he described its relevance and importance in similarity to that of the battered child syndrome; all too often, things have been occurring around us without us knowing it, despite clear indicators. Sensemaking is often, and simply, the ability to see what is truly going on before our very eyes.[310]

Hamel, et al. discuss changes in organizational survival. In previous years, a company simply had to maintain status quo to stay in business. Now, staying in business requires a much different process than maintaining the status quo: "Continued success no longer hinges on momentum. Rather, it rides on resilience— on the ability to dynamically reinvent business models and strategies as circumstances change."[311] It is the "renewal" that should be the natural consequence of a company's resilience; that is, the company should robustly work toward its future rather than rest on its past successes.

Measuring Resilience

Five little words have proven meaningful when talking about the core attributes of a resilient organization: positive, focused, flexible, organized and proactive. You will have more information on these five a little later in this section. Having the ability to measure resilience is really important. You need it to prove the doubters wrong. Because you are on the verge of creating or fighting something less understood by most, you must have the ability to stand tall, with absolute confidence, and tell others how to prove the existence of resilience beyond simple newspaper clippings. You have to get down to the nuts and bolts of actually measuring resilience. O'Neal[312] notes various methods developed to measure resilience, which he refers to as hardiness. Note: hardiness and resilience are often used interchangeably throughout existing research on resilience. Some of these "measures" of resilience include the following:

1. **Personal Views of Survey III**, created by the Hardiness Institute in 1985
2. **Cognitive Hardiness Scale**, by K. Nowack in 1989
3. **Psychological Hardiness Scale**, by S. Youkin and N. Betz in 1986
4. **Resilience Scale**, by G. Wagnild and H. Young in 1993
5. **Resiliency Scale**, by C. Jew in 1999
6. **Personal Resilience Questionnaire and Organizational Resilience Questionnaire**, by Conner in 1992
7. **Family Hardiness Index**, by McCubbin in 1996.

O'Neal stated, "Although only a few references can be found prior to the mid-1980s, the volume of studies has grown tremendously in the last few years."[313] Of the seven measures listed, Conner's Organizational Resilience Questionnaire appears best suited for organizational studies since the others focus on individuals rather than organizations.

O'Neal's scale for organizations measures five key areas:

1. It displays a sense of security and self-assurance that is based on a view that life is complex but filled with opportunity **(Positive)**;
2. It provides a clear vision of what to achieve **(Focused)**;
3. It demonstrates a special pliability when responding to uncertainty **(Flexible)**;
4. It takes a structured approached to managing ambiguity **(Organized)**;
5. It engages change rather than defends against it **(Proactive)**[314]

Simply having the knowledge that these various measures exist places you leaps and bounds above others. Relying on the good work of others and citing their findings allows you to build the better mousetrap we discussed in the book's chapters. As you propose the battle plan and strategy to go after a resilient organization by building your own resilient organization, you can talk about what others have done in measuring resilience, to set the stage for your proposals and your arguments. By doing so, you are not flying blind; rather you are flying in the dark but by the use of instruments created by others. Soon, that dark will turn into light as evil is exposed and diminished.

Modeling Resilience within a Devastated Industry

In Rosenman and Handelsman's[315] research regarding modeling resiliency in a community devastated by man-made catastrophe, the authors found that a devastated community can rally to its immediate needs of food, water, shelter and so forth and quickly rebuild basic community infrastructure for traveling on roads, obtaining clean water, and other needs. However, the key thing needed for this success is the leadership's ability to lift the morale of the citizenry and workers. A good example of community resilience was observed, to some degree, with the rise, decline and resurgence of the American auto industry.

Franko[316] studied the American auto industry's movement from the 1980s through the 1990s. He compared the American auto industry's resilience with that of the Japanese auto industry and found that the American auto industry developed the ability to become "lean and mean." He explained:

> *refocusing on core businesses after disastrous de-worisifications in the 1970s and 1980s was surely part of the continued success of a number of American firms...important motors of improved U.S. performance (include) innovation...and the development of a global outlook (the need to compete with Japanese).[317]*

Franko found that the Japanese, during the 1970s, were equally resilient to product failure and company collapse, because the Japanese used the same notions of innovation and they needed to compete with the Americans. The respective auto companies found a way to survive. Carl, et al.[318] believed that a resilient system has the ability to create opportunity for growth and learning.

Shared Risk

Comfort[319] described the concept of shared risk and how vital it is to effective emergency management. Shared risk "means a community's capacity to mitigate risk and respond to damaging incidents when they occur. [Shared risk] depends upon [the community's] ability to assess its own vulnerabilities, monitor its own performance, and mobilize resources in response to threat."[320] This concept is essential in our understanding of evil and whether it operates in an environment of shared risk.

Sensemaking and Mindfulness in Organizations

Pay close attention to this portion of the appendix. These two profound concepts are absolutely required for an organization to become resilient—no ifs, ands, or buts about it. Period.

Consistently, Weick rises to the top of the research list in the review of resiliency concepts.[321] He coined the phrase "sensemaking" and applied it to a variety of organizational settings and situations.[322] In his 1998 article, "Enacted

Sensemaking in Crisis Situations," he defines crises as "characterized by low probability/high consequence events that threaten the most fundamental goals of an organization"[323] and argues that, in order to counteract catastrophes, one must "reduce tight coupling and interactive complexity."[324]

Smith[325] supports Weick's theory on sensemaking and its relationship to resilience, and theorizes the importance of developing routines and role structures. Smith explains the significance of these routines and role structures in halting the eroding of organizational resilience by inhibiting an effective response from those responsible for controlling events.

Similar to the idea of sensemaking is the idea of mindfulness. Fiol and O'Connor describe mindfulness as "a way of seeing the information gained by scanning, a way of evaluating that information, and a way of acting on it that contrast[s] with many of the assumptions of traditional approaches."[326] McCann[327] connects organizational resiliency to an organization's agility through four characteristics, one of which is sensemaking. He describes sensemaking, in the organizational resiliency context, as the process of scanning and interpreting large amounts of diverse data and then rapidly creating a hypothesis and mental model about what the organization is experiencing. This ability to connect the variable of organizational agility to the sensemaking construct of organizational resiliency is supported by research.

In contrast, Comfort[328] argues that sensemaking can fail in organizations. She describes the 9/11 attacks in terms of the flights from Boston and Dulles, which were controlled by hijackers. The passengers and crews were unable to make sense of the immediate situation because they were coerced into following the hijacking procedures, and were thus unable to make sense of what was going on to act differently. "In each instance, the crews and passengers on these planes faced unimaginable events. They did not recognize the risk and were unable to act to avert danger."[329]

However, Saveland's[330] study found that sensemaking is an evolutionary aspect of organizational change and explained it as being the most important factor in situational awareness and the mindfulness of high-reliability organizing. In this case, United Airlines Flight 93, which crashed into the Pennsylvania field, exhibited sensemaking. The passengers became aware of the situation and the hijackers' intent, and acted appropriately. These brave passengers acted together, almost like an organization, making sense of their environment and chances of survival.

Hinrichs and Tenkasi state, "Organizational systems, structures and relationships provide a foundation for effective sensemaking."[331] Organizations are susceptible to stress. Drabek states "Organizational environments are uncertain and contain important patterns of strain."[332] He credits managers for learning to be aware of various organizational complications and developing methods in overcoming those complications. Hence, organizations "morph" into their environments; they have the ability to adapt. Hatch[333] describes isomorphism (also called requisite variety), which is a belief that organizations match the complexity of the environments they find themselves within—even those environments that are extremely challenging or out of the ordinary. Lagadec explains, "Our ability to deal with chaos depends on structures that have been developed before the chaos arrives. When the chaos arrives, it serves as an abrupt and brutal audit; at a moment's notice, everything that was left unprepared becomes a complex problem and every weakness comes rushing to the forefront. The breach in the defenses opened by the crisis creates a sort of vacuum."[334]

In high-risk industries, failures, mistakes and errors will often not be tolerated due to the potentially catastrophic outcome associated with mistakes. To overcome these problems, such organizations prudently develop alternatives to experimentation and trial-and-error learning. They must learn as much as possible from problems, transfer learning across organizations and develop their processes based on proactive learning.[335] There are two elements that distinguish complex systems from other system forms: (1) the capacity to avoid the harshness of entropy by importing energy and information and (2) the capacity for "self-organization." Self-organization concerns the ability to internally produce the means for renewal and regeneration.[336]

At the end of the day, if an organization has failed to become mindful of threats, it will be unable to make sense of them. Making sense of threats requires one to be smart enough to first see the challenge. Its goes back to the age-old adage "You can't fix a problem unless you first acknowledge one exists." An organization must see a threat, like a deer seeing a hunter in the forest—be "mindful." Being mindful of the threat allows the deer to go to the next step of survival—making sense of the threat and taking action. Organizations are no different, although those that are not resilient organizations look more like a deer being caught in the headlights, awaiting its fate.

The High-Reliability Organization (HRO)

As we reach the end of understanding the basic functionality of a resilient organization, let's visit the interchangeable term, called a highly reliable organization (HRO). While some may differ with my opinion, I see both as one-in-the-same as we talk about resilient organizations. At the end of the day, if it looks like a duck and walks like a duck, it's a duck! An HRO, referenced in some research, is a resilient organization. Why the difference in terms? You say "tomato," I say "tomahto." Now you decide.

HROs according to Aase are "characterized by the overall demand for high reliability because of their unique potential for catastrophic consequences."[337] He provides the following examples of HROs: nuclear power plants, energy utility plants, transportation systems (aircraft, space shuttles, shipping freights), chemical plants, offshore installations and large construction projects. Similarly, Weick[338] defends HRO's placement in organizational writings because it allows the reader to understand these types of organizations and their effectiveness during difficult times. Aase advises that "the relations between high-risk organizations and organizational effectiveness, organizational learning or organizational knowledge should be explored in further depth."[339]

Scott[340] asserts that high-reliability theory is valuable for organizations to explore because it allows industries working in dangerous environments (nuclear power plants, etc.) to remain alert and successful. These organizations focus more on the things that could destroy them than on how to advertise or market a product. They are always at risk of failure[341] and find themselves in complex, rapidly changing and tightly coupled environments that demand their utmost attention because their first error can destroy their entire organization. This is often referred to as a tightly coupled system, "spun so tightly"[342] that few possible substitutions or buffers exist to release strain. Therefore, it becomes reliability seeking[343] to prevent failure.[344]

Weick and Sutcliff's book, *Managing the Unexpected,*[345] promotes key concepts that organizations may adopt to manage uncertainty including cultivating humility, being glad when you're having a bad day (so you can learn from it), creating an error-friendly learning culture, developing skeptics (who can point out things others may not see), being suspicious of good news, seeking out bad news, treating all unexpected occurrences as information and spreading this information widely.[346] Weick presented a workshop on HRO tactics for the U.S. Forest Service,[347] stating, "Mindfulness is the passkey into high reliability organizing."[348] It's imperative that workers in an HRO strive to see more, view more, learn more, do more and, most importantly, not to become complacent. HROs can accomplish this through five central processes that encourage self-awareness and the willingness to learn: failures, simplifications, operations, resilience and distributed expertise.

Weick[349] provides further details on the fourth item—resilience. The HRO will maintain a commitment to resilience, seek out what may go wrong, and prepare plans and contingencies to work out catastrophic events. Weick interchanges the word "resilience" with "reliability" and describes viable actions that a reliable system follows in order to sustain its existence. These actions include: conducting a short study, developing a speedy trust, conducting just-in-time learning, fostering psychological stimulation and working with fragments of potential relevant preceding incidents. Weick supports the notion that HROs actually need "near misses" to learn how to react and act regarding the unexpected. HROs are successful when they trust others with more experience and expertise to make decisions.

Clarke[350] states that HROs have almost certain safety; that is, organizations operating in this capacity are error-free. He maintains that HROs contain certain characteristics that presume that the organizations are learning from themselves (or intrinsically).

O'Connor and Fiol[351] support Clarke's contention that HROs encourage reporting of errors in order to learn to improve their organizations. These types of organizations are decentralized and tend to push decisions down to the lowest level in order to bring about a quick decision.

La Porte and Consolini define redundancy as "the ability to provide for the execution of a task if the primary unit fails or falters."[352] They describe the landing of military craft on the deck of an aircraft carrier and how almost everyone on board bears some responsibility for each landing's success, They explain that this process is part of a continuous loop of confirmation and communication that occurs at once over many channels. Redundancy enhances organizational reliability/resiliency.

Smart states, "The theory of HRO design is well placed to inform organizational design where performance reliability and safety are critical and that failure is simply not an option."[353] His work lists catastrophic tragedies—including Chernobyl, Exxon Valdez, Bhopal and the Challenger—and posits that these types of events have led to efforts to understand them better. Within the high-risk organization, one might presume that leadership from a certain individual was responsible for the organization's resilience, but Schulman's 1996 study, "Heroes, Organizations and High Reliability," found that not to be the case. Schulman reviewed extensive interviews conducted at a nuclear power plant and found that no heroic tales existed. In fact, the findings concluded that the culture of the organization was antiheroic and the message of the organization was "don't be a hero." A hero was thought of as a "cowboy," a rough individual who could bring more damage to the organization than good. Rather than depending on heroes, organizational resiliency appears to depend on an organizational preparedness among all members of that organization.

Perrow's[354] Normal Accident Theory (NAT) postulates that when organizations are involved in dangerous work, failure is to be expected. That is, failure is inevitable in tightly coupled systems. In contrast, Roberts[355] later cited a work conducted at Berkeley's school on HRO theory and concluded that when certain organizational strategies are set in place, one can achieve outstanding results without failure. Sagan[356] concluded that NAT offered the best explanation of the study of U.S. nuclear weapons. He felt comfortable in his research because the nuclear close calls (i.e., near misses) could have escalated into full-blown nuclear war, but "good luck" prevented near catastrophes. While NAT is a theory that justifies failure, HRO offers substance for helping to prevent failure.[357]

High-Reliability Theory (HRT)

Smart et al.[358] reviewed research and case studies on HROs. They spanned the globe looking for an existing study on high-reliability theory based on their assumption that findings must exist on tragedies such as Exxon Valdez, Chernobyl, the Challenger, etc. They found that scholars had indeed studied these types of incidents. The general consensus was that HROs, which they also refer to as "failure-free," feel "the need effectively to pursue seemingly paradoxical courses of action simultaneously."[359] Simply stated, personnel are trained to perpetuate and accept the fact that if they see a problem, they "own" it and must find a way to fix it or find somebody else who can. Taking full responsibility is a hallmark of a high-reliability culture (HRC). The HRC creates a value system that rewards, rather than punishes, a member for finding failure or fault.

Smart et al.[360] credit a group of researchers working at the University of California, Berkeley, for being largely responsible for high-reliability theory (HRT). The Berkeley researchers identified key design features that they believe can form a template for catastrophe aversion:

1. The political and organizational leadership prioritizes extreme reliability.
2. The prime cultural norm labels any action jeopardizing reliability as "a disgrace."
3. Standard operating procedures and clear hierarchies are specified (i.e., a task-based approach is taken to organizational design).
4. Zero tolerance is applied to any feature impacting this task-based view in order to eliminate cascading error.
5. Continuous organizational learning is practiced using trials without major errors.
6. System redundancy is achieved by resourcing to peak rather than average loading.
7. Collegiality and inverted hierarchy occur in periods of high loading.
8. Continuous innovation occurs in times of average loading.
9. Continuous training emphasizes coordination through shared ideology.
10. Interdependence and reciprocal coupling are key structural features.
11. "Alertness," "attention," and "care" are emphasized as key operational performance characteristics[361] leading to the creation of a "collective mind."[362]

Smart et al.'s research found that despite all efforts to avoid catastrophic events, errors do occur and serious accidents are rare but, over time, inevitable. According to Brown's[363] theory, the best one can hope for is a near-error-free environment. Sutcliffe and Vogus[364] found that a near-error-free environment can be accomplished by optimistically adjusting to present adversity, which in turn, strengthens the organization's capabilities to make future adjustments.

Complex Adaptive Systems

I learned through my doctoral studies the concept of complex adaptive systems. These can also be construed as organizations that are resilient or on the cusp of becoming resilient. To begin this conversation, let's look at California's Northridge earthquake, which caused severe damage and killed many in Southern California in 1994. The disaster response system that took effect, according to Comfort,[365] illustrates the "vital characteristics of a complex, adaptive system—a capacity for learning from one set of conditions and actions and incorporating those new facts into the decision-making process for the next stage of action."[366] During this process, the system balances chaos and order, anticipation, and resilience.

Some believe that "the environments are largely invented by organizations themselves [because]...they select their environments from ranges of alternatives, then they subjectively perceive the environments they inhabit."[367] Arizona State University Center for Environmental Studies[368] found that resilience researchers are interested in complex adaptive systems and that these types of units are unique in developing resiliency within organizations.

Comfort defines self-organization as the "capacity to adapt to new information and reallocate resources and action accordingly."[369] In her research, she cites Kaufman's study describing all types of systems as operating on a continuum between order and chaos. Systems at either end move toward the center, known as the edge of chaos, "where there is sufficient order to hold and exchange information, but sufficient flexibility to adapt to changing environment...at the edge of chaos, organizations are able to adapt most successfully to changing demands for the environment."[370] Kaufman describes this process as self-organization, where change in behavior was initiated by the actor, not by any outside entity.

The purpose of this book is to explore how the aforementioned elements play into evil's ability to operate in situations described as a chaotic state under severe distress. A major goal of this book is to determine if evil is able to learn from incoming data in this dynamic environment and, in turn alter significantly the operating context of the organization's ability to respond to threats. But we have much work to do; a lot yet to learn.

Systematic and extensive social science disaster research has been going on for nearly five decades now. Much worthwhile work has been done. A very large number of empirical generalizations have been produced. Yet, I am troubled. In view, the field more and more is producing less and less of what might be characterized as major advances in new knowledge and understanding of disaster related phenomena.[371]

References

Aase, K. and G. Nybo, eds. 2002, April 5. Organizational knowledge in high-risk industries: What are the alternatives to model based learning approaches. Third European Conference on Organizational Knowledge. Athens, Greece. 1–22.

Aitken, S. 1999, January/February. How Motorola promotes good health. *The Journal for Quality and Participation* 54–57.

Americas: The end of the Arellano's; Drugs in Mexico. 2002, March 16. *The Economist,* 43.

DEA offers $5M bounty for trafficker arrest. 2003. *Crime Control Digest* 37(39): 3.

Ashmos, D.P. and G.P. Huber. 1987. The systems paradigm in organization theory: Correcting the record and suggesting the future. *Academy of Management Review* 12(4): 607-622.

Audet, M., M. Landry, and R. Dery. 1986. Science et resolution de probleme: Liens, difficultes et voies de depasement dans le champ des sciences de l'administration [Science and problem solving: Similarities, dissimilarities, and extensions in the field of administrative science]. *Philosophy of the social Sciences/Philosophie des Sciences Sociales* 16:409–440.

Baig, J. 2000. Mexico's most feared family. Retrieved on January 8, 2011 from http://news.bbc.co.uk/2/hi/americas/780040.stm

Bandura, A. 1989. Human agency in social cognitive theory. *American Psychologist* 44(9):1175–1184.

Becerra, O. 2002, December. Tijuana cartel fights for its future. *Jane's Intelligence Review.*

Beers, R. 1999, March 4. Assistant Secretary for International Narcotics and Law Enforcement Affairs testimony before the Subcommittee on Criminal Justice, Drug Policy, and Human Resources House Government Reform and Oversight Committee. Retrieved on May 2, 2005, from http://www.globalsecurity.org/security/library/congress/1999_h/99022514_1 gi.htm

Bell, M. 2002. The five principles of organizational resilience. Retrieved on January 8, 2011, from

http://www.gartner.com/resources/103600/103658/103658.pdf

Berliner, P. 1994. *Thinking in jazz: The infinite art of improvisation.* Chicago: University of Chicago Press.

Beunza, D. and D. Stark. 2003. *A desk on the 20th floor: Survival and sensemaking in a trading room.* Unpublished manuscript. Madrid, Spain: University of Pompeu Fabra, Department of Economics and Business.

Bigley, G. and K. Roberts. 2001. The incident command system: High-reliability organizing for complex and volatile task environments. *Academy of Management Journal* 44(6):1281–1299.

Biscoe, B. 1999. *A closer look at resilience: Rebounding from the pain of the past.* Norman, Oklahoma: The University of Oklahoma, College of Continuing Education.

Brafman, O. and R. Beckstrom. 2006. *The starfish and the spider.* New York: Penguin.

Braverman, M. 2001. *Applying resilience theory to the prevention of adolescent substance abuse.* Davis, CA: University of California Davis, Department of Psychology.

Brown, A. 1993. *High reliability organizations: A review and critique of the Berkeley group* (MRP/93/9). Templeton Management research paper.

Caldwell, Robert. 2007a, July 1. Cartel secrets: Top-level insider reveals the cartel's most guarded info. *San Diego Union Tribune* G2, G4–5.

Caldwell, Robert. 2007b, July 1. Cold-blooded killers. *San Diego Union Tribune* G5.

Caldwell, Robert. 2007c, July 1. The evidence. *San Diego Union Tribune* G6.

Caldwell, Robert. 2007d, July 1. The narco bosses. *San Diego Union Tribune* G4.

Carl, F., S. Carpenter, and T. Elmqvist, eds. 2002, April. Resilience and sustainable development: Building adaptive capacity in a world of transformation. Paper presented at the World Summit on Sustainable Development.

Carley, K. 1993. Coding choices for textual analysis: A comparison on content analysis and map analysis. In P.V. Marsden, ed. *Sociological methodology* 23:75–126. American Sociological Association.

Carter, S. 2006, January 24. Armed standoff along U.S. border. *Inland Valley Daily Bulletin* A1, A7.

Cash, T. 1993. The illicit drug situation in Colombia: Drug intelligence report. Washington, DC: U.S. Drug Enforcement Administration.

Ciudad, J. October 31, 2004. Carillo Fuentes suffers highest losses. Retrieved December 18, 2004, www.diario.com.mx/

Clarke, L. 1993. Drs. Pangloss and Strangelove meet organizational theory: High reliability organizations and nuclear weapons accidents. *Sociological Forum* 8(4):675–689.

Cole, R. 2001. From continuous improvement to continuous innovation. *Quality Management Journal* 8(4):24–36.

Collins, J.C. and J.I. Porras. 1994. *Built to last: Successful habits of visionary companies.* New York: Harper.

Comfort, L. 1994. Risk and resilience: Inter-organizational learning following the Northridge earthquake of 17 January 1994. *Journal of Contingencies and Crisis Management* 2(3):157–170.

Comfort, L. K. 2001, January 18. Governance under fire: Organizational fragility in complex systems. Symposium conducted at the meeting on Governance and Public Security, Campbell Public Affairs Institute, Maxwell School of Public Affairs and Administration, Syracuse University, Syracuse, NY.

Conner, D. 1992. *Managing at the speed of change.* New York: Villard.

International organized crime syndicates and their impact on the United States: Hearing before the Senate Foreign Relations Committee, Subcommittee on the Western Hemisphere, Peace Corps, Narcotics, and Terrorism.104 Cong., (1998) (testimony of Drug Enforcement Administrator Constantine).

Congressional Research Service, The Library of Congress. (2001). *Mexico's counternarcotics efforts under Zedillo and Fox, December 1994–March 2001.* Washington, DC: Author.

Constantine, T. 1998. International organized crime syndicates and their impact on the United States. Senate Foreign Relations Committee. Retrieved on January 8, 2011 from

http://www.justice.gov/dea/pubs/cngrtest/ct980226.htm

Coutu, D. 2002, May. Confronted with life's hardships, some people snap, and others snap back. How resilience works. *Harvard Business Review* 46-55.

Creswell, J. 1998. *Qualitative inquiry and research design.* Thousand Oaks: Sage Publications.

Grove, K. 1997. *Architecture for a resilient organization: Survive, grow, and prosper in a downsized environment.* Cincinnati, Ohio: The Union Institute and University. Organizational Behavior Studies.

D'Aveni, R. 1994. *Hypercompetition: Managing the dynamics of strategic maneuvering.* New York: Free Press.

Defense Intelligence Agency. 2003. Arellano Felix Organization. Retrieved August 7, 2004, from

http://164.185.231.21/finishprod/dia_interpol/dtors/mexico_dto_chart_sep03.jpg

Denzin, N. 1984. *The research act.* Englewood Cliffs, NJ: Prentice Hall.

Dettmer, J. 2001. Mexico's real war on drugs. *Insight on the News,* 17(34):18–19.

Dettmer, J. and T. Maier. 1998, August 10. Eavesdropping experts get their men. *Insight on the News* 14:6.

Doe, P. 1994. Creating resilient organizations. *Canadian Business Review,* 21(2):1–5.

Dougall, A.L., H.B. Herberman, D.L. Delahanty, S.S. Inslicht, and A. Baum. 2000. Similarities of prior trauma exposure as a determinant of chronic stress responding to an airline disaster. *Journal of Consulting and Clinical Psychology* 68(2):290–295.

Drabek, T. 1989. Strategies used by emergency managers to maintain organizational integrity. *Environmental Auditor* 1(3):139–152.

Drug Enforcement Administration. 1987. Intelligence collection and analytical methods. Washington, DC: Author.

Drug Enforcement Administration. 1997. Ramon Arellano Felix named to FBI's ten most wanted fugitives. Retrieved August 10, 2004, from www.usdoj.gov/dea/pubs/pressrel/pr 970918.htm

Drug Enforcement Administration. 2002. Drug intelligence brief. Mexico: Country brief July 2002. Retrieved on August 10, 2004, from www.usdoj.gov/dea/pubs/intel/02035/02035. html

Drug Enforcement Administration. 2003. Country profile for 2003 Mexico (DEA Publication No. 03047 November 2003). Washington, DC: Author.

Drug Enforcement Administration. 2003. Beginning of the end of Arellano Felix Trafficking organizations (2000–2002). Retrieved October 25, 2004, from http://www.usdoj.gov/ dea/pubs/pressrel/pr070903a.html

Drug Enforcement Administration. 2004. Major cartel lieutenants arrested in Mexico. Retrieved August 10, 2004, from 8/10/04 from http://www.usdojgov/dea/major/united_ eagles/index.html

Durkin, T. 1997. Using computers in qualitative strategic research. In G. Miller and R. Dingwall, eds. *Context and method in qualitative research* 92–105. Thousand Oaks, CA: Sage.

El Universal. 2004. Major drug trafficking organizations form alliances. Retrieved December 18, 2004 from

www.fbis.cia.ic.gov/cgibin/cqcgi...11+12+13&TrackDocID=:A {20041011000070

Ellingwood, K. 2010, August 31. Mexico fires 3,200 federal police officers. *Los Angeles Times.* Retrieved September 2, 2010 from http://articles.latimes.com/2010/aug/31/world/ la-fg-mexico-police-fired-20100831

Ellis, P. 1998. *Chaos in the underground: Spontaneous collapse in a tightly coupled system.* Vol. 6. Hung Hom, Kowloon: Hong Kong Polytechnic University, Department of Business Studies.

Egeland, B., E. Carlson, and L.A. Sroufe. 1993. Resilience as process. *Development and Psychopathology* 5(4):517–528.

Eisenhardt, K.M. and J.A. Martin. 2000. Dynamic capabilities: What are they? *Strategic Management Journal* 21(10–11):1105–1121.

Fiol, M. and E. O'Connor. 2002, July. Future planning + present mindfulness = strategic foresight. Paper presented as the International Conference at the University of Strathclyde Graduate School of Business in Glasgow, UK.

Fanning, K. 2002. 9/11/2001: The day that changed America. Firefighters fight on. New York Fire Department prepared for the future. Retrieved October 20, 2002, from

http://teacher.scholastic.com/scholarsticnews/indepth/911/nation_firefighters.htm

Feagin, J., A. Orum, and G. Sjoberg, eds. 1991. *A case for case study.* Chapel Hill, NC: University of North Carolina Press.

Federal Bureau of Investigation. 2003. Top leadership of Arellano Felix Drug trafficking organization indicted. Retrieved August 10, 2004, from www.fbi.gov/page2/july03/070903arellano.htm 217

Fifth of Mexico's top agents are facing criminal probes. December 5, 2005. *The San Diego Union Tribune* A12.

Franko, L. 2002, May–June. Global competition in the 1990s: American renewal, Japanese resilience, and European cross-currents. *Business Horizons* 25–38.

Fraenkel, J.R. and Wallen, N.E. 2000. *How to design and evaluate research in education.* Boston: McGraw Hill Higher Education.

Freeman, S., L. Hirschhorn, and M. Maltz. 2002. *Moral purpose and organizational resilience: Sandler, O'Neil & Partners in the aftermath of September 11, 2001.* Cambridge, Massachusetts: Massachusetts Institute of Technology. Sloan School of Management.

Garmezy, N. 1991. Resilience in children's adaptation to negative life events and stressed environments. *Pediatric Annals* 20(9):459–466.

Goble, G., H. Fields, and R. Cocchiara. 2002, September. Resilient infrastructures: Improving your business resilience. *IBM Global Services.*

Goldway, T. 2002. *So others might live: A history of New York's bravest—The FDNY from 1700 to present.* New York: Basic Books.

Gordon, E. and L.D. Song. 1994. Variations in experience of resilience. In: M. Wang and E. Gordon, eds. *Educational Resilience in Inner-city America: Challenges and Prospects,* 27-43, Hillsdale, NJ: Erlbaum.

Greene, R. 2002. *Holocaust survivors: A study in resilience.* Indianapolis, Indiana: Indiana University, School of Social Work.

Grotberg, E. 1995. *The international resilience project: Research, application and policy.* Civitan International Research Center, UAB. Institute for Mental Health Initiatives.

Grove, K. 1997. *Architecture for a resilient organization: Survive, grow, and prosper in a downsized environment.* Cincinnati, Ohio: The Union Institute and University. Organizational Behavior Studies.

Guba, E.G. 1978. *Toward a methodology of naturalistic inquiry in educational evaluation.* Monograph 8. Los Angeles: UCLA Center for the Study of Evaluation.

Guidimann, T. 2002, September. From recovery to resilience. *The Banker* 3–6.

Hamel, G. and L. Valikangas. 2003, September. The quest for resilience. *Harvard Business Review* 52-63.

Hammonds, K. 2002, May. 5 habits of highly reliable organizations: *Fast Company* 58:124.

Hannan, M.T. and J. Freeman. 1984. Structural inertia and organizational change. *American Sociological Review* 49(2):149–164.

Hatch, M. J. 1997. *Organization theory: modern symbolic and postmodern perspectives.* New York: Oxford University Press.

Heyman, J. and H. Campbell. 2004. Recent research on the U.S. Mexico border. *Latin American Research Review,* 39:205.

Hind, P. 1996. The resilience audit and the psychological contract. *Journal of Managerial Psychology* 11(7):18–29.

Hinrichs, G. 2002. Enactment, sensemaking and social agreement: An interpretive model of implementing high performance work systems. Paper presented at the Midwest Academy of Management Meetings in Lisle, Illinois.

Hodder, I. (1994). The interpretation of documents and material culture. In N. K. Denzin and Y. S. Lincoln, eds. *Handbook of qualitative research.* Thousand Oaks, CA: Sage.

Hoffman, B. 2004, January. What we can learn from the terrorists. *Global Horizons* 2:32–39.

Horne III, J. 1997, Spring–Fall. The coming age of organizational resilience. *Business forum* 24-28.

Huber, G.P. and A.H. Van de Ven, eds. 1995. *Longitudinal field research methods: Studying process of organizational change.* Thousand Oaks, CA: Sage.

Husserl, E. 1913. *Ideas: General introduction to pure phenomenology.* W. R. Boyce Gibson. trans. NY: Collier.

Hutchinson, A. 2002. Statement of Asa Hutchinson, Administrator, before the Senate Judiciary Committee, Subcommittee on Technology, Terrorism and Government Information. Retrieved on January 8, 2011 from http://www.justice.gov/dea/pubs/cngrtest/ct031302.html

Iverson, D. 2002. Book review: Managing the unexpected. *Fire Management Today* 62(4):36–37.

Johnson, L. and F. Kloman. 1999, October. Dealing with disaster: Examine approaches for small public entities, non-profit organizations and businesses to reduce losses and overcome the effects of extreme events. Paper presented at Dealing with Disaster: A Public Risk Institute Symposium.

Kaufman, J., A. Cook, L, Amy, B. Jones, and T. Pittinsky. 1994. Problems defining resilience: Illustrations from the study of maltreated children. *Development and Psychopathology* 6:115–147.

Kendra, J. and T. Wachtendorf. 2001. *Elements of community resilience in the World Trade Center attack.* Newark, Delaware: University of Delaware, Disaster Research Center.

Kenney, M. 2001. *Out-smarting the state: A case study of the learning capacity of Colombian narcotics organizations.* Gainesville, Florida: University of Florida.

Kenney, M. 2003. Intelligence games: Comparing the intelligence capabilities of law enforcement agencies and drug trafficking enterprises. *International Journal of Intelligence and Counterintelligence* 16:212–243.

Kiel, L.D. 1994. *Managing chaos and complexity in government. A new paradigm for managing change, innovation, and organizational renewal.* San Francisco: Jossey-Bass.

Klein, M. 2002, 9/11. Fear yields to New York resiliency. *The Journal News.* Retrieved on October 22, 2002, from

www.thejournalnews.com/9- 11/11wtc01.htm

Kleiman, M., P. Reuter, and J. Caulkins. 2002. The "war on terror" and the "war on drugs": A comparison. *The Journal of the Federation of American Scientists* 55:1–5.

Kobasa, S.C. 1982. Commitment and coping in stress resistance among lawyers. *Journal of Personality and Social Psychology* 42(4):707–717.

Kobasa, S.C., S.R. Maddi, and S. Kahn. 1982. Hardiness and health: A prospective study. *Journal of Personality and Social Psychology* 21:168–177.

Kraul, C. 2002, March 16. The collapse of Mexico's invincible drug cartel. *The Los Angeles Times.* Retrieved on August 10, 2004, from www.theantidrug.com/drugs_terror/news_ collapse.asp

Kumpfer, L.K. 1999. Factors and processes contributing to resilience: The resilience framework. In M.D. and J.L. Johnson, eds. *Resilience and development: Positive life adaptations* 179–224. New York: Academic/Plenum.

Kumagai, Y. 2002. *Local strategies for accelerating sustainability: Case studies of local government success.* Toronto, Canada: ICLEI World Secretariat.

La Cronica. 2004, December 4. PGR, PGJE investigate murder of drug traffickers linked to 'El Gillio'. Retrieved on December 12, 2004, from www.lacronica.com/EdicionImpresa/Hoy/General/Home.asp

La Frontera. 2004a, November 6. Cafes besieges PGJE offices, arrests PME officer linked to CAF. Retrieved December 18, 2004, from http:www.frontera.info/EdicionImpresa/Hov/General/Home.asp

La Frontera. 2004b, November 12. Court upholds indictment, order to stand trial handed down for CAF kingpin. Retrieved December 19, 2004, from www.frontera.info/EdicionImpresa/Hov/General/Home.asp

La Frontera. 2004c, November 19. Authorities capture 5 CAF gunmen in La Mesa. Retrieved December 12, 2004, from

www.frontera.info/EdicionImpresa/Hoy/General/Home.asp

Lagadec, P. 1993. *Preventing chaos in a crisis.* London: McGraw-Hill.

La Porte, T. and P. Consolini. 1991. Working in practice buy not in theory: Theoretical challenges of high-reliability organizations. *Journal of Public Administration Research and Theory,* 1(1):19–47.

Levinthal, D.A. and J.G. March. 1981. A model of adaptive organizational search. *Journal of Economic Behavior and Organization* 2:307–333.

Levinthal, B. and J.G. March. 1988. Organizational learning. *Annual Review of Sociology* 14:319–340.

Lincoln, Y. and E. Guba. 1985. *Naturalistic Inquiry.* Newbury Park, California: Sage.

Losel, F., T. Bliesener, and P. Koferl. 1989. On the concept of invulnerability: Evaluation and first results of the Bielefeld Project. In M. Brambring, F. Losel and H. Skowronek, eds. *Children and risk assessment, longitudinal research and intervention* 186–219. New York: Walther de Gruyter.

Maddi, S. R. 1987. Hardiness training at Illinois Bell Telephone. In J. P. Opatz, ed. *Health Promotion Evaluation: Measuring the Organizational Impact* 101–115. Stevens Point, WI: National Wellness Association.

Mallak, L. 1997. Putting organizational resilience to work. *Industrial Management* 40(8):8–13.

Mallak, L. 1998. Measuring resilience in health care provider organizations. *Health Manpower Management* 24(4):148–152.

Mallak, L., H. Kurstedt Jr., and G. Patzak. 1997. Planning for crises in project management. *Project Management Journal* 28(4):14–20.

Marks, M. 1977. Organizational adjustment to uncertainty. *The Journal of Management Studies* 14(1):1–7.

Marion, R. and J. Bacon. 2000. Organizational extinction and complex systems. *Emergence,* 1(4):71–96.

Marosi, R. 2005, May 22. Tijuana awash in wave of violent crime. *The Los Angeles Times* B1.

Martin, T. 2004, November. A model for business resiliency. *Continuity Insights* 1:30–34.

McCann. 2004. Organizational effectiveness: Changing concepts for changing environments. *HR. Human Resource Planning* 27(1):42–50.

McKinsey. 2002. Increasing FDNY's Preparedness. Retrieved March 19, 2004, from www.nyc.gov/html/fdny/html/mck_report/index.html.

Mellow, G. and T. Rosemary, T. 2005, May-June. Creating the resilient community college. *Change Magazine* 58–66.

Merriam, S.B. 1998. *Qualitative Research and Case Stud Application in Education.* San Francisco: Jossey-Bass.

Mexico Attorney General's Office. 2004, December 2. Jude orders five alleged CAF members to stand trial on organized crime charges. Retrieved November 29, 2004, from Department of the Pentagon, FBIS report LAP20041129000069 [100].

Mexico City Contralinea. 2004, November 2. Expert affirms PGR losing drug trafficking fight. Retrieved December 18, 2004 from, Department of Defense, FBIS report LAP20041122000017 [100] p 1-5. Drug kingpins Arellano Felix, Osiel Cardenas expand alliance to South America, join cartels to ship 30 tons of cocaine to the United States (2004, December 13). Mexico City Reforma.

Meyer, A.D. 1982. Adapting to environmental jolts. *Administrative Science Quarterly* 27(4):515–537.

Miles, M.B. and A.M. Huberman. 1994. *Qualitative data analysis: An expanded sourcebook.* 2nd ed. Thousand Oaks, CA: Sage Publications.

Mitchell, J.C. 2000. Case and situation analysis. In R. Gomm, M. Hammersley and P. Foster, eds. *Case study method,* 165–186. Thousand Oaks, CA: Sage.

Monday, J. and M. Myers. 1999, October. Coping with disasters by building local resiliency. Dealing with Disaster: A Public Risk Institute Symposium, 9–13. Public Entity Risk Institute.

Moustakas, C. 1994. *Phenomenological Research Methods.* Thousand Oaks, CA: Sage.

Murnighan, J. 1993. *Social psychology in organizations. Advances in theory and research.* Englewood Cliffs, NJ: Prentice Hall.

Murray, K. 2004, July 22. Two top Mexican drug cartels join forces. *Reuters News Service.* Retrieved on July 22, 2004, from http://today.reuters.com/news/home.aspx

Nadler, D.A., M.S. Gerstein, and R.B. Shaw. 1992. *Organizational architecture: Designs for changing organizations.* CA: Jossey-Bass.

O'Brien, K. 2002, September 9. One nation under stress. For many indirectly affected by September 11, emotional recovery is a struggle. *The Star Ledger.*

O'Connor, E. and C.M. Fiol. 2002. *Diving into white lightning: Herd behaviors in healthcare.* Denver, Colorado: University of Colorado Denver, Graduate School of Business Administration.

Office of National Drug Control Policy. 2003. *Debriefing report. High Intensity Drug Trafficking Area Program. California Regional Partnership Southwest Border HIDTA. July.* Washington, DC: Author.

Office of National Drug Control Policy. 2004a. *Debriefing report. III. Mexican trafficking and transportation for the ONDCP Office for State and Local Affairs report for the study of domestic market disruption. July.* Washington, DC: Author.

Office of National Drug Control Policy. 2004b. *Los Angeles HIDTA.* Retrieved on August 10, 2004, from

http://www.whitehousedrugpolicy.gov/hidta/la-content.html

Office of National Drug Control Policy. 2005. *Oregon HIDTA FY 2005 Initiative Request, Portland Metro Heroin HIDTA Initiative.* Washington, DC: Author.

Office of National Drug Control Policy. (2004c). *Southwest Border HIDTA.* Retrieved on August 10, 2004, from

http://www.whitehousedrugpolicy.gov/ hidta/ca-content.html

Office of National Drug Control Policy. 2004d. *Program policy and budget guidance. Performance management process (PMP). Section XIII.* Washington, DC: Author.

Office of National Drug Control Policy. 2004e. *FY 2004 HIDTA priority targeting project (CPOT) request matrix.* Unpublished manuscript. Washington, DC: Author.

One year after 9-11: Disaster recovery emerges as key challenge. 2002, September. *Electronic Commerce News* 7(19):1–5.

O'Neal, M. 1999. *Measuring resilience*: Point Clear, AL: NA.

Pappalardo, J. 2004. Asa Hutchinson watchful of the diplomacy of security. *National Defense*, August 2004.

Perrow, C. 1984. *Normal accidents: Living with high risk technologies.* New York: Basic Books.

Perrow, C. 1999. *Normal accidents: Living with high-risk technologies.* 2nd ed. Princeton, NJ: Princeton University Press.

Porter, M. 1985. *Competitive advantage: Creating and sustaining superior performance.* London: The Free Press.

Prosecutor accuses drug cartel hit man of having secret list of jury witnesses. 2004, August 8. *San Diego Union Tribune.*

Public Broadcasting System. 2000. Interview Heidi Landgraff and Vince de la Montaigne. *Frontline.* Retrieved August 10, 2004, from

http://www.pbsorg/wgbh/pages/frontline/shows/drugs/interviews/landgraff montaigne.html

Public Broadcasting System. 2000. The Arellano Felix Tijuana cartel: A family affair. *Frontline.* Retrieved August 10, 2004, from http:///www.pbs.org/wgbh/pages/frontline/shows/drugs/business/afo/afosum mary.html

Putnam, T. 1995, February. *The collapse of decision-making and organizational structure on Storm King Mountain.* Missoula, Montana: Missoula Technology and Development Center, USDA Forest Service.

Pyecha, J. 1988. *A case study of the application of noncategorial special education in two states.* Chapel Hill, NC: Research Triangle Institute.

Quarantelli, E.L. 1987. Disaster studies: An analysis of the social historical factors affecting the development of research in the area. *International Journal of Mass Emergencies and Disasters* 5:285–310.

Quarantelli, E.L. 1994. *Draft of a sociological disaster research agenda for the future: Theoretical, methodological and empirical issues.* Newark, Delaware: University of Delaware.

Ravelo, R. 2004, June 27. Race for governor. Retrieved on June 1, 2004, from FBIS, Pentagon, Reference number 1.LAP20040701000016). *Proceso.*

Redman, C.L. 2002. ASU joins resilience alliance. *Center for Environmental Studies Newsletter* 5(1):1–2.

Rerup. C. 2001. Houston, we have a problem: Anticipation and improvisation as sources of organizational resilience. *Comportamento Organizacional E Gestao* 7:27–44.

Resa-Nestares, C. 1999. Transnational organized crime in Spain: Structural factors explaining its penetration. In E.C. Viana, ed. *Global Organized and International Security*, Ashgate, Altershot.

Richards, J. 1999. Transnational Criminal Organizations, Cybercrime and Money Laundering. Boca Raton, Fl.: CRC Press.

Rijpma, J. 1997. *Complexity, tight-coupling and reliability: Connecting normal accidents theory and high reliability theory.* Leiden, Netherlands: Leiden University, Department of Public Administration, Crisis Research Center, Department of Public Administration.

Robb, D. 2000. Building resilient organizations. *OD Practitioner* 32:27–32.

Roberts, K., S. Stout, and J. Halpern. 1994. Decision dynamics in two high reliability military organizations. *Management Science* 40(5):614–624.

Robinson, L. 1998, September 28. A Mexican firing squad. *U.S. News and World Report* 49.

Rosenman, S. and I. Handelsman. 1992. Rising from the ashes: Modeling resiliency in a community devastated by man-made catastrophe. *American Imago* 49(2):185–226.

Rubiin, H. and I. Rubin. 1995. *Qualitative interviewing: The art of hearing data.* Thousand Oaks, CA: Sage Publications.

Rudolph, J. and N. Repenning. 2002, March. Disaster dynamics: understanding the role of quantity in organizational collapse, *Administrative Science Quarterly* 47:1–30.

Rummler, G. and A. Brache. 1990. *Improving performance: How to manage the white space on the organization chart.* San Francisco: Jossey-Bass Publishers.

Rusk, M.C., W.A. Schoel, and S.M. Barnard. 1995. Psychological resiliency in the public sector: Hardiness and pressure for change. *Journal of Vocational Behavior* 46(1):17–39.

Sagan, S. 1993. *The limits of safety: Organizations, accidents and nuclear weapons.* Princeton: Princeton University Press.

Saveland, J. 2005, April 26–28. Integral leadership and signal detection for high reliability organizing and learning. Paper presented at the Eighth International Wildland Fire Safety Summit, Missoula, Montana.

Savona, E. 1995. Harmonizing policies for reducing the transnational organized crime risk trans-crime. Working Paper 2, Toronto, Canada: University of Toronto.

Scott, W.R. 1994. Open peer commentaries on accidents in high-risk systems. *Technology Studies* 1:23–25.

Seidman, E.E. 2006. *Interviewing as qualitative research: A guide for researchers in education and the social sciences.* 3rd ed. New York: Teachers College Press.

Sitkin, S.B. 1992. Learning through failure: The strategy of small losses. In B.M. Staw and L.L. Cummings, eds. *Research in Organizational Behavior* 14:231–266.

Strategic Forecasting Incorporation. 2007. *Mexican drug cartels: The evolution of violence.* Washington, DC: Author.

Stumpfer, D. 2001. *A model of intrapersonal resilient functioning in adults.* Manuscript submitted for publication.

Schulman, P. 1996. Heroes, organizations and high reliability. *Journal of Contingencies and Crisis Management* 4(2):72–82.

Schulman, P., E. Roe, M. Van Eeten, and M. Bruijne. 2004. High reliability and the management of critical infrastructures. *Journal of Contingencies and Crisis Management* 12(1):14–28.

Schwandt, D. and M. Marquardt. 2000. *Organizational learning: From world-class theories to global best practices.* Boca Raton, Florida: CRC Press.

Seidman, E.E. 1998. *Interviewing as qualitative research: A guide for researchers in education and the social sciences.* 2nd ed. New York: Teachers College Press.

Shannon, E.1988. *Desperados: Latin drug wars, U.S. lawmen, and the war America can't win.* New York: Penguin Group.

Shannon, E. 2001, June 11. The border monsters. *Time Magazine* 23:69–70.

Smart, P., D. Tranfield, and P. Deasley. 2003. *Integrating 'lean' and 'high reliability' thinking.* Cranfield, UK: Cranfield University, School of Management, Advanced Management Research Center.

Smith, D. 2002. Crisis management. Retrieved October 6, 2003, from www.http://216.239.53.100/search?q=cache:RQzGXuasmh0C:www.shef.ac.uk/~ mcn/6810/reading/crisisessay.pdf 231

Smith, G. 2002, November 25. In this war, Fox is actually winning some battles. His anti-narcotics drive is drawing applause from Washington. *Business Week* 57.

Spagat, E. 2006, January 27. Two tons of marijuana found in border tunnel. *Inland Valley Daily Bulletin* A6.

Staglin, D. 1997, June 23. Border alert. *U.S. News and World Report* 16.

Stake, R. 1995. *The Art of Case Study Research.* Thousand Oaks, CA: Sage.

Starbuck, W.H. 1976. *Organizations and their environments. In Handbook of industrial and organizational psychology.* Vol. 18. Chicago: Rand McNally.

Staudinger, U.M., M. Marsiske, and P.B. Baltes. 1993. Resilience and levels of reserve capacity in later adulthood: Perspectives from life-span theory. *Development and Psychopathology* 5:541–566.

Steinman, Alan, P. Mulholland, and A. Palumbo. 1991. Resilience of logic ecosystems to light-elimination disturbance. *Ecology* 72:1299–1313.

Stockstill, M. 2006, January 17. Border drug war backfiring. *Inland Valley Daily Bulletin* A1, A8.

Strasser, S. 1969. *The Idea of Dialogal Phenomenology.* Pittsburgh, PA: Duquesne University Press.

Strumpfer, D.J.W. 2001. *A model of intrapersonal resilient functioning in adults.* Unpublished manuscript. Johannesburg, South Africa: Rand Afrikaans University, Department of Human Resource Management.

Sullivan, K. and M. Jordan. 2002, October 31. U.S. Called the Loser in War on Drugs. *The Washington Post* A1, 232.

Sutcliffe, K. and T. Vogus. 2003. *Organizing for resilience.* Draft. Ann Arbor, Michigan: University of Michigan, Department of Management and Organizations.

Sutcliffe, K. and T. Vogus. 2003a. *Organizing for resilience.* K. Cameron, J.E. Dutton, R.E. Quinn, eds. San Francisco: Berrett-Koehler, 2003, 94–110.

Sutcliffe, K. and T. Vogus. 2007. Organizing or resilience: Towards a theory of research and agenda. In ISIC. IEEE International Conference on Systems, Man and Cybernetics, 3418–3422, 7–10 Oct. 2007.

Teece, D.J., G. Pisano, and A. Shuen. 1997. Dynamic capabilities and strategic management. *Strategic Management Journal* 18(7):509–533.

Tenkasi, R. 2002. *Enactment, sensemaking and social agreement: An interpretive model of implementing high performance work systems.* Lisle, IL: Benedictine University, Program in Organizational Development.

Tierney, K. 2001. *Strength of a city: A disaster research perspective on the World Trade Center attack.* Social Science Research Council.

United Nations, Office of Drugs and Crime. 2003. *Mexico 2003 country profile.* New York, NY: Author.

U.S. Department of Agriculture, Rocky Mountain Research Station. 2004, May 10–13. Managing the unexpected in prescribed fire and fire use operations. A workshop on the high reliability organization, 1–74.

U.S. Department of Health and Human Services. 2006. Code of federal regulations. Title 45 public welfare. Part 56. Protection of human subjects. Revised June 2005.Retrieved on August 18, 2006, from http://www.hhs.gov/ohrp/humansubjects/guidance/ 45cfr46.htm#46.102

U.S. Department of Justice, National Drug Intelligence Center. 2001. *Mexican drug trafficking organizations: A national threat assessment.* (Product No. 2001-C0428-001). Washington, DC: Author.

U.S. Department of Justice, National Drug Intelligence Center. 2002. *Mexican drug trafficking organizations: A national threat assessment.* (Product No. 2003-J0403- 001). Washington, DC: Author.

U.S. Department of Justice, National Drug Intelligence Center. 2004. *National threat assessment 2004: Domestic drug flows.* (Product No. 2004-QO317-007). Washington, DC: Author.

U.S. Department of Justice, National Drug Intelligence Center. 2008, April 11. Situation report: cities in which Mexican DTOs operate within the United States. (Product No. 2008-S0787-005). Retrieved on August 30, 2010, from

http://www.justice.gov/ndic/pubs27/ 27986/ index.htm

U.S. Department of State. 2003a. Arellano Felix organization. Rewards offered for members of Arellano Felix organization. Retrieved on August 10, 2004, from

http://www.state.gov/g/inl/narc/rewards/26369.htm

U.S. Department of State. 2004a, March 13. International drug trafficking and terrorism. Testimony before the Senate Judiciary Committee Subcommittee on Technology, Terrorism, and Government Information. Retrieved April 14, 2005, from http:www.state.gov/g/inl/rls/rm/2002/9239.htm.

U.S. Department of State. Bureau of International Narcotics and Law Enforcement. 2004b. *International national control strategy report 2003: Report on Canada, Mexico, and Central America.* Washington, DC: Author.

U.S. Department of State. 2004c. Benjamin Arellano Felix captured. Retrieved August 10, 2004, from

http://www.state.gov/g/inl/narc/rewards/8707.htm

U.S. Department of Treasury. 2004. Recent OFAC actions. Office of Foreign Assets Control. Retrieved August 10, 2004, from http://www.ustreas.gov/offices/eotffc/ofac/actions/20040601.html

U.S District Court, Southern District of California, Grand Jury. 2003. *Indictment Criminal Case 97CR2520K, 7th Superseding.*

Vogus, T. and T. Welbourne. 2002. Structuring for high reliability: HR practices and mindful processes in reliability-seeking organizations. *Journal of Organizational Behavior* 24(7):877–903.

Walker, W. 1995. *The use of scenarios and gaming in crisis management planning and training*. Santa Monica, California: RAND/European-American Center for Policy Analysis.

Webster's Dictionary. 2003. Retrieved February 3, 2003, from http://dictionary.reference.com/search?q=resilience

Weekly Compilation of Presidential Documents. 2002. *Research Library Core* 38(12):464.

Weekly Compilation of Presidential Documents. 2002. *Research Library Core* 38(48):2099.

Weick, K.E. 1976. Educational Organizations as Loosely Coupled Systems. *Administrative Science Quarterly* 21:1–9.

Weick, K.E. 1979. *The psychology of organizing*. New York: McGraw-Hill.

Weick, K.E. 1993a. The Collapse of Sensemaking in Organizations: The Mann Gulch Disaster. *Administrative Science Quarterly* 38(4):628--652.

Weick K.E. and R. Quinn. 1999. Organizing Change and Development. *Annual Review of Psychology*. 50:361–386.

Weick K.E. and K. Roberts. 1993. Collective mind in organizations: interrelating on flight decks. *Administrative Science Quarterly* 38(3):357–381.

Weick, K.E. 1988. Enacted sensemaking in crisis situations. *Journal of Management Studies* 25(2):305–317.

Weick, K.E. 1993. Sensemaking in organizations: Small structures with large consequences. *In Social psychology in organizations: Advanced theory and research*. Englewood Cliffs: Prentice-Hall.

Weick, K.E. 1995. *Sensemaking in organizations*. Thousand Oaks, CA: Sage.

Weick, K.E. and K.M. Sutcliffe. 2005. Managing the unexpected. The Second Managing the Unexpected Workshop. Jacksonville, Florida, 1–20.

Weick, K.E. and K.M. Sutcliffe. 2001. *Managing the unexpected: Assuring high performance in an age of complexity*. San Francisco: Jossey-Bass.

Weick, K.E., K.M. Sutcliffe, and D. Obstfeld. 1999. Organizing for high reliability: Processes of collective mindfulness. *Research in Organizational Behavior* 21:81–123.

Werner, E.E. and R.S. Smith. 2001. *Journeys from childhood to midlife: Risk, resilience, and recovery.* Ithaca, NY: Cornell University Press.

Westman, M. 1990. The relationship between stress and performance: The moderating effect of hardiness. *Human Performance* 3(3):141–155.

White House, Office of National Drug Control Policy, High Intensity Drug Trafficking Area Program. 2004. *High Intensity Drug Trafficking Area program annual report.* Washington, DC: Author.

White House. 2002, March 1. *Mexico Report.* Washington, DC: Author.

White House. 2004. Statement of Presidential Designation of Foreign Narcotics Kingpins. The White House. Retrieved August 10, 2004, from

www.whitehouse.gov/news/ releases/2004/06/20040601-5.html

Wiersma, W. 2000. *Research methods in education: An introduction.* 7th ed. Boston: Allyn and Bacon.

Wildavsky, A. 1988. *Searching for safety.* New Brunswich: Transportation Books.

Wilkes, G. 2002. Introduction: A second generation of resilience research. *Journal of Clinical Psychology* 58(3):229–232.

Williams, P. and R. Godson. 2002. Anticipating organized and transnational crime. *Crime, Law and Change* 37(4):311–355.

Wolin, S. J., W. Muller, F. Taylor, and S. Wolin. 1999. *Three spiritual perspectives on resilience: Buddhism, Christianity, and Judaism.* New York: Guilford Books.

Wood, R. and A. Bandura. 1989. Impact of conceptions of ability on self-regulatory mechanisms and complex decision making. *Journal of Personality and Social Psychology* 56(3):407–415.

Woods, D. 2004. *Creating foresight: Lessons for enhancing resilience from Columbia.* Draft. Columbus, Ohio: The Ohio State University, Institute of Economics, Cognitive Systems Engineering Laboratory.

Yin, R.1984. *Case Study Research: Design and Methods.* 1st ed. Beverly Hills, CA: Sage Publishing.

Yin, R.1989. *Case Study Research: Design and Methods.* Rev. ed. Newbury Park, CA: Sage Publishing.

Yin, R. 1994. *Case Study Research: Design and Methods.* Thousand Oaks: Sage.

Yukl, G. 2002. *Leadership in organizations.* Upper Saddle River, New Jersey: Prentice Hall.

Zapf, D., C. Dormann, and M. Frese. 1996. Longitudinal studies in organizational stress research: A review of the literature with reference to methodological issues. *Journal of Occupational Health Psychology* 1(2):145–169.

*Bible quotations are from the King James Version, unless indicated otherwise.

End Notes

[1] Drug Wars: Silver or Lead, "Plata O Plomo," a Gary "Rusty" Fleming film, Renavatio Productions, Inc., 2008.

[2] http://www.time.com/time/world/article/0,8599,2005135,00.html

[3] http://www.foxnews.com/world/2010/08/22/decapitated-bodies-hung-bridge-mexican-city-besieged-drug-gang-infighting

[4] http://www.pbs.org/wgbh/pages/frontline/shows/warriors/contractors/highrisk.html

[5] Edgar Valdez Villarreal was captured by Mexican authorities on August, 30, 2010. But the drug violence continues unabated.

[6] http://www.foxnews.com/world/2010/08/25/mexican-government-migrants-dead-ranch-killed-zetas-drug-gang/

[7] http://www.wthr.com/story/13057320/families-of-massacred-migrants-couldnt-pay-ransom?clienttype=printable&redirected=true

[8] U.S. Department of Justice, National Drug Intelligence Center (2003)

[9] U.S. Department of State (2004c)

[10] United Nations (2003)

[11] Heyman, J. and Campbell, H. (2004): Recent research on the U.S. Mexico border. *Latin American Research Review, 39,* 205–220.

[12] American Heritage Dictionary of the English Language, online: http://education.yahoo.com/reference/dictionary/entry/cartel

[13] *Drug Wars: Silver or Lead, "Plata O Plomo"*

[14] *International Organized,* 1998, p. 3

[15] Cook, C., ed. (2007, October). Mexico's drug cartels. *CRS Report for Congress.* Congressional Research Service. Retrieved August 29, 2010 from, http://www.fas.org/sgp/crs/row/ RL34215.pdf.

[16] Williams, P. and Godson, R. (2002), p. 311-355

[17] Ibid., p. 333

[18] Ibid., p. 339

[19] Sovona (1995)

[20] Williams and Godson, p. 337

[21] Strategic Forecasting Incorporated (2007). *Mexican Drug Cartels: The Evolution of Violence,* p. 10

[22] Kenney M. (2003), p. 230

[23] Ibid., p. 232
[24] Ibid.
[25] Ellingwood, K. (2010)
[26] Becerra, O. (2002)
[27] Brooks, R. (1999), p. 16
[28] DEA Offers (2003), p. 20
[29] Willoughby (2003)
[30] Shannon, E. (2002), p. 69, *Times Magazine*
[31] Weekly Compilation of Presidential Documents (2002), Nov. 26, p. 2,099
[32] Ibid, p. 464
[33] Golden (1997)
[34] Dettmer, J. and Maier, T. (1998)
[35] Ibid., p. 6
[36] Ibid.
[37] Ibid., p. 25
[38] Beers, R., 1999, p. 16
[39] Ibid.
[40] Brooks, p. 4
[41] PBS *Frontline* (2000) conducted an interview with FBI De La Motaingne, who supervised the AF-DTO Task Force.
[42] Baig (2000), p. 16
[43] *Congressional Research Service Report for Congress* (2001)
[44] Office of National Drug Control Policy Southwest Border HIDTA (2004)
[45] ONDP (2004e)
[46] ONDP (2004e), p. 4
[47] Murray, K. (2004)
[48] Ibid.
[49] Americas: The end of the Arellanos: Drugs in Mexico (2002, March 16) *The Economist*, 43
[50] Willoughby (2003)
[51] U.S. Department of Justice, National Drug Intelligence Center (2001)
[52] DEA Offers (2003)
[53] Ibid.
[54] Ibid.
[55] Ibid., p. 20
[56] ONDCP (2003)
[57] U.S. Department of State (2003a)
[58] Ibid. (2002)
[59] Ibid. (2003b)
[60] Ciudad Juarez El Diario (2004)
[61] Mexico Attorney General's Office (2004)
[62] La Frontera (2004b)

[63] Ibid. (2004c)
[64] Ravelo, R. (2004)
[65] La Cronica (2004)
[66] *Mexico City Reforma* (Drug Kingpins, 2004)
[67] Mexico City Contralinea (2004)
[68] Mexico City Contralinea (2004)
[69] White House (2004)
[70] U.S. State Department (2004b)
[71] Hutchinson, as quoted in Pappalardo, J. (2004), p. 66
[72] Ibid.
[73] ONDCP (2004), p. 140
[74] Southwest Border HIDTA, HIDTA strategy (2004c)
[75] Marosi, R. (May 2005), *Los Angeles Times*, p. B9
[76] Staglin, D. (1997), *U.S. News and World Report*
[77] Dettmer, J. (2001)
[78] *El Universal* (2004)
[79] Becerra, O. (2002)
[80] U.S. Department of Justice, National Drug Intelligence Center (2001)
[81] Ibid., (2003).
[82] Caldwell, R. (2007a)
[83] Stockstill, M. (2006)
[84] Carter, S. (2006)
[85] Caldwell, R. (2007c), p. G6
[86] Ibid.
[87] Ibid., (2007b), p. G5
[88] Caldwell (2007d)
[89] U.S. District Court (2002)
[90] Ibid., p. 4
[91] Ibid.
[92] Ibid., (2003), pp. 4-11
[93] Kraul, C. (2002), *Los Angeles Times*
[94] Ibid., p. 1
[95] Sullivan, K. and Jordan, M. (2002)
[96] White House (2002), p. 20
[97] Spagat, E. (2006)
[98] Caldwell (2007a), p. G2
[99] Ibid.
[100] Ibid.
[101] Ibid.
[102] Ibid., p. G4
[103] Ibid., p. G5
[104] Ibid.

[105] Strategic Forecasting Incorporated (2007), p. 9
[106] Ibid.
[107] Constantine (1998), p. 8
[108] Ibid.
[109] Resa-Nestares (1999)
[110] Ibid., p. 4
[111] Patron Saints of the Mexican Drug Underworld, DVD (2009). Robert Almonte, producer
[112] www.narcoticstraining.com (2009)
[113] Patron Saints of the Mexican Drug Underworld
[114] Ibid.
[115] Ibid.
[116] Ibid.
[117] Weick et al. (1999)
[118] Braverman (2001)
[119] Weick (1976)
[120] Weick (1999)
[121] Robb, D. (2000)
[122] Weick's work on sensemaking (1999)
[123] Schwandt, D. and Marquardt, M. (2000)
[124] Caldwell, R. *The Evidence* (July 2007c)
[125] Ibid., p. G6
[126] Caldwell, *The Narco Bosses* (July 2007d)
[127] Ibid., p. G4
[128] Weick et al. (1999)
[129] Weick (1993)
[130] Weick et al. (1999)
[131] Schwandt and Marquardt (2000)
[132] Sutcliffe and Vogus (2003)
[133] Smart et al. (2003)
[134] Scott, W.R. (1994)
[135] Hinrichs, G. (2002)
[136] Hamel, G. and Valikangas, L. (2003)
[137] Garmezy, N. (1991)
[138] Weick (1993), p. 628
[139] Sutcliffe and Vogus (2003), p. 7
[140] Weick (2001)
[141] Lagadec, P. (1993), p. 54
[142] Wildavasky, A. (1998)
[143] Weick (2004)
[144] Sutcliffe and Vogus, 2003
[145] O'Connor, E. and Fiol, C.M. (2002), p. 13

[146] Weick (1988)
[147] Weick (1979)
[148] Weick (1993)
[149] Schwandt and Marquardt (2000)
[150] Ibid, p. 7
[151] Rerup (2001)
[152] Weick (2004)
[153] Monda, J. and Myers, M. (1999), p. 5
[154] Carroll (1998a) ; Weick et al. (1999)
[155] Beunza, D. and Stark, D. (2003)
[156] Weick (2001)
[157] Yukl, G. (2002), p. 37
[158] Kendra and Wachtendorf (2002), p. 102
[159] Braverman (2001)
[160] Wood, R. and Bandura, A. (1989)
[161] Weick and Quinn, R. (1999)
[162] Perrow, C. (1984)
[163] Weick and Sutcliffe (2005)
[164] Mallak, L. (1997)
[165] Hamel et al. (2003), p. 53
[166] McCann (2004)
[167] Weick et al. (1999)
[168] Weick (1995); Weick et al. (1999)
[169] Rerup (2001)
[170] Heyman and Campbell (2004)
[171] Hutchinson, (2002)
[172] Hoffman, B. (2004)
[173] Horne, III, J., and Orr, J. (1998). Assessing behaviors that create resilient organizations. *Employment Relations Today, Winter,* 29-39.
[174] Bruneau, M., Change S., Eguchi, R., Lee, G., O'Rourke, T., Reinhorn A., Shinozuka, M., Tierney, K., Wallace, W., and Von Winterfelt, D. (2002). *A framework to quantitatively assess and enhance seismic resilience of communities.* Buffalo, NY: Multidisciplinary Center for Earthquake Engineering Research.
[175] Horne III, J. (1997, Spring-Fall). The coming age of organizational resilience. *Business forum,* 24-28.
[176] Kleiman et al., 2002
[177] D'Aveni (1994)
[178] Hinrichs, G. (2002), p. 3
[179] Bigley, G. and Roberts, K. (2001)
[180] Kenney, M. (2001), p. 1
[181] Webster, (2003), p. 1,003
[182] Sutcliffe and Vogus (2003)

Dr. Paul R. Chabot

[183] Mallak, (1997)
[184] O'Connor, E. and Fiol, C.M. (2002)
[185] Wildavsky (1988)
[186] Ibid. (1991)
[187] Sutcliffe and Vogus (2002), p. 7
[188] Wildavsky (1991)
[189] Collins, J.C. and Porras, J.I. (1994)
[190] Rusk, Schoel, and Barnard (1996); Maddi (1987)
[191] Aitken, S. (1999); Guidimann, T. (2002)
[192] Sutcliffe and Vogus (2003)
[193] Carl et al. (2002)
[194] Sutcliffe and Vogus (2002)
[195] Weick and Sutcliffe
[196] Grotberg, E. (1995), p. 2
[197] Braverman, p. 2
[198] Greene, R. (2002), p.1
[199] Sutcliffe and Vogus (2003), p. 1
[200] Ibid., 2003
[201] Johnson, L. and Kloman, F. (1999), p. 3
[202] Hoffman (2002), p. 32
[203] Ibid., p. 34
[204] Hamel et al. (2003)
[205] Ibid., p. 55
[206] Ibid., p. 63
[207] Quarantelli (1987)
[208] Horne, p. 27
[209] Ibid.
[210] Ibid.
[211] Walker, W. (1995), p. 1
[212] Lagadec (1993)
[213] Ibid., p. 3
[214] Ellis, P. (1998)
[215] Rudolph and Repenning (2002)
[216] Tierney, K. (2001), p. 1
[217] One year after 9/11 (2002)
[218] Carl and Elmqvist (2002)
[219] Fanning, K. (200)
[220] O'Brien, K. (2002)
[221] McCann (2004), p. 48
[222] Ibid., pp. 48-49
[223] Bell (2002), p. 1
[224] Robb, D. (2000)

[225] Ibid., p. 28
[226] Ibid.
[227] Ibid., p. 30
[228] Ibid., p. 32
[229] Ibid., p. 30
[230] Sutcliffe and Vogus (2003)
[231] Ibid., p. 28
[232] Ibid., (2003)
[233] Garmezy (1991)
[234] McCann (2004)
[235] Bruneau et al. (2002)
[236] Kendra and Wachtendorf (2001), p. 102
[237] Bigley and Roberts (2001)
[238] Ibid., p. 1,297
[239] Ibid. (2001)
[240] Ibid., p. 1,298
[241] Martin, T. (2004)
[242] Ibid., p. 30
[243] Horne and Orr (1998)
[244] Ibid., p. 31
[245] Horne and Orr, p. 32).
[246] Ibid.
[247] Rerup (2001)
[248] Ibid., p. 27
[249] Ibid.
[250] Ibid, p. 3
[251] McKinsey (2002)
[252] Goldway, T. (2002
[253] Kendra and Wachtendorf (2002)
[254] Freeman, Hirschhorn, and Maltz (2002)
[255] Ibid.
[256] Woods, D. (2004)
[257] McCann, p. 49
[258] Meyer, A.D. (1982)
[259] Strumpher, D.J.W. (2001), p.5
[260] Ashmos and Huber (1987), p. 135
[261] Weick (1993)
[262] Kumagai, Y. (2002)
[263] Kenney (2001)
[264] Ibid., p. 3
[265] Ibid., p. 6
[266] Ibid., p. 30

267 Ibid., p. 1
268 Ibid., p. 226
269 Ibid., p. 227
270 Cash, T. (1993)
271 Kenney (2003)
272 Ibid., p. 112
273 Constantine (1998), pp. 4-5
274 Marion, R. and Bacon, J. (2000)
275 Fortune (2005)
276 Wildavsky (1988)
277 Smart (2003), p. 736
278 Schwandt and Marquardt (2000)
279 Ibid., p. vii
280 Comfort (2001)
281 Ibid, p. 121
282 Ibid., p. 124
283 http://www.foxnews.com/world/2010/10/12/mexican-police-official-investigating-border-lake-shooting-dead
284 ONDCP (2004)
285 Strategic Forecasting Incorporated (1997)
286 Sutcliffe and Vogus (2007), p. 3,418
287 Wildavsky, A. (1988), p. 147
288 Smith, G. (2002), pp. 4-5
289 Mallak et al. (1997), p. 17
290 Ibid.
291 Grove (1997)
292 Goble, Fields, and Cocchiara (2002)
293 Ibid., p. 5
294 Ibid., p. 6
295 Horne (1997), "The Coming Age of Organizational Resilience"
296 Ibid., p. 27
297 Yukl (2002), p. 37
298 Kumpfer, L.K. (1999)
299 Sutcliffe and Vogus (2003), p. 8
300 Werner and Smith (2001)
301 Braverman (2001), p. 1
302 Ibid.
303 Ibid., p. 2
304 Hind, p. (1996), p. 19
305 Ibid., p. 23
306 Coutu, D. (2002), p. 48
307 Comfort, L.K. (2001)

[308] McCann (2004)
[309] Weick, (1999)
[310] Weick (1995)
[311] Hamel and Valikangas (2003), p. 53
[312] O'Neal, M. (1999)
[313] Ibid., p. 3
[314] Ibid., p. 10
[315] Rosenman and Handelsman (1992)
[316] Franko, L. (2002)
[317] Ibid., p. 36
[318] Carl et al. (2002)
[319] Comfort (2001)
[320] Ibid., p. 118
[321] Hammonds (2002)
[322] Weick and Sutcliffe (2005)
[323] p. 305
[324] p. 316
[325] Smith (2002)
[326] Fiol and O'Connor (2002), p. 13
[327] McCann (2004)
[328] Comfort (2001)
[329] Ibid., p. 116
[330] Saveland, J. (2005)
[331] Hinrichs, G. and Tenkasi, R. (2002), p. 224
[332] Drabek, T. (1989), p. 151
[333] Hatch, M.J. (1997)
[334] Lagadec, p. 54
[335] Carroll (1998a); Weick et al. (1999), p. 1
[336] Kiel,L. D. (1994)
[337] Aase, K. and Nybo, G. (2002), p. 7
[338] Weick, (1999)
[339] Aase and Nybo, p. 7
[340] Scott, W. R. (1994)
[341] Vogus and Welbourne (2003)
[342] Perrow, C. (1999)
[343] Vogus and Welbourne
[344] D'Aveni, R. (1994)
[345] Weick and Sutcliff (2001)
[346] Iverson, D. (2002)
[347] USDA (2004)
[348] Weick and Sutcliff (2001), p. 14
[349] Ibid.

[350] Clarke, L. (1993)
[351] O'Connor and Fiol (2002)
[352] La Porte and Consolini (1991), p. 84
[353] Smart (2003), p. 735
[354] Perrow (1984)
[355] Roberts (1993)
[356] Sagan (1993)
[357] Rijpma, J. (1997)
[358] Smart et al. (2003)
[359] Ibid., p. 736
[360] Ibid., (2003)
[361] Weick (1993)
[362] Smart et al. (2003), p. 736
[363] Brown, A. (1993)
[364] Sutcliffe and Vogus (2003)
[365] Comfort (1994)
[366] Ibid., p. 168
[367] Starbuck, W.H. (1976), p. 1,069
[368] ASU Joins (2002)
[369] Comfort (2001) p. 119
[370] Kaufman (1993) p. 120
[371] Quarantelli, E.L. (1994b), p. 1

About the Author

Dr. Paul Chabot, President and CEO of Chabot Strategies LLC *www.chabotstrategies.com* is an Iraq war veteran and began his military intelligence career in 2001, serving first at the Office of Naval Intelligence, later with the Defense Intelligence Agency, in conjunction with an assignment in the Pentagon working for the Joint Chiefs of Staff in the National Military Command Center assessing immediate national security threats. In 2008, Paul returned from Iraq where he served as an intelligence officer with Joint Special Operations Forces. Today he serves with the U.S. Navy 3rd Fleet and holds the rank of Lieutenant Commander.

In 2010, Paul sought the Republican nomination for California's 63rd Assembly District. Despite being significantly outspent, he placed second in the primary (out of seven candidates), defeating three elected officials, including the mayors of the two largest cities in the region. Paul earned the endorsements of numerous associations, including the California Police Chiefs' Association, the California Peace Officers' Association and the California Narcotic Officers' Association. Visit *www.paulchabot.com* for more campaign information. Immediately following his primary campaign, Paul served as the statewide California Veterans Chairman for Carly Fiorina's bid for the U.S. Senate.

Immediately prior to his campaign, Paul was appointed by the Governor and confirmed by the Senate as Commissioner to the State Parole Board for three consecutive terms. He is proud of his strong public safety record and dedication to protecting California's communities by keeping dangerous criminals behind bars.

Paul has over 15 years of law enforcement experience; serving as a Reserve Deputy Sheriff for the San Bernardino County Sheriff's Department with specialized assignments to the narcotics and street gangs division. Paul also served full-time as a police officer at the University of Southern California.

Paul had the privilege of interning for Congressman Jerry Lewis and was later selected for the Nation's prestigious Presidential Management Fellowship Program working for the White House Office of National Drug Control Policy. He was promoted to White House Senior Advisor for Law Enforcement, Justice and Drug Control Programs. During his nearly 6 years in the White House, he completed two rotational assignments, one with the U.S. Attorney's Office in Los Angeles targeting methamphetamine production and one later with the U.S. State Department Office of Inspector General, assessing counter-terrorism and counter-narcotics programs.

Paul has founded several organizations dedicated to his passions to promote American values, youth mentorship and the deterrence of substance abuse, including; Stars and Stripes United, Inc. *www.starsandstripesunited.com*, the Freestyle Foundation, Inc. *www.freestylefoundation.org*, the Inland Valley Drug Free Community Coalition (www.ivdfc.org), and the Coalition for a Drug Free California *www.drugfreecalifornia.org*, a state-wide collaborative organization of law enforcement, government and volunteers dedicated to preventing the sale and abuse of illegal drugs. He performs a number of pro-bono speaking programs for youth, through his website *www.drchabotconsulting.com*.

Significant presentations include keynotes at the U.S. Naval Academy, U.S. Military Academy at WestPoint, as well as a number of White House conferences, nationwide. He has provided keynote speeches in 48-states. Paul has been a guest on CNN and Fox cable news channels and quoted in local, national and international print media, radio and TV including: Fox News, CNN, al Jazeera, CBS, ABC, Los Angeles Times, Wall Street Journal, among others.

Paul holds a B.A. in administration from California State University at San Bernardino, a M.A. in public administration from the University of Southern California, and a doctorate (Ed. D) in executive leadership from George Washington University. Paul holds a certificate in legislative studies from Georgetown University and is a graduate and guest lecturer of the Delinquency Control Institute at the University of Southern California.

Dr. Chabot can be reached through his national security firm's website at *www.chabotstrategies.*com and via email at *info@chabotstrategies.com*

###

Dr. Chabot on Fox News Channel debating drug legalization with
Host John Stossel – 2010

Dr. Chabot on al Jazeera discussing U.S. efforts combating
terrorists, worldwide – 2010

Dr. Chabot on CNN discussing the harm brought to communities
by drug legalization efforts – 2009

Dr. Chabot holds a news conference regarding a state-wide (California)
military coalition he created addressing War Vet concerns – 2010

Dr. Chabot taped by CNN addressing illegal drugs and the failure of political leaders to protect youth from drug legalization efforts – 2009

Dr. Chabot on al Jazeera – 2010

Ensign Paul Chabot with officers at Pensacola Naval Base 2001

Dr. Chabot speaks to 4,000 cadets at the U.S. Naval Academy 2005

LTjg Paul Chabot with other naval intelligence officers 2003

White House Advisor Dr. Chabot keynotes annual law
enforcement conference 2004

Candidate for State Assembly, Dr. Chabot at statewide political conference 2010

White House Advisor Dr. Chabot keynotes presentation at
WestPoint Military Academy 2003

Law Enforcement Officer Dr. Chabot combating crime in New Orleans following Hurricane Katrina 2005

Law Enforcement Officer Dr. Chabot on patrol 2000

Law Enforcement Officer Dr. Chabot helping youth 1998

Dr. Chabot in front of White House 2001

Dr. Paul R. Chabot

Dr. Chabot in front of the West-Wing of the White House 2003

Congressional Intern Dr. Chabot with Congressman Jerry Lewis 1995

Parole Board Commissioner Dr. Chabot worked with California's violent Prison System 2009

California Assembly Candidate Dr. Chabot with fellow gun supporters 2010

Iraq War Veteran Dr. Chabot speaks to fellow military personnel
on Veterans Day 2010

Iraq War Veteran Dr. Chabot speaks to fellow military personnel
on Veterans Day 2010

Dr. Chabot, a Life Member of the Veterans of Foreign War
fighting for U.S. Military Veterans – 2010

Dr. Paul R. Chabot

LT Paul Chabot, Special Operations Intelligence Officer – Baghdad, Iraq 2008

354

CPSIA information can be obtained at www.ICGtesting.com
Printed in the USA
266330BV00001B/21/P